Patriotism in America

Books by John J. Pullen

PATRIOTISM IN AMERICA
A SHOWER OF STARS
THE TWENTIETH MAINE

Patriotism in America
A Study of Changing Devotions
1770-1970
by John J. Pullen

AMERICAN HERITAGE PRESS NEW YORK

Book Design: Elaine Gongora

Library of Congress Catalog Card Number: 78-142981

07-050916-6

The author wishes to make appreciative acknowledgment for permission to use material from the following sources:

"Construction Workers Tackle the Protesters," *The National Observer,* May 18, 1970. Copyright © 1970 by Dow Jones & Company, Inc.

Merle Curti, *The Roots of American Loyalty* (New York, Columbia University Press, 1946). Copyright 1946 by Columbia University Press.

J. William Fulbright, *The Arrogance of Power* (New York, Random House, Inc., 1966). Copyright © 1966 by J. William Fulbright.

Eric F. Goldman, *The Tragedy of Lyndon Johnson* (New York, Alfred A. Knopf, Inc., 1969). Copyright © 1968, 1969 by Eric F. Goldman.

To Move a Nation, by Roger Hilsman. Copyright © 1964, 1967 by Roger Hilsman. Excerpt reprinted by permission of Doubleday & Company, Inc.

Kenneth Keniston, *Young Radicals* (New York, Harcourt, Brace & World, Inc., 1968). Copyright © 1968 by Kenneth Keniston.

Irving Kristol, "American Intellectuals and Foreign Policy," *Foreign Affairs,* July, 1967.

Ernest C. Marriner, *The History of Colby College* (Waterville, Maine, Colby College Press, 1963). Copyright © 1962 by Colby College Press.

Shailer Mathews, *Patriotism and Religion* (New York, The Macmillan Company, 1918). Copyright 1918 by The Macmillan Company.

Margaret Chase Smith, "Defense Spending: Changing Attitudes," *Defense Management Journal,* Winter, 1970.

Harlan Fiske Stone, "The Conscientious Objector," *Columbia University Quarterly,* October, 1919.

Carola Oman, *Nelson* (Garden City, New York, Doubleday & Company, Inc., 1946). Copyright 1946 by Doubleday & Company, Inc.

Lieutenant Robert C. Ransom, Jr., *Letters from Vietnam.* Copyright © 1968 by Robert C. Ransom.

Carl Sandburg, *Abraham Lincoln: The War Years,* Vol. II (New York, Harcourt, Brace and Company, Inc., 1939). Copyright 1939 by Harcourt, Brace and Company, Inc. Copyright 1936, 1937 by Carl Sandburg.

L. N. Tolstoy, *Christianity and Patriotism,* translated by Constance Garnett (London, Jonathan Cape Limited, 1922).

The author is also grateful to these publications for permission to use material from the following issues:

Air Force Magazine, July, 1970.

Army, April, 1970.

The Colby Alumnus, Summer-Fall, 1969.

The Gallup Opinion Index, June, 1969, and January, 1970. Copyright © 1969 and 1970 by Gallup International, Inc. Excerpt reprinted by permission.

The New York Times, F. D. R. Editorial, April 12, 1970. © 1970 by The New York Times Company. Excerpt reprinted by permission.

Opinion Research Corporation Public Opinion Index, April 15, 1969. Copyright © 1969 by Opinion Research Corporation.

The Washington *Post,* May 18, 1970. © 1970 by the Washington *Post.*

TO RUTH

Acknowledgments

In these pages Colby College of Waterville, Maine, has served as one of the principal vantage points from which to view the patriotic attitudes of several generations of young people. Part of the book is based on letters written by Colby men who fought for their country: Zemro Smith and Nathaniel B. Coleman in 1862–65, and Robert C. Ransom, Jr., in 1968. The first words of acknowledgment and appreciation should therefore go to those who have made these letters available: William J. Pollock of the Colby class of 1921, who donated the Smith and Coleman letters to the college; and Louise and Robert Ransom, mother and father of Lieutenant Ransom, whose letters were privately published by his parents in the moving little volume, *Letters from Vietnam.*

It should also be acknowledged that *Patriotism in America* had its inception at Colby. When the Civil War letters from Mr. Pollock arrived at the college early in 1969, it occurred to the Alumni Secretary, Sid Farr, that they might form the basis for a commentary related to the attitudes of American youth today. He wrote to ask if I would care to write such a commentary for *The Colby Alumnus.* It appeared in the 1969 summer-fall issue under the title "Patriotism Then and Now"; whereupon another Colby man, one who has been a valued friend for many years, attorney Asa H. Roach, suggested that something be done to seek wider circulation for the article. He was joined in this idea by Richard N. Dyer, Assistant to the President of Colby, who brought the article to the attention of Richard M. Ketchum, Senior Editor for Book Publishing at American Heritage Publishing Company. It was at Mr. Ketchum's invitation and with his skillful creative guidance—plus that of Kenneth Leish, Editor-in-Chief of American Heritage Press—that the article was expanded into this book.

During the preparation of both the article and the book I was fortunate in having the almost continuous help and advice of another friend, Flint O. DuPre, whose experience as a professional writer and knowledge of informational sources were of invaluable service.

In making use of polling results I was aided by a group of individuals and organizations who left me with the impression that generosity is uniformly characteristic of people who work at or are associated with public opinion research. Joseph C. Bevis, W. Phillips Davison, Hazel Erskine, LeBaron R. Foster, and Philip K. Hastings were especially helpful, although an immediate disclaimer should be entered in their behalf: none of them is responsible for the interpretation of data to which they have directed my attention. On a corporate plane, I received prompt and friendly cooperation from American Institute of Public Opinion, Louis Harris and Associates, The Louis Harris Political Data Center, Opinion Research Corporation, and Roper Research Associates. Lloyd A. Free, President of the Institute for International Social Research, was good enough to read the manuscript.

For research privileges and assistance my sincere thanks go to the Yale University Library and to staff members in several of its components, particularly to Gretchen A. Swibold in the Political Science Research Library. And at the excellent Acton Public Library in Old Saybrook, Connecticut, Mary Goodrich and her staff have been helpful in several ways.

Under the heading of appreciation for miscellaneous favors and services come my sister Ruth Pullen and an old friend and former associate, Dwight C. Van Meter.

Finally and far from least, Jean A. Pullen has borne with and sustained me through the difficult process that only authors' wives are called upon to endure and has helped me with that trying task, the Index, in a manner that is deserving of special acknowledgment and gratitude.

—J. J. P.

Contents

"Our country! In her intercourse with foreign nations may she always be in the right; but our country, right or wrong!" Stephen Decatur's toast at a dinner in Norfolk, Virginia, April, 1816.

Question asked of 852 people by Opinion Research Corporation in 1959: "Do you think that whatever our federal government does is right?" Answers: 66 per cent NO; 24 per cent YES; 10 per cent NO OPINION.

"Anyone who says patriotism is 'my country right or wrong' ought to have his head examined." Jane Fonda addressing an antiwar rally in Columbia, S.C., as reported by the Washington *Post,* May 18, 1970.

CHAPTER ONE

Different Kinds of Love

★ Thomas Jefferson once wrote, "I hold it that a little rebellion now and then is a good thing, and as necessary in the political world as storms in the physical." Whether or not the stormy period in the United States from April 30 to about July 4, 1970, was a good thing, perhaps only a Jefferson could decide, but certainly it did make nearly every American newly aware of a strong, deep, mysterious, and often divisive emotion: patriotism.

In fact, it provided a laboratory of patriotism unique in our history—an opportunity to study this quality not in the abstract, nor as it exists in Russia, China, or the world generally, but here in America, concentrated in vivo, so to speak.

It was on the evening of April 30 that President Nixon told the nation he had ordered American troops into Cambodia, causing an explosion of public opinion that split the country not just in two but into several parts, the cracks of the division, like those of a shattered mirror, zigzagging through almost every segment of our society. So many people declared themselves *against* the war, *against* the President, *against* the policies of the government, that it simply was not possible to call them all unpatriotic, for if such they were, we had no country. And on the other hand, there were so many people supporting the war, the President, and the government that it was equally impossible, for the same reason, to impugn *their* patriotism. We had at one end of the spectrum young men whose consciences and deeply held beliefs were leading them to a painful decision: to accept jail or exile rather than to engage in a war that they thought wrong and not in the best interests of the country. And at the other end, a President who, in the words of one commentator, put patriotism ahead of political survival in order to do what he thought was best for the nation.

To review some of these dramatic events, it will be recalled that nearly everyone was astonished by President Nixon's Cambodian decision. Events of the preceding days had given very little warning of this move. Speaking to the nation on television and radio on April 20, the President had announced plans for the withdrawal from Vietnam of additional troops, which by the spring of 1971 would bring the total reduction in force since he had taken office to 265,500 men. But he had pointed out that the forcible imposition of a communist government upon the people of South Vietnam would mean humiliation and defeat for the United States, and, he said, "This we cannot and will not accept." And he warned that if the enemy attempted to jeopardize the remaining forces by increased military action in Vietnam, Laos, or Cambodia, he would take "strong and effective measures."

The American people probably did not regard these warnings very seriously. Somehow the impression had grown that what the President was conducting was a sort of tableau, and his performance had been watched with some admiration. He had inherited a war that was not of his doing. With lack of public support for this war so evident to the enemy as well as to everyone else, he was sitting down to a poker table with most of his cards showing. Yet he had played with considerable skill and effectiveness. He had developed a technique of keeping both the enemy in Vietnam and his opponents at home at bay. He had reassured the American public with announcements of substantial troop withdrawals to be completed within specific times, a proposal for moving from the draft to an all-volunteer armed force, and a concept for "Vietnamization," or turning the fighting over to the

South Vietnamese. And he had from time to time issued stern warnings to the enemy that the United States would not be put upon during the process of disengagement.

Many people thought that all this put as good a face upon the withdrawal as could be expected; it was hard to see how any President could do better; an excellent show! But at the same time many believed that surely Mr. Nixon could not be serious about threats of added military measures in Southeast Asia if the enemy did not behave. He was a practical politician, and there were signs of his political peril everywhere. According to the polls, public approval of his handling of the Presidency had declined since January, more than half of those with opinions wanted troops withdrawn from Vietnam immediately or within eighteen months, a majority wanted the withdrawals to continue even if the South Vietnam government collapsed, and six out of ten people wanted the United States to stay out of Laos and Cambodia even if it appeared that the communists were going to take over those countries.

In his speech announcing the attacks into Cambodia, President Nixon indicated full awareness of the political danger he was incurring. He admitted that his decision might cost him the next presidential election. This remark and others showed that the President was well aware of the state of public opinion, and stories to the effect that he had become isolated from the people were not entirely realistic. It seems more probable that he was acting as did Lord Nelson at the naval battle of Copenhagen when having been flagged to leave off action, he said to those on deck around him, "You know . . . I have only one eye. I have a right to be blind sometimes. I really do not see the signal."

He was also accused of being withdrawn and secretive in his relations with Congress and with his own cabinet. But for a commander in chief about to launch a surprise attack, this attitude is understandable; perhaps Mr. Nixon had learned something from the example of Stonewall Jackson, who usually did not even tell his staff where he planned to strike until the march to his chosen objective was well under way and who once said that mystery is the secret of success.

3

The explanation of the action is much more likely to be found in President Nixon's character and career. He had risen to the White House through great adversity; he had borne the whips and scorns of the press on many occasions and had developed, one might think, a thick skin; he was not charismatic and knew it —knew also that effectiveness as a President does not depend on being a charmer; he had seen the success of well-laid plans that had been carried through with diligence and determination. Finally, he had long been a passionate foe of communism and was part of a generation of politicians and statesmen, including Eisenhower, who had firmly believed in the policy of its "containment."

Later reports had it that the Cambodian attacks had been urgently requested by the commander in Vietnam, General Creighton W. Abrams, as a military necessity if withdrawal was to proceed on schedule, and, indeed, the great stores of arms, ammunition, and equipment captured—all within easy striking distance of vital centers in Vietnam—indicated valid reasoning behind the request. The precautionary nature of the blow had been emphasized by the President in his April 30 address, but as is usual in such matters, the rationale was overcolored by the emotional content. This emotion reflected what is the substance of one kind of American patriotism as it exists today: pride in and love for the country, concern for its future, a belief that it is threatened from without and within by alien forces, and a determination to resist these inroads on every front.

Thus the President said that we would be conciliatory at the conference table but that "we will not be humiliated. We will not be defeated." And, "If when the chips are down, the United States acts like a pitiful, helpless giant, the forces of totalitarianism and anarchy will threaten free nations and free institutions throughout the world."

In the speech he also gave North Vietnam further warnings and spoke of domestic enemies. "We live in an age of anarchy both abroad and at home. We see mindless attacks on all the great institutions which have been created by free civilizations in the last five hundred years. Here in the United States, great universities are being systematically destroyed."

Even as he spoke, United States forces in cooperation with those of South Vietnam were moving across the Cambodian border. The fact that the President had sent armed forces into a sovereign state without consulting Congress and contrary to the wishes of a majority of Americans was, in itself, enough to have precipitated a considerable uproar. But there were added factors present to aggravate the situation. Warm spring weather had come to the college campuses—riot weather—and several demonstrations were already going on or were about to start. During the night of April 29–30, students had been fighting with the police and the National Guard at Ohio State University, where several students had received wounds from shotgun fire. Stanford had been having the worst riot in its history, with forty-two injured, and Yale was getting ready to demonstrate on behalf of Black Panthers imprisoned in New Haven. Many of the demands of the demonstrators had to do with increased advantages for black students, amnesty for past rioters, and so on—the usual things—but protests against R.O.T.C. and war-related campus research were also in evidence, and it was certain that Vietnam was not very far beneath the surface of the turmoil. Besides being in a riotous mood, students had a very practical reason for getting excited about any extension of the conflict. Thousands of men of their age were getting it in the neck in this war. They made up a disproportionately small part of the population to be bearing the burden of death and wounds, and one that was almost without power politically. About 75 per cent of our servicemen are inducted into the armed forces or enlist while still under twenty-one, and in the 1968 fall elections nearly 30 per cent of the total force was below voting age.

Even so, it would not be correct to say that the antiwar protest was entirely a revolt of youth. Opinion studies of the fifteen months or so prior to April 30, 1970, had not shown any clear pattern relating age to attitude toward the war. It was only when college students were studied (and it is easy to forget that everyone who is young is not in college) that a body of opinion somewhat more adverse to the Vietnam war than that of the general public was detected. It was apparently this increment of the explosive charge that went off with the loudest bang when the Cambodian incursion was announced. The potential for trouble on the college campuses was one aspect of the situation that the President may not have understood; otherwise he might not have conducted himself exactly as he did.

The President had spent the entire night of April 29–30 preparing his Cambodian speech, catnapping as he worked. He had evidently slept little or badly on the following night, that of his TV appearance, for he looked tired and haggard when he appeared at the Pentagon on the morning of May 1. There, speaking with people in a corridor of the building and remarking upon the more radical college rioters in contrast with the young men in Vietnam, he said something about "bums . . . burning up the books, storming around about this issue, I mean . . . you name it." To anyone who saw the incident on television it was evident that the President did not know he was being recorded; he was standing with his back nearly toward the camera, the corridor was badly lighted for the purpose, and the whole affair was obviously unplanned. However, a politician of Nixon's experience even in deep fatigue probably should have known better.

Then came the tragedy of Kent State University, most vividly recalled by three unforgettable news photographs: a boy silhouetted against a cloud of tear gas, his long hair flying, his arm upraised in the act of throwing something . . . a group of national guardsmen, gas-masked and helmeted, with leveled rifles, firing . . . and a girl, her mouth widely opened in a scream, kneeling over a boy from whose body blood was flowing. The toll at Kent State: two young men and two girls shot to death and several wounded. It was the Boston Massacre of the youth rebellion, and the whole country recoiled from it in shock and horror.

Within the next few days the United States went through a disturbance that for scope and divisiveness had not been paralleled since the Civil War. In fact, had the division been regional, as it was in 1861, instead of running through home, community, office, school, union, church, and practically every other unit of society, a civil war or a secession might very well have resulted. What President Nixon had hoped would be accepted as a limited action to clear the flank of our troops in Vietnam and speed their departure, and which he had carefully explained as such, touched off a mushrooming cloud of protest. Some of the criticism, as was to be expected, was not altogether fair or rational. For example, it was asserted that the tone of Nixon's remarks about the radical college demonstrators had encouraged the guardsmen to fire at Kent State. And the cry on campuses, "We're Nixon's bums," was raised with an alacrity indicating an undue desire to take offense. On the other hand, the President was being somewhat less than tactful or compassionate when he said of the Kent State shootings that they "should remind us all once again that when dissent turns to violence it invites tragedy."

From Maine to California, college communities rose in revolt. Thirty-four alarmed college presidents sent Nixon a letter that read in part, "We implore you to consider the incalculable dangers of an unprecedented alienation of America's youth and to take immediate action to demonstrate unequivocally your determination to end the war quickly."

By May 12 about 450 of the nation's approximately 2,500 two-year and four-year colleges and universities were reported to be on strike.

There were innumerable incidents of violence and confrontation with law enforcement officials. Vandalism was widespread. At least thirty R.O.T.C. buildings were firebombed.

One student, carrying a sign that said, "For God's Sake, End the War," doused himself with gasoline and set himself afire in protest, and as he lay dying asked his mother to write to President Nixon telling him that her dead son had felt that the President was contributing to violence and chaos, and his mother wrote the letter as requested.

There were reverberations all around the world. Moscow and Peking denounced the United States; that was to be expected. But there were also protests in friendly countries. In London the heads of pigs were dumped in front of United States corporation offices. A crowd of students in West Berlin gathered and compared the United States with Nazi Germany. In Sydney 100,000 demonstrated. There were clouds of tear gas in Manila, sniper shots in Caracas—all related to the Cambodian attack.

As though taken aback by all the hell raised by his decision (although how far aback he had been taken is by no means certain) President Nixon made extraordinary efforts at conciliation. When 60,000 to 100,000 college students came to Washington to demonstrate on May 9, he allowed them to use the Ellipse, an area near the White House. That morning, after another nearly sleepless night, he arose at 4 A.M. and went to the Lincoln Memorial, where he held a remarkable predawn conference with about 50 students. During the day members of his staff and of government departments sought out and talked with hundreds more. Nevertheless there was great uneasiness among the youngsters and among many of their elders. For although the President was willing and anxious to discuss the matter with youthful dissenters, his conciliatory efforts did not extend as far as expressing any remorse about Cambodia. The whole affair was an awesome demonstration of the powers of the United States Presidency; people had known, of course, in general what these powers are; but they had also realized that in a democracy rulers who do not do as the majority wishes get thrown out of office when their terms expire, and the consciousness of this possible fate on the part of elected officials had always been thought sufficient to restrain them from disregarding the majority will.

Now—and no one could think of another case quite like it in our history—here was a President who had completely slipped the bonds of this restraint! So what next? Into the Middle East with troops? Or into communist sanctuaries in North Vietnam or China? What was to prevent it?

It was this disregard of the Congress and of the public that came as such a shock to the country. All modern governments, even the totalitarian, depend to some extent upon the consent of the governed. Even Hitler did not dare launch his foreign adventures until he was sure he had the majority of the German people

8

behind him, nor did he ever completely disregard public opinion. In the captured archives of the Third Reich were found records of a system of reports designed for keeping Nazi leadership constantly informed on the state of the public mind. And it does not necessarily follow that when a nation is taken over by a communist government all activity of this sort comes to a halt and concern about what people are thinking ceases; there is, for example, a Czechoslovak Institute of Public Opinion. All this is not to suggest that the President of the United States has taken on Nazi or Red dictatorial powers—an implication that would be ridiculous —but to point to one of the problems of American patriotism that emerged very clearly in May, 1970: the fact that the President is boss of United States foreign policy under our system as it is currently operating, and if your idea of what is best for the country is not the same as his, there is not much that you and those who share your opinion can do about it until the next presidential election comes around.

President Nixon, with the information available to him, did what he thought was right. There were many who agreed with him or who came to agree with him after they had shared some of his information. And there were many who, once the decision had been made, decided that they ought to support him—the traditional reaction of the American public in times of crisis. All this added up to an after-the-fact majority of support for the President, although the slimness of the majority was also a measure of the great division of opinion within the country. In a Gallup Poll conducted right after the Cambodian incursion, 57 per cent of the respondents gave Mr. Nixon a vote of confidence for his handling of the Presidency—up four points from a similar poll in March. Results of a nationwide Harris survey announced on May 25 might have been interpreted as saying that Mr. Nixon's supporters outnumbered his opponents, but it, too, indicated the tremendous rift in America: 50 per cent of the respondents thought Nixon was right on his Cambodian decision, 43 per cent had serious doubts, and 7 per cent were not sure; and there were deep divisions between the old and the young, small town and city

9

dwellers, men and women, and people of the South and the West versus those of the Northeast (the first-named being the strongest supporters of Nixon in each case).

One might have thought after exposure to the mass media that denunciation of the President's action was virtually universal. But the polls proved what has often been proved before: that the American people have a way of rallying around the President after an important foreign policy decision.

The amount of support that Nixon received was not surprising to political scientists or to people who have served on a White House staff; they point out that although the President is the central target for complaints, he traditionally has strong emotional support from the people—and that this allegiance goes to the office, not just to the man who is holding it.

As for the chasms in public opinion that developed, the most important was between two classes: those who supported the President and those who did not. But the Cambodian decision had also opened a Pandora's Box of other divisive issues. There were questions of general foreign policy, of the influence of the military, of the powers of the Executive versus those of Congress, and so on, and these were far from being merely side-bar arguments. For the American who wishes to be patriotic, they raised the more general question: To whom should I be loyal and to what?

There was also some indication of blacks splitting away from whites, not so much because of Cambodia as because the whole uproar was diverting attention away from a vision of America in which the lot of the socially and economically disadvantaged would be improved and from efforts to achieve that improvement. This view was typically expressed in a position paper of the Black Student Union at the University of Maryland, which said, "While whites engage in infantile disorders, black student and community needs go untended." Less than two weeks after the Kent State shootings, police fired into a crowd of stone-throwing Negro youths at Jackson State College in Mississippi, killing two and wounding others. The Kent State shootings had made front page headlines all across the country, while public attention and concern for the Jackson State victims was visibly much less, and the black students commented upon this contrast bitterly.

By mid-May it would have been hard to find any classification of our society not affected by serious disunity as a result of the Cambodian decision.

The normal amount of not seeing eye-to-eye that exists between the Executive and the Congress widened into a deep gulf. Splits also developed within the Congress itself and within the Executive branch. The Senate Committee on Foreign Relations, which for some years had been trying to arrange a Runnymede that would bring the monarch in the White House to book, fell back upon a drastic measure—evidently the only effective one its investigations had revealed as being reliable. It approved an amendment to cut off funds for future military operations in Cambodia.

This was followed by proposals for other amendments and resolutions denying funds for combat in Vietnam after a certain date, repealing Congressional approval of the war as expressed in the Tonkin Gulf Resolution, forbidding future use of troops anywhere abroad without the consent of Congress, and so on—all haunted by the possibility that Congress might at some time in the future be castigated for having tied the President's hands at a critical point in some unforeseen military operation. Also to be faced was the accusation that for the first time in our history in the middle of a war the Congress had attempted to discredit an American President and embarrass him in the eyes of the world. Thus at some hazard Congress struggled to bring into the open long-standing and perplexing constitutional issues having to do with the powers of a President to make foreign commitments and involve the nation in war. Rifts also appeared in the President's official family. In a letter that leaked to the press, the Secretary of the Interior chided the President for allegedly cutting himself off from the nation's youth and from members of his own cabinet. More than 250 State Department and foreign aid employees signed a letter criticizing the Cambodian adventure.

The business community, normally thought of as a stronghold

11

of Republican conservatism, also gave evidence of alarm and divisiveness. More than a thousand New York lawyers stopped work for a day in order to go to Washington to urge immediate withdrawal from Indochina, and another thousand attorneys in Washington joined them. In other communities lawyers and businessmen contributed to funds solicited by young people for the purpose of financing protest trips. The heads of three of America's largest corporations, throwing aside their usual caution concerning stockholder and governmental relations, publicly condemned the prolongation of the war, while the stock market, refuting a belief widely held, especially among the young, that wars are for the benefit of big business, dropped like a shot duck.

As might have been expected, the American flag became a center of controversy and interest, and this situation was one that had been building up for several months. The nationwide appearance of small flag decals in the windows of cars, houses, and shops had begun to be extremely noticeable in 1969. Accordingly, the agents of polltaker Louis Harris had gone around interviewing those who were showing the flag in order to find out what they intended to declare through this display.

In one way the results were reassuring. In many quarters the little flags had been interpreted as meaning support for something reactionary, warlike, or even sinister, such as "law and order" repression of the blacks and the young, dedication to the Vietnam war, or even a widespread plot to establish the dominance of rightist factions. But when the people behind the window flags were asked what they thought they were symbolizing, only 2 or 3 per cent said they meant to convey antiradical or prowar sentiments; the ascribed meanings had mostly to do with faith and pride in the United States, devotion to freedom, and other uncontroversial ideas. And the flag people were not found to be significantly concentrated in any particular groups, schools of thought, or localities.

However, when a national cross section was questioned at the same time as to whether patriotism in America was thought to be declining, 55 per cent said yes, and the reasons given illuminated one widely accepted meaning of patriotism in this country today.

The stated reasons for the decline included draft evasion, disrespect for the government and the President, disenchantment with the war in Vietnam, youth riots, and racial turmoil. Thus by a sort of obverse impression, there was evidence of what might otherwise have been suspected: that a certain body of belief had captured the flag and made it stand for unquestioning loyalty to the government, readiness to support or serve in whatever war the government wishes to engage in, and general allegiance to the social, political, and economic status quo. This was confirmed by the attitudes of certain contending factions in May, June, and July, 1970. For example, the more violent of the youthful dissenters, sworn foes of "the establishment," spat and stamped upon the flag, while their opponents clung fiercely to the national banner and often defended it with clubs and fists.

Nowhere was the clash between these schools of patriotism more dramatic than in New York City. Here on May 8 a crowd of construction workers, wearing their helmets (and adding the phrase "hard-hat patriotism" to the language), charged behind a cluster of flags, somewhat in the manner of a Civil War infantry regiment, and routed student antiwar demonstrators in a melee that left seventy persons injured. Then they stormed City Hall and forced officials to raise to full staff a flag that had been flying at half staff in memory of the Kent State students who had been killed by the national guardsmen. The workers also tried to tear down the flag of an Episcopal church, under the impression, the rector thought, that it was a Vietcong flag. Marches and demonstrations by construction workers and longshoremen—who displayed American flags and signs such as "America, Love It or Leave It"—continued almost daily through the rest of May, mainly in the financial district, where the Dow-Jones average was dropping to a seven-year low. The spectacle of Wall Street bankers and brokers cheering the workmen represented a somewhat unusual coalition, and the leftist labor press did not fail to remark upon this, warning the construction workers and longshoremen that these Wall Street wolves were only waiting to slash their misguided throats when the opportunity presented itself. But actually, there was less difference between the workers and the brokers than their costumes might indicate; *The New York Times Magazine* ran a feature article about one of the hard-hat patriots and presented him as earning from $15,000 to $18,000 a year and owning a $40,000 two-family home.

Labor was less unanimous in its opinion than these demonstrations might suggest. On May 21 there was an antiwar rally by members of several New York City unions joining with students. And on May 24 the head of the 417,000-member Amalgamated Clothing Workers of America, one of the nation's largest trade unions, broke with the pro-Administration AFL-CIO leadership and condemned the President's Cambodian incursion. Also, around the country, union leaders reported that the backlash by workers was not entirely because they were prowar but because they were reacting to the violence of student protests.

As one worker put it, "If those kids want to be against the war it's okay by me. I might even agree with them. But when they spit on the flag and call the President a pig, that's where I get off."

The effect of student incivility was otherwise apparent. A *Newsweek* poll conducted by Gallup in mid-May asked the question, "Who do you think was primarily responsible for the deaths of four students at Kent State University?" and 58 per cent responded, "Demonstrating students." This result was not surprising to polltakers who had sampled public opinion following the August, 1968, antiwar demonstrations in Chicago and who had found that the general attitude was strongly against the youthful protesters in spite of largely sympathetic media coverage. In late May a referendum in Oregon to lower the voting age from 21 to 19 was roundly defeated, and reaction to campus disorders was thought to have been the reason. In June the voters in Maine turned down a large bond issue for their relatively innocent state university, where the most conspicuous demonstration had taken the form of a mass blood donation, and the chancellor of the university told a congressional subcommittee he thought that public irritation over campus violence had had something to do with the rejection. All across the country, state legislators, college alumni, corporate donors, and other sources of funds also reacted to the unrest, and the reduction of appropriations and giving, coming at the worst possible time—just when the collapse in Wall Street had cut investment values—was a near-disaster for many colleges and universities. Soon there were reports that some might have to close and others would need to shut down whole departments. For several years development officers had been pressing alumni and legislatures hard, and many of the potential benefactors, some of whom may have been looking for an out anyway, took the demonstrations as excuses for tightening the purse strings. In this respect, there was a crumb of comfort for college officials in Kenneth Keniston's *Young Radicals,* the intensive study of protesting youth published in 1968. Keniston had pointed out that demonstrations were taking place only on a very few of the nation's hundreds of campuses, and that it is mainly an institution's reputation for academic excellence, not for radicalism, that attracts protest-prone students to it. Possibly the colleges and universities struck by demonstrations in May, 1970—which are considerably more than a few—will now be able to display their scars as marks of academic prestige and as additional evidence that they are worthy of financial support.

At any rate, it was the relative few that received most of the attention from the media, to the extent that the much larger and more conservative part of the college population was largely overlooked. For example, with their attention focused on campuses where riots were going on, people tended to begin thinking of all college students in America as being opposed to the R.O.T.C. The National Association of State Universities and Land-Grant Colleges sent questionnaires to its 101 members in the spring of 1970 to find out what the score was. (Contrary to popular belief, R.O.T.C. is not required by law at land-grant colleges, and in only five of the universities questioned had it been made compulsory.) The result showed that in most of the schools the continuation of R.O.T.C. was assured. In fact, student referendums or polls at such widely separated campuses as the University of Montana, Purdue, and the University of Virginia showed that majorities of students wanted to keep the program. At Rutgers 79 per cent favored keeping it in some form. At the

University of Colorado the majority was more than three to one. It was overwhelming at Michigan State and Pennsylvania State. The only university reporting a referendum showing a majority in favor of removing R.O.T.C. was the State University of New York at Buffalo. On many campuses the program was in the process of undergoing extensive changes, but quantitatively at least R.O.T.C. seemed to be in no serious trouble in its relations with a large and important part of the college population.

So there was division in the world of education, more than met the eye, more than one would gather from reading the newspapers, watching television, or listening to radio. And this was true even in the lower echelons of education. At the high school from which one of the Kent State martyrs had graduated, the controversy had a most pathetic note; one faction wanted to fly the flag at half staff for the dead girl, another objected. They compromised by flying one flag for the girl at half-staff and another for the Vietnam war dead at full staff on a second pole.

One of the most interesting situations of all had to do with opinions within the churches. There exists a strange relationship between patriotism and religion. Both are characterized by symbols (for example, the flag and the cross), rituals, sacred writings and music, relics, and hallowed grounds. Also, it seems, by heatedly disputed doctrines. And both are capable of generating about the same high degree of intolerance, except that in the United States, under the precedents of the Constitution and a sort of gentleman's agreement, we have accommodated ourselves to respecting the other fellow's religion, no matter how outlandish we may privately think it is. (Unless we are to engage in internecine holy wars revolving around questions of national loyalties, the time may have come for us to develop a similar respect for the other fellow's patriotism.)

There is also a natural-seeming correlation between certain schools of patriotism and kinds or degrees of religious belief. This was illuminated in the spring and summer of 1968 by studies covering nine denominations of Protestant clergymen in California. Even at that time, months prior to the Cambodian uproar, this survey revealed a great division of opinion on the Vietnam war among the clergymen, with hawks slightly outnumbering the doves and a great range of attitudes from the fundamentalists (very hawkish) through the conservatives (somewhat less hawkish) to the neo-orthodox and liberal ministers (dovish). This range was somehow not surprising when considered along with attitudes toward the war in the conservative-to-liberal spectrum generally. As between Catholics and Protestants, a Gallup Poll in October, 1969, indicated that there was no tremendous difference when it came to believing that the Vietnam war was a mistake; 53 per cent of the Catholics thought so and 59 per cent of the Protestants, with the prowar people about 35 per cent in each case and the "no opinions" roughly comparable.

Such figures indicated substantial disunity as the year 1969 ended, and in May, 1970, differences within the churches were further exacerbated as they were everywhere else by the Cambodian affair. Typically, in New Britain, Connecticut, when two students delivered antiwar messages at a Sunday mass in St. Mary's Church, 150 parishioners walked out and began circulating a petition asking for the removal of the pastor who had allowed the students to appear. And at a convention of the Episcopal Diocese of Connecticut a proposal for a resolution urging the withdrawal of United States troops from Vietnam and Cambodia was tabled after heated controversy.

There was trouble in the military as well as in the civilian world. A Concerned Officers' Movement had been organized as an outlet for dissent, and one of its leaders estimated that a substantial number of junior officers in all the services were now opposed to the war. NBC-TV reported that a number of men in one company when ordered into Cambodia had been on the point of revolt. On CBS-TV it was reported that military morale was low, and the muttering of one soldier, shown as he boarded a helicopter for the troop movement, was almost mutinous. In Washington the draft director said that the Cambodian campaign was going to make his job "an awful lot tougher." It was tough enough already. A few days previously the Oakland draft center, which handles draftees for all of northern California, had reported that more than half of those ordered to report for induction were not even showing up, and that 11 per cent of those who did report were refusing to serve. It was about the same story in New York City, where many men had failed to appear in April and the city had not met its quota. The recalcitrants probably would not be taken to court for a couple of years, if ever, because prosecutors were swamped under a backlog of accumulated draft cases. By this time draft-avoidance counseling had become a nationwide industry, with thousands of attorneys handling draft cases and hundreds of groups offering counseling services. Draft boards were bogged down under the load of objections and appeals; many were further impeded by raiders who destroyed or disarranged their files.

Outside one induction center, prospective draftees who were arriving by bus were met by young women who gave them leaflets explaining how they might avoid conscription. One young man refused with the statement that his country needed him, and he loved his country. The girl offering the draft-counseling service assured him that she loved her country too. The boy then remarked that they must be talking about two different kinds of love and went through the door into the induction station.

That was about it—different kinds of love and visions of a different kind of America. Undoubtedly there were a few people abroad during these troubled days who hated America and wished to do it harm. Most, however, seemed to be expressing some kind of devotion even in dissent. The very intensity of these emotions constituted the chief danger. McGeorge Bundy, whose advice had had something to do with putting our increased forces into Vietnam in 1965, said of the Cambodian decision that anything like it again would tear the country to pieces and the chances of a serious and general domestic upheaval would be real.

The tidal wave of emotion and concern took many people by surprise, including those furthest left among the college radicals. If they had had more warning, with their talent for organization and communication, the radicals could have undoubtedly produced confrontations and disturbances much larger and more spectacular than those that took place. As it happened, much of the aroused college population rushed on past them and escaped their manipulative efforts; these were the masses of hitherto moderate students who had previously not been conspicuous in The Movement. At the mass demonstration on May 9 in Washington it was observed that many young people were bored with speeches being made by the radicals. Although demonstrations continued, one of the most important efforts took the form of pressure applied through established political procedures. Large groups of students and faculty members (in the case of Haverford, nearly the whole college) went to Washington to buttonhole congressmen and press for an end to the war. More than a thousand Princeton students began working for antiwar candidates as part of a New Congress Movement, and the plan spread to more than three hundred other campuses. By the middle of May the capital was full of youngsters lobbying for peace and organized into at least twenty-five different groups, not to speak of many independent delegations. Besides these direct meetings with the legislators, many planned to work in the home districts of congressmen to defeat those who would not pledge their efforts toward the ending of the war. How successful these efforts could be, with the elections only a few months away, was problematical. And how successful an antiwar congressman could be was also in question. But if the staying power of the young people could match their initial energy, this turn of events promised great hope for the Republic.

There was also evident in many aspects of the college reaction a surge of patriotism that transcended the more immediate concerns of previous demonstrations. True, it was antigovernment, at least anti-Administration with respect to the current policy. But it was very much procountry, and this often came out in words.

For example, in a strike meeting at Bowdoin College a professor who was protesting Nixon's decision said, "It's not his country, it's our country!" And Parsons School of Design in Manhattan tried to convey the idea in pictures as well as words; it canceled a scheduled showing of student work and replaced it with a new exhibit entitled, "My God! We're Losing a Great Country!"

In very little of the dissent could it be said that the students were being unpatriotic if we believe that it is a service to criticize one's country and to try to set it right when one is convinced that it is wrong.

One thing people learned—or were strongly reminded of—in the months of May and June, 1970, is that it is very difficult to be patriotic without getting angry. Patriotism is a subject that is hard to write about or discuss objectively: try as he will, the writer or speaker will at times slip off his tightrope and betray a little animus, or set of mind, one way or the other. Patriotism is very personal and very emotional. And it appears to be particularly so in America, where we do not enjoy the comfort, the freedom from anxiety and doubt, that come from the direct, single-minded allegiance to the state that is the desideratum of totalitarian government.

It is the flare of anger, the blur of emotion, that often obscures recognition of something that should be obvious but that is at times difficult to see: the fact that patriotism in America is such an individual matter. That being so, it probably cannot be defined in a way that will satisfy everyone, but the events of May to July, 1970, added to others in our history, have almost dictated a definition: *love of country and readiness to act in its best interests as indicated by individual conscience and judgment.*

This definition, whatever its failings may be, rests upon a devotion that must be genuine. It allows that we may think of the radical as a patriot if his schemes are motivated by love and seem to have, in his mind at least, some constructive purpose. It also allows us to judge, as any prudent person must, an individual whose expressions are those of hate and destruction and who has no plan for replacing the edifice he hates and wishes to destroy.

To illustrate: in May, 1970, on the Yale campus, two slogans were seen painted on walls. One said, "SMASH THE STATE," and the other said, "SMASH AMERICA." By a liberal stretch of the imagination, it is possible to concede that the first might have been written in a spirit of patriotism, if the writer had in mind replacing the demolished state with something better. But most people cannot bring themselves to believe that the fellow who wrote the second was in a patriotic mood. Once upon a time we would have said that the idea is ridiculous anyway; you cannot smash the Rocky Mountains and the Mississippi River and everything else that is America. But today it apparently is physically possible to smash everything about it that matters, and this is one reason why patriots should be more concerned about the country than they ever have been.

In our definition the word "country" is chosen for the reason that it seems to stand for something all-embracing and a great deal larger than the word "nation." In America we have not always been a nation. But we always have been, and always will be, we hope, a country. When Nathan Hale said he regretted that he had but one life to lose for his country, there was no nation in the sense that we know it today—just a collection of colonies struggling to be free—and no national government except that of the British, in whose eyes Hale was a traitor. Use of the word "country" also avoids the difficulties of attaching patriotism to a particular government or part of government, which is often impossible and nearly always inappropriate. For example, Nathan Hale's words, had they been, "I only regret that I have but one life to lose for George Washington and the Continental Congress," would certainly not have come ringing down through the years with such credibility. President Wilson once told a large crowd of foreign-born people who had just been naturalized, "You have just taken an oath of allegiance to the United States. Of allegiance to whom? Of allegiance to no one, unless it be God. Certainly not of allegiance to those who temporarily represent this great Government. You have taken an oath of allegiance to a great ideal, to a great body of principles, to a great hope of the human race."

Finally, in its recognition of individual conscience and judgment, the definition denies that patriotism can be made the exclusive property of any class, group, or school of thought. A review of our history will show, in fact, that no such group has ever been able to corral patriotism and keep it—which should be encouraging to those who may now consider themselves to be on the wrong side of the tracks patriotically. If patriotism were otherwise, it might in the long run prove to be a fatal virtue; deeply entrenched in one habit of thought, the country might fail to recognize the variants that nature provides to adapt, save, and preserve its favored organisms.

CHAPTER TWO

God and/or Country

★   While the previously recorded events were going forward, a very curious piece of business was nearing its climax in the Supreme Court. It had to do with the draft law and the conscientious objector, and the outcome would demonstrate how, in the eyes of the Court, the meaning of conscience has been widened to include intellectual judgments as well as religious or purely moral convictions—hence its relationship to our definition that recognizes these qualities as essentials of patriotism in America.

A bit of historical background may serve to illuminate the significance of the decision.

In the Civil War—the first war in which the draft became a major factor—the problem of the conscientious objector was alleviated by the fact that a conscripted man could hire a substitute or pay a sum of money to the government to be excused. But there were many who refused to take this way out. Stonewall Jackson had a few conscientious objectors in his command, but not for long. He said they obeyed orders well enough even to the point of taking aim with their muskets, but getting them to take *correct* aim was another matter; therefore, his advice was that these people be left at home where they could work and produce supplies for the Army.

On the Union side, by the end of the war a firm policy had been evolved. The federal draft law as it stood in 1864 allowed exemptions for objectors who were members of religious denominations opposed to the bearing of arms and who were prohibited from doing so by the articles of faith of their denominations. An incident of the postwar years as related by Peter Brock in his book *Pacifism in the United States* indicates that official concern for the conscientious objector was not always completely altruistic. It seems there was a large group of Mennonites in Russia who were alarmed by a czarist conscription law passed in 1871 that put an end to the exemption from military service that they had enjoyed for a number of years. Mennonite delegates were sent to the United States and Canada, and since these were desirable immigrants—honest and hard-working—there was competition for them. Certain states even passed legislation freeing them from the liability for military duty if they would simply register as conscientious objectors. Russia realized its mistake and amended the rule to allow conscripted Mennonites to choose forestry as an alternative to military service. But it was too late. About ten thousand came to the United States and eight thousand to Canada. To what extent the many peace sects of England and Europe were attracted to the United States, both before and after the Civil War, because they thought they might have more freedom from the military authorities here would probably be difficult to determine, but this incident suggests that this idea may have been among the important considerations.

For World War I, Congress passed a draft act that included a provision similar to that of the Civil War: combat service was not to be required of members of any recognized, established religious sect that had a creed forbidding participation in war and whose convictions were against war, but persons so exempted were not to be excused from noncombat duty, and President Wilson by an executive order designated the Medical, Sanitary, Quartermaster, and Engineering Corps as noncombat services. Then the President's order went on to do something that had not been contemplated by Congress. It directed that persons certified by their local boards as exempt from combat services because of religious objections or *those who objected because of conscientious scruples* should be assigned to these noncombat duties when they reported to their military units.

Thus Wilson (and this was characteristic of the man whether it was his idea or not) had introduced something that was ahead of his time: the possibility that an individual could be exempted from combat duty on grounds of his own beliefs—not just by reason of a religious creed.

However, the Army still found itself with a group of obdurate and intractable young men on its hands. This was not a large group—never more than a few thousands—but it was a troublesome one because these were men who refused to wear the uniform or to perform even noncombat duty, which they considered as contributory to killing and to war. They were not punished summarily but were segregated in areas of the various camps they were in while a board appointed by the Secretary of War went around to examine them and report on who was really a conscientious objector and who was not. If a man proved to be the real McCoy, he could be given a "farm furlough," that is, sent to work on a farm in lieu of regular duty.

One of the members of the three-man board that went traveling around the country to the camps was Harlan Fiske Stone, later to take his place on the Supreme Court, and Stone thought it might be helpful to future Americans, particularly those serving on comparable boards, if he left a record of his experiences. This was published in the October, 1919, issue of *Columbia University Quarterly*.

Stone estimated that more than 80 per cent of the objectors appearing before the board belonged to well-organized religious sects. Those who made the best impression on him were the Quakers, because of "their high intelligence and their evident desire to render service to the country in its time of need so far as possible within the limits of their religious convictions." Other sects from isolated communities "presented a depressing example of dense ignorance of what was going on in the world." Undoubtedly the sect making the worst impression was represented by a church organized in Salt Lake City at the time the draft act was passed. Its principal article of faith was nonparticipation in war, and it had two members. Both, naturally, were conscientious objectors. Stone reported that there were many fanatics among the religious objectors, but the board found that it accomplished very little by trying to prove they were illogical, "for, after all, human experience teaches us that religious belief when firmly held refuses to surrender to logic or to science." The best that could be done was to test by whatever means were appropriate the sincerity of the fanatic in his belief, and presumably, since he was a fanatic, he was about as sincere as he could get.

It was the group of nonreligious objectors, however, that gave the board its real headaches. As Stone noted, "The President's order expressly recognized that scruples against participating in war might be conscientious although not religious. How to detect the presence of such scruples and to distinguish them from the mere extremist support of more or less novel social or political theories and from mere individualistic resistance to the will of the majority, such as one sometimes sees in the petulant disobedience of an ill-disciplined child, was the difficult task."

Few overt cowards or slackers were encountered. And the professed pacifists presented no real problem; each of them either had or had not a track record as a pacifist in civilian life. Young men from the colleges were the hardest to deal with in Stone's opinion. He criticized them as being egoists, glib, supremely confident of being right, and wholly indifferent to the record of human experience. They refused the farm furlough, yearned for martyrdom, complained when denied imprisonment. Nearly all, Stone noted, had been carefully reared in good families, but their experience had been confined to college or university life, and he was inclined to the belief that they were products, if not the victims "of an educational system which too often encourages dabbling in the social sciences and in the problems of contemporary civilization . . . without insisting on rigorous methods in the verification of data and in subjecting them to analysis. Education had taught these men to read and to talk; it had stirred their emotions and had given them information and opinions on almost every conceivable subject; but neither it nor the hard knocks of experience, which were lacking in their lives, had ever forced them to weigh evidence or to reach conclusions by the process of thought."

Also numerous among the nonreligious objectors, although not quite as difficult to handle, were the socialists, who considered the war a capitalistic and therefore immoral enterprise. Another and a pathetic group consisted of men to whom the prospect of bloodshed was pathologically repugnant and who often broke down during the interviews. Stone noticed that nearly all of these came from Russia or were of Russian descent, and he supposed they might have been affected by the violence that had recently occurred in that country. Of all the men examined by the board, only about four hundred were subjected to court-martial. They were usually convicted of disobeying orders and sentenced to prison terms, but clemency was extended to many after the war had ended.

This was the story of the nation's first experience with objectors who (thanks to President Wilson) were given an out for nonreligious as well as religious convictions. The draft act passed in 1940, with World War II approaching, made no allowance for the nonreligious; however, the act was more liberal than previous legislation; it did not require membership in a pacifist religious sect if the claimant's own opposition to war was based on "religious training and belief." In 1948 there was a further liberalization; Congress amended the language of the draft act to read that "religious training and belief" was to be defined as "an individual's belief in a relation to a Supreme Being involving duties superior to those arising from any human relation, but does not include essentially political, sociological, or philosophical views or a merely personal moral code."

All of these laws, of course, were on extremely shaky ground. The First Amendment to the Constitution says that Congress "shall make no law respecting an establishment of religion," and here was legislation that provided a religious benefit. Yet to declare the law unconstitutional would be to introduce massive confusion. When confronted with the issue, the Supreme Court chose to obliterate the constitutional infirmity of the law by removing the theistic requirement—"a remarkable feat of judicial surgery," as Justice John M. Harlan called it.

One of the most important tests was United States v. Seeger. In 1957 Daniel A. Seeger declared that he was conscientiously opposed to war in any form because of his religious beliefs; but he put quotation marks around the word *religious;* said that he preferred to leave the question as to his belief in a Supreme Being open rather than answer *yes* or *no;* and that his was a belief in and devotion to goodness and virtue for their own sakes and a religious faith in a purely ethical creed. He cited Plato, Aristotle, Spinoza, and others for support of his ethical belief in intellectual and moral integrity "without belief in God, except in the remotest sense." In 1965 the Court found in favor of Seeger and got around the challenge to God as follows:

"We have concluded that Congress, in using the expression 'Supreme Being' rather than the designation 'God,' was merely clarifying the meaning of religious training and belief so as to embrace all religions and to exclude essentially political, sociological, or philosophical views. We believe that under this construction, the test of belief 'in a relation to a Supreme Being' is whether a given belief that is sincere and meaningful occupies a place in the life of its possessor parallel to that filled by the orthodox belief in God of one who clearly qualifies for the exemption. Where such beliefs have parallel positions in the lives of their respective holders we cannot say that one is 'in a relation to a Supreme Being' and the other is not." And the Court concluded that Seeger's beliefs met these criteria.

Another customer, however, was considerably tougher. This was Elliott A. Welsh II. In applying for conscientious objector status, Welsh crossed out the words on the application "religious training and. . . ." Thus by implication he also rejected the words "Religious training and belief in this connection means an individual's belief in a relation to a Supreme Being involving duties superior to those arising from any human relation, but does not include essentially political, sociological, or philosophical views or a merely personal moral code."

Welsh made things even more difficult by coming very close to saying that his belief was what Congress said it could *not* be, essentially political, sociological, and so forth. In a letter to his local draft board he had written, "I can only act according to what I am and what I see. And I see that the military complex wastes both human and material resources, that it fosters disregard for (what I consider a paramount concern) human needs and ends; I see that the means we employ to 'defend' our 'way of life' profoundly change that way of life. I see that in our failure to recognize the political, social, and economic realities of the world, we, *as a nation,* fail our responsibility *as a nation.*"

For a fellow who had so readily placed his head so far within the noose, what could be done except to hang him? Not much, most people would say, and yet the Court managed the seemingly impossible in its opinion, announced in mid-June, 1970. It ruled in favor of Welsh in a five-to-three decision, Mr. Justice Harlan concurring with the result but not with the reasoning. Whereas Harlan had referred to the Seeger opinion as "surgery," he called this one a "lobotomy." The term may have been suggested to him by one passage of the opinion that almost seemed to say that Welsh needed a brain operation because his mind was not functioning properly on this question. [In the following, 6 (j) is the section of a Selective Service act providing the exemption.] "When a registrant states that his objections to war are 'religious,' that information is highly relevant to the question of the function his beliefs have in his life. But very few registrants are fully aware of the broad scope of the word 'religious' as used in 6 (j), and accordingly a registrant's statement that his beliefs are nonreligious is a highly unreliable guide for those charged with administering the exemption."

The opinion in favor of Welsh said in part, "If an individual deeply and sincerely holds beliefs which are purely ethical or moral in source and content but which nevertheless impose upon him a duty of conscience to refrain from participating in any war at any time, those beliefs certainly occupy in the life of that individual 'a place parallel to that filled by . . . God' in traditionally religious persons. Because his beliefs function as a religion in his life, such an individual is as much entitled to a 'religious' conscientious objector exemption under 6 (j) as is someone who derives his conscientious opposition to war from traditional religious convictions."

The Court also said, "We certainly do not think that 6 (j)'s exclusion of those persons with 'essentially political, sociological, or philosophical views or a merely personal moral code' should be read to exclude those who hold strong beliefs about our domestic and foreign affairs or even those whose conscientious objection to participation in all wars is founded to a substantial extent upon considerations of public policy. The two groups of registrants which obviously do not fall within these exclusions from the exemption are those whose beliefs are not deeply held and those whose objection to war does not rest at all upon moral, ethical, or religious principle but instead rests solely upon considerations of policy, pragmatism, or expediency."

The unusual way in which these conclusions have been arrived at—that is to say, many would consider, through a shoring up with added meanings of a law that is constitutionally imperfect —does not detract from their importance as related to patriotism. What has taken place has been a remarkable exercise in theology as well as jurisprudence. Thus we now see in the history of draft act legislation and interpretation an evolving concept of God, which is extremely liberal. He has tended to fade as a being "up there" or "out there" somewhere and to reappear in a more humanistic form—as a presence within the heart and mind, the spark of "celestial fire" that George Washington urged us to keep alive in our breasts.

If we take this interpretation of a guiding power that the Supreme Court now allows—that of an internal working of intellect and conscience—the old familiar saying of "God and Country" has more relationship to patriotism in America than it might at first seem to have. In recognizing that the individual does not need to follow certain of its orders if his moral and intellectual judgments forbid him to do so, the government also implies that if like judgments urge him to agree with its course of action, he will be all the more loyal and effective from being convinced that he is right. This latitude for individual decision as it has been discussed here applies, of course, to one of the hardest tests of patriotism: that of using lethal weapons in defense of the country. Yet a review of our history will indicate that both in peace and in war patriotism in America has never been a matter of blind obedience; in this, as in so many things, the American is a free man, with all the perplexities and problems that freedom entails.

CHAPTER THREE

When Patriots Were Rebels

★ In his book *The Loyal and the Disloyal*, Morton Grodzins points to an important difference between patriotism in a democracy and in a totalitarian state. In a democracy the individual is loyal to several groups and idea systems. The family, the school, the church, clubs, work organization, sports team, other groups with whom he is in frequent contact, along with their ideas, ideals, and standards, are objects of his allegiance and reward him by enriching his life in one way or another. And somehow all these loyalties, if they produce the desired life-satisfactions, merge and combine into loyalty to the nation. In a totalitarian state, on the other hand, every attempt is made by the government to capture or destroy all intermediate loyalties so that the individual's primary allegiance is directly to the state. The destruction of normal family life under the Nazi rule in Germany is a good example. (If we accept the Grodzins thesis, it must also follow that one of the best ways to undermine patriotism in a democracy is to make the citizen dissatisfied with as many as possible of the institutions that serve him, all the way from his Tuesday night bowling league to the great university to which he sends his children.)

Mr. Grodzins's concept seems to stand up every way it is

looked at in America, including historically. Allegiance to the United States grew up in increments. The two thousand or so Massachusetts militiamen and minutemen who on April 19, 1775, rushed from Essex, Middlesex, Norfolk, Suffolk, and Worcester counties to attack a British column on the Boston–Concord road had no nation to fight for. In fact, it is doubtful if they had any thought of independence at the time. Even when they had been gathered into the semblance of an army, the first American flag that flew above General Washington's headquarters at Cambridge had the alternating red and white stripes that are seen on the present flag, but instead of the field of stars in the corner, it displayed the British Union Jack, indicating that the colonies still hoped for some sort of continued association with the mother country. What the colonists were fighting for at the outset at least was simply their rights as Englishmen, the welfare of their communities, and for their homes. Many of them were unreliable soldiers for that very reason. The minutemen who had swarmed to Lexington came and went like bees. If there was a need for them at home, then home came first; planting and harvesting would not wait, and there was no welfare department to take care of a family whose head had not provided for it. In a larger way, the same concern for the near rather than the distant affected the whole genesis of the United States. First we were a group of colonies with an increasing commonality, then a wartime association, then a confederation of states, and only after several years a union. And even for decades after that, there was small loyalty to a national government in the sense that patriotism includes today.

The process by which we became a nation was gradual. In fact, what we like to call the Revolution was really a rebellion against King George and his Tory ministers resulting in separation, not a revolution in the sense of the French Revolution, which overturned and destroyed many social institutions. Americans had inherited from England a deep devotion to certain ideas, principles, and institutions, and these continued largely unchanged. For example, there were precedents in England for much that was written into the American Constitution—the most interesting being that of a strong President (monarch) operating under restraints of a Congress (Parliament).

So although there was a free and easy way about the new Republic, less pomp and ceremony, more liberal customs, and greater emphasis on democratic equality, it might be argued that the change was more one of manners than of political realities. Nevertheless, the severing of allegiance to the Crown wrenched many people badly. Merle Curti has written, "In many hearts the old ties of loyalty were broken with great difficulty and in many more—a majority, no doubt—there was no enthusiasm and much downright opposition to what Paine called 'the new method of thinking that hath arisen.' Families, friends and neighbors divided; some among the least-privileged classes took the Tory side, and many among the most aristocratic ranks threw themselves into the patriot cause."

"Into the patriot cause. . . ." The use of words is significant. It has always been customary to regard the rebels of 1775 as patriots and the loyal colonists as the nonpatriots, and this was the habit of thought, apparently, in the late eighteenth century in both America and France. But today the needle has swung to the other side of the dial, and patriotism has come to be associated more with those who support the national government and the general status quo than with those who want to make drastic changes. This suggests that patriotism does not always live on the same side of the street, and that people who have the most widely accepted concept of what is best for the country are most likely to be considered "patriotic."

Yet there is always plenty of room for argument. The new government of the United States had not been in existence more than five years when it discovered that rebellion was still very much a part of the American character. A levy on whiskey caused an uprising in western Pennsylvania among farmers who disposed of their surplus grain through distilling, and President Washington had to put the insurrection down by the use of military force. A rumor, which was never entirely laid to rest, had it that Alexander Hamilton had proposed the excise tax not just to obtain revenue but also to provoke a resistance that would give the new federal government an opportunity to demonstrate its strength.

Another early instance of patriots in opposition to one another was the War of 1812, which gave us the word "hawks" and the phrase "Mr. Madison's War" as a precedent for Mr. Johnson's and Mr. Nixon's War. The early school book story of this war and the one, in fact, on which President Madison based his message to Congress asking for a declaration of war was that Great Britain was impressing our sailors on the high seas, attacking our commerce, and blockading our ports while engaged in her struggle with Napoleon. But some of the facts did not fit the story. For example, the New England states, which had most of the shipping interests, were strongly against the war, while the western states, with no ships or ports, were strongly for it. The main reason for the war, of course, was that the "war hawks" of the West wanted to drive the British out of North America and take possession of Canada, wanted also to have a free hand in subduing the Indians who faced them on the frontier and who, they thought, were being protected in across-the-border sanctuaries and stirred up by the British. In the opinion of Samuel Eliot Morison, it was the most unpopular of all the wars the country has ever fought, including that in Vietnam. Dissent although not confined to New England was at its greatest there. The Yankees recognized the phoniness of the war slogan, "Free trade and sailors' rights," because their trade had not been greatly interfered with and they believed Britain was impressing few sailors other than those who were her actual subjects; further, it seemed wrong to be attacking England when she was standing as a bulwark of freedom against the tyrannous Napoleon. One of the hotbeds of feeling was Harvard College, and one of Harvard's protests took the form of awarding at the 1814 commencement honorary degrees to four men who had defied and obstructed the federal government in a number of ways. There were charges to the effect that New Englanders were plotting to secede from the Union, and if the war had not ended in 1814, there might indeed have been serious internal trouble.

One of the points of interest about the War of 1812 concerns what people could do to resist an unpopular war that they cannot do now. In 1970 the Massachusetts legislature passed a bill that provided that Massachusetts servicemen need not participate in a war that is undeclared and therefore unconstitutional, meaning, of course, the war in Southeast Asia. This had no hope of being effective. But in the War of 1812, when the cry "On to Canada" was ringing through the country, Massachusetts (and other New England states as well) refused to provide quotas of militia called for by the national government and in most cases made the refusal stick. The grounds were very simple: the Constitution said that the militia could be called into service of the United States for three specific purposes, to execute the laws of the Union, suppress insurrection, and repel invasion; and an attack into Canada certainly did not fall into any of these categories.

Madison asked for a conscription law toward the end of the war, and Daniel Webster responded with one of his thundering orations. "Is this, sir, consistent with the character of a free government? Is this civil liberty? Is this the real character of our Constitution? No, sir, indeed it is not. The Constitution is libelled, foully libelled. The people of this country have not established for themselves such a fabric of despotism. They have not purchased at a vast expense of their own treasure and their own blood a Magna Carta to be slaves. Where is it written in the Constitution, in what article or section is it contained, that you may take children from their parents, and parents from their children, and compel them to fight the battles of any war in which the folly or the wickedness of the government may engage it? Under what concealment has this power lain hidden which now for the first time comes forth, with a tremendous and baleful aspect, to trample down and destroy the dearest rights of personal liberty? Who will show me any constitutional injunction which makes it the duty of the American people to surrender everything valuable in life, and even life itself, not when the safety of their country and its liberties may demand the sacrifice, but whenever the purposes of an ambitious and mischievous government may require it?"

Webster went on to say that if the Congress could do such a thing as this based on its constitutional power to "raise armies," then based on its power to "borrow money" it could take a person's funds by force and make him take a note in return. He would be shocked to return today and see the government taking both our men and our money with equal facility and ease. It was an age of innocence in federal-state relationships. The War of 1812 did, however, demonstrate a quality of American patriotism that would endure: the fact that support would not be extended automatically to the national government for any sort of enterprise in which it might wish to become involved. The invasion of Canada was a flop; the land war, except for General Jackson's victory at New Orleans and a few other successes, went very badly; and had it not been for the triumphs of our Navy and the fact that Francis Scott Key wrote "The Star-Spangled Banner" after seeing the American flag survive a British bombardment of Fort McHenry, the War of 1812 would have added very little to our stock of patriotic lore.

But on the whole, the early years of the Republic were gloriously patriotic. The success of the War of Independence, as evidenced in both the material well-being and the spiritual happiness of Americans, had an exhilarating effect comparable to that of a shot of bourbon on an empty stomach, and, better than bourbon, the effect lasted for several decades. The Founders, who included some of the most brilliant men America has ever produced, were around for many years to lend the inspiration of their presence. Getting the Presidency off to a strong start, Washington came as close to being deified as any man in our history has ever come. He was idealized in person and in memory. As late as 1860 Artemus Ward, in his piece on the strong points of famous men, wrote, "Old George Washington's Fort was not to hev eny public man of the present day resemble him to eny alarmin extent. Whare bowts can George's ekal be fownd? I ask & boldly anser no whares, or eny whare else." When Lafayette revisited the country in 1824–25, his progress was marked by a continuous ovation while he was being enriched by gifts of $200,000 and a township of land.

People were singing Scott Key's new song about the flag, those who could remember the words, and the flag itself was everywhere in evidence. All the church bells were rung on the Fourth of July, an almost sacred holiday, and it was noted with awe, almost as a sign from heaven, that Thomas Jefferson and John Adams both died on July 4, 1826, the fiftieth anniversary of the Declaration of Independence. The glories of the new Republic and the heroic deeds of its soldiers and sailors were celebrated in song and story.

What also seems to have been extremely important in stimulating American patriotism was the physical beauty and distinctiveness of the country. If it be asked, Can a man love a country almost as he does a woman? the answer is probably *yes*. The physical importance of any given land is best exemplified by the situation of the Jews. A people so well integrated both religiously and racially could possibly have settled and formed the State of Israel in some other place—as a people—and could have done so with less peril to themselves and the world. But no other place would do. For two thousand years there had been a special meaning to the verse of the Psalms: "By the rivers of Babylon, there we sat down, yea, we wept, when we remembered Zion."

In hundreds of both insensible and sensible ways the tendrils of the land entwine themselves about the heart. The angle at which the light in a particular latitude falls at different times of day and year . . . the memory of a cowbell echoing over a pasture now deserted . . . the moving shine of wind-waves running over a wheatfield in August . . . the smell of lilacs . . . the color of a distant mountain or forest . . . the recollections that loved relatives or friends have left inseparably attached to a town, a street, a garden . . . of such stuff is love of country made to a greater degree than we may imagine.

For many years, mostly in the first half of the nineteenth century, leading writers worried about our failure to achieve literary independence from England, and they hoped that physical America itself—the majestic Rockies, the broad Mississippi, the vast plains, the rampaging herds of buffalo, and so on—would inspire the grand, distinctive, and truly American literature they were looking for. It never exactly happened that way, and Long-fellow pointed out why in his *Kavanagh:* A man does not become a great writer, he said, just because he happens to live next to a great mountain; literature deals with people not with landscapes. And yet once in a while this love of the land and its relation to American patriotism has been expressed in great passages of our literature. Most recently it has been reflected in the growing and widespread interest in conservation of our natural resources and the beauties of our environment, such as remain.

Although they still felt inferior to England in some ways—few of which they were willing to admit—the Americans who began the nineteenth century in this country did so with high hopes because they were living in a land of great natural wealth and opportunity under a constitution that promised the most rational and enlightened government the world had ever seen. But there was a flaw in their society—a fault that was to prove nearly fatal. The Declaration of Independence had been a white declaration; close to a million black people did not qualify for liberty and the pursuit of happiness. In his original draft of the Declaration, Thomas Jefferson referred to the slave trade in terms so severe that they might have been expanded into a denunciation of slavery itself, but in the discussions of the draft with the Continental Congress the opposite direction was taken: the condemnatory sentences were struck out. Again, during the Constitutional Convention in 1787, slavery was attacked on both moral and economic grounds; at one point only two Southern states were strongly defending it, and these upheld it not as anything good but as a necessary evil. Later, after the cotton gin and the industrial revolution in the textile business had fastened slavery upon the South much more firmly, it would be too late to abolish it with a piece of paper, so we must wonder in vain what blood and treasure might have been spared if America's original documents of incorporation had said that all men, black, white, or of any other color, were to be forever free within its boundaries. Because it has seemed that the patriotic support of Americans for their government depends to a very large degree on a belief that the government is doing what is right and good, this is pointed to as an instance of temporizing on a moral issue that did result in much confusion and suffering.

There was plenty of indication in the years 1846–48 that a large part of the American public would blow the whistle on an action by the government that they considered unjust. In 1846, in what was primarily a land grab, President James K. Polk ordered troops under General Zachary Taylor into a piece of territory "in dispute" between Texas and Mexico. This naturally provoked an attack by the Mexican Army, whereupon Polk asked Congress to pass a war and appropriations bill to support the soldiers in the field, a request that Congress did not dare refuse. (Does this situation sound familiar?) Even so, there was strong opposition in the Senate and in the House, where Congressman Abraham Lincoln spoke against the war, and widespread dissent expressed by editors, writers, and other leading citizens. In protest against the war, Henry Thoreau refused to pay his poll tax and the authorities jailed him for a night. But although they put Henry in the jug, they failed to bottle up his ideas. His famous essay "Civil Disobedience" was to live on through the years to become a manifesto of modern dissenters.

However, it was Albert Gallatin who commented on the war with Mexico in terms of the moral sense that seems to underlie American patriotism in times of its greatest ardor and that, when absent, seems to leave it without firmness or foundation. He told the people of the United States, "Your mission was, to be a model for all other governments and for all other less favored nations, to adhere to the most elevated principles of political morality, to apply all your faculties to the gradual improvement of your own institutions and social state, and, by your example, to exert a moral influence most beneficial to mankind at large. Instead of this, an appeal has been made to your worst passions; to cupidity, to the thirst of unjust aggrandizement by brutal force; to the love of military fame and of false glory; and it has even been tried to pervert the noblest feelings of your nature. The attempt is made to make you abandon the lofty position which your fathers occupied, to substitute for it the political morality and heathen patriotism of the heroes and statesmen of antiquity.

"I have said, that it was attempted to pervert even your virtues. Devotedness to country, or patriotism, is a most essential virtue, since the national existence of any society depends upon it. Unfortunately, our most virtuous dispositions are perverted, not only by our vices and selfishness, but also by their own excess. Even the most holy of our attributes, the religious feeling, may be perverted from that cause, as was but too lamentably exhibited in the persecutions, even unto death, of those who were deemed heretics. It is not, therefore, astonishing, that patriotism, carried to excess, should also be perverted. In the entire devotedness to their country, the people, everywhere and at all times, have been too apt to forget the duties imposed upon them by justice toward other nations. It is against this natural propensity that you should be specially on your guard."

In the years that have elapsed since Gallatin wrote these words, it has been demonstrated several times that morality and patriotism are not unconnected and that the American people respond to a national challenge most patriotically and therefore most effectively when they are convinced that their cause is just and right. Unfortunately, people have not always been as right as they thought they were, or have been "right" on opposite sides, as was the case in the Civil War.

CHAPTER FOUR

Abraham Lincoln's Tonkin Gulf

★ It cannot be said that consanguinity makes for harmony, at least not in the Anglo-Saxon race. Within a period of eighty-five years a people primarily of that descent was engaged in two major divisive conflicts: the War of Independence and the American Civil War.

The Civil War was a strange affair that must stand in many respects as the patriotic ideal in revealing the full depth of dedication of which Americans are capable. When it was over, half a million or more servicemen had died, hundreds of thousands had been wounded or invalided for life, and it was estimated that ten billion dollars had been spent—a trifle nowadays, but at that time twice as much as would have been necessary to purchase and free every slave in the South under a plan advocated in 1862. And what made it a war so distinguished for patriotism was that element that seems essential to a high degree of patriotic ardor— belief in a cause.

Just what the supreme difference consisted of is hard to say, as is so often the case after or even during a war. Historians are not in entire agreement as to an exact catalogue of reasons for the conflict, which grew out of a mixture of antagonisms. Few, however, would argue with the assertion that it was slavery that colored the prewar years with their most passionate emotions. Among many people in the North, the abolitionists in particular, slavery was a religious issue. Slave owners were told they were not Christians, and some were refused Communion, and the rage that this sort of thing engendered was certainly not the least of the causes of the war. In his Cooper Institute speech in 1860, Lincoln commented on the phenomenon of both sides being so passionately convinced that they were beyond reproach. The only thing that would satisfy the South, he said, was "this, and this only: cease to call slavery wrong and join them in calling it right." And in the same speech, "Their thinking it right and our thinking it wrong is the precise fact upon which depends the whole controversy. Thinking it right, as they do, they are not to blame for desiring its full recognition as being right; but thinking it wrong, as we do, can we yield to them?"

The Civil War was to some extent a holy war, which is the very worst kind, and the sense of this as it applied to the North is well exemplified by the "Battle Hymn of the Republic," the words of which are highly religious and which has God himself marching along at the head of the emancipating columns. In fact, the antislavery feeling on the part of many northern people was more ethical and religious than it was a genuine concern for the economic and social well-being of the blacks, as events of the next hundred years were unhappily to prove, but it was a strong emotion, nevertheless. On the part of the southerners there was an answering backlash of resentment against this overweening righteousness, a devotion to a life-style and culture that they felt was superior to northern industrial society, and a belief that the very principles that had justified the parting of America from Britain entitled them to go their own way. Both sides thought they were right. Both, as Lincoln remarked, read the same Bible and prayed to the same God, and each invoked His aid against the other.

To fan the blaze higher, talented sentimentalists, remarkable martyrs and madmen and fiery orators and propagandists were abroad. Harriet Beecher Stowe made millions weep with her *Uncle Tom's Cabin,* and upon meeting her Lincoln said, "So you're the little woman who wrote the book that made this great war." Elijah Parish Lovejoy lost his life at the hands of a mob and his name became sacred to the cause of abolition. John Brown awakened fear and hate by his murderous raid on Harper's Ferry. William Lloyd Garrison, in protest against slavery, set a precedent for draft card burners by burning the Constitution itself, calling it "a covenant with death and an agreement with hell."

Legend has it that the war was begun, appropriately enough, by one of the most fanatical patriots of either side, Edmund Ruffin, a grim old man with shoulder-length gray hair who would kill himself when the South was finally defeated. In the half darkness of early morning on April 12, 1861, Ruffin pulled the lanyard of a cannon on the shore of Charleston Harbor that was pointed at Fort Sumter; the muzzle flash, while illuminating the sand and surf in the near vicinity, also ignited the whole nation. And it very quickly put President Abraham Lincoln to the point of a decision. Troops and property of the United States had been attacked. How should he respond?

The situation was not unlike that which would confront President Lyndon B. Johnson in August, 1964, when United States destroyers were reportedly attacked in the Gulf of Tonkin. On that occasion Johnson ordered retaliatory action, and shortly afterward Congress passed a joint resolution approving and supporting the President in his determination "to take all necessary measures to repel any armed attack against the forces of the United States and to prevent further aggression" and then going on to say other things that were interpreted as congressional approval for later and more massive intervention in South Vietnam.

In Lincoln's case, however, there was no Congress to turn to for quick approval, for Congress (what there was left of it after the secession) was not in town, nor would it be until called to convene in July, 1861, nor did Lincoln seem to be in any particular hurry to call it to Washington.

Instead he went forward on his own initiative and authority with a series of actions that would make those of President Johnson in 1964-65 and even those of President Nixon on April 30,

1970, seem like deeds of gentle persuasion. By the time Congress met, he had a full-scale war in progress and 230,000 men under arms.

Of course there had to be the 1861 equivalent of the Tonkin Gulf Resolution in order to make an honest man of the President, and a joint resolution intended to legitimatize Lincoln's unconstitutional acts was introduced in the Senate on July 6. What had been Lincoln's transgressions in the preceding three months? We may listen to the indignant voice of Senator John C. Breckinridge: "The Constitution declares that the Congress alone shall have power 'to declare war.' The President has made war. Congress alone shall have power 'to raise and support armies.' The President has raised and supported armies on his own authority. Congress shall have power 'to provide and maintain a navy.' The President has provided an immense Navy, and maintains it without authority of law. The Constitution declares that no money shall be taken from the Treasury except in pursuance of appropriations made by law. The President has taken money from the Treasury without appropriations made by law for the purpose of carrying out the preceding unconstitutional acts." Nor was that all that Lincoln had done, and Breckinridge went on ticking off the charges: he had suspended the writ of habeas corpus in places, made unreasonable searches and seizures, taken people's property without due process of law, and even deprived citizens of their liberty unlawfully. Breckinridge denied that a President could violate the Constitution on the grounds of necessity. He declared that the joint resolution condoning Lincoln's actions would be valueless. "I deny, Mr. President, that one branch of this Government can indemnify any other branch of the Government for a violation of the Constitution or the laws."

In support of the stand taken by Breckinridge, Senator Anthony Kennedy asserted that to approve Lincoln's acts would be to establish "a precedent that may be seized upon hereafter, under the plea of necessity, for gross and palpable aggressions upon the Constitution of the country itself."

These are sentiments that would have sounded completely *au courant* in recent hearings of Senator J. William Fulbright's

Committee on Foreign Relations. Had the opponents of the resolution wanted to go further, piling personal upon legal embarrassment, they could have quoted from an autobiographical sketch that President Lincoln had written for use in his 1860 presidential campaign. In it Lincoln had said that he had opposed the war with Mexico because, for one reason, it was "unnecessarily and unconstitutionally begun by the President of the United States" and that it was unconstitutional "because the power of levying war is vested in Congress, and not in the President." And digging further back, into a speech that Lincoln had made on the Mexican War in Congress in 1848, they could have caught him on record as believing in a principle that condoned the action of the South: "Any people anywhere, being inclined and having the power, have the *right* to rise up and shake off the existing government, and form a new one that suits them better. This is a most valuable, a most sacred right—a right which, we hope and believe, is to liberate the world. Nor is this right confined to cases in which the whole people of an existing government may choose to exercise it. Any portion of such people that *can may* revolutionize and make their *own* of so much of the territory as they inhabit."

However, these stands that had been taken and the constitutional rules that had been established made no more difference than a wisp of cobweb that is brushed aside by a fireman rushing into a house to extinguish a blaze. No one made many bones about this.

In supporting the actions of the President, Senator Timothy O. Howe said, "I am going to vote for the resolution, and I am going to vote for it upon the assumption that the different acts of the Administration . . . were illegal, and not upon the assumption that they were legal and valid . . . I vote for these measures; and I approve them . . . all the more because the taking of them involved the President in some personal hazard. I will not approve them more; but I admire them the more because he did not hesitate to save the Republic, although the act of saving it might be attended by some personal risk to himself."

Howe then spread his oratorical wings and launched into one

of those great flights of classical eloquence of which modern senators have so deprived us. He cried, "Why, sir, I have heard that when a chasm opened in the Forum of Rome, it was said by the oracles that whatever was most precious in Rome, must go into it to close it; and a soldier, with his armor on, mounted his horse, and spurred him into the chasm; and I am told that the conscious earth closed over him. Sir, while your flag floats from yonder dome, let no man who loves the Republic ever forget that, in the year 1861, the President of the United States saw a horrid chasm opening to the Union of the States, and he did not hesitate a moment, clothed with all that was precious to him in the way of name or fame, to plunge himself into the chasm."

And Senator Henry S. Lane said, "I sanction and approve everything that the President has done during the recess of Congress, and the people sanction and approve it, and there is no power this side of Heaven that can reverse that decision of the American people."

Breckinridge recognized the inevitable with a wonderful oratorical flourish of his own: "I am quite aware that in the present temper of Congress, one might as well oppose his uplifted hand to the descending waters of Niagara as to reason or to appeal against the contemplated proceedings. . . . We can only hope that this flash of frenzy may not assume the form of chronic madness."

The resolution was passed and incorporated as the third section of an Act of August 6, 1861, to increase the pay of privates in the Army "and for other purposes" and read as follows: "That all the acts, proclamations, and orders of the President of the United States, after the 4th of March, 1861, respecting the army and navy of the United States, and calling out or relating to the militia or volunteers from the States, are hereby approved and in all respects legalized and made valid, to the same intent and with the same effect as if they had been issued and done under the previous express authority and direction of the Congress of the United States."

The congressman who had said that "no power this side of

Heaven can reverse that decision of the American people" told the whole story. From a distance of more than a hundred years it may seem as if for a few days following the firing on Sumter, Lincoln had the power of war or peace in his hands. That is extremely doubtful. The course he took was probably less dangerous to him personally and politically than a decision to ignore the insult to the national sovereignty would have been. Lincoln was acting on a powerful emotional mandate from the people of the North. In fact, when the war was nearly over, he would say, "I claim not to have controlled events, but frankly admit that events have controlled me."

The contrast between the situation of President Lincoln in April, 1861, and that of President Johnson in 1965, or more particularly that of President Nixon in April, 1970, is striking. All three executives exercised strong and unusual initiative, with Lincoln far outdistancing Johnson and Nixon in that respect. And all three did what they believed was best for the country. In response, the people reacted to Johnson's and Nixon's decisions with anger (slow in one case, fast in the other). But the people of the North rallied overwhelmingly behind Lincoln. For a few months at least, even the Democratic party in the North gave its full support to the war, and its leader, Stephen A. Douglas, visited the White House to give Lincoln this assurance personally. All over the North there were patriotic speeches, parades, and war meetings. Recruiting stations could not begin to accommodate all the men who wanted to enlist.

Recalling our definition of patriotism in America—that it is love of country and readiness to act in its best interests as indicated by individual conscience and judgment—it is perfectly apparent that the reason the people supported Lincoln so wholeheartedly was that his ideas and theirs as to what was best for the country were very nearly in complete accord. (It must also be concluded that when this condition prevails, constitutional impediments are stepped over very lightly.)

There was another element making for patriotic unity in 1861, and that was the fact that the national government was taken to be so representative of the country as a whole; in fact, a desire to preserve the integrity of that government became the North's strongest motivation once the war had begun.

There was apparently no such devotion to the Confederacy, as a government, in the South. Nevertheless there was as great a patriotism, with just as distinct a country as the object of allegiance. Somehow the South attained the status of a separate nation, even though it was not supposed to. The federal government in Washington took care never to recognize the Confederate government, and on that basis the conflict should have always been called an "insurrection" or a "rebellion"—never a war. But the grandeur of the struggle made it a war in spite of all that. It would come to be known as the Civil War, or the War Between the States. And its records would finally be published by the Government Printing Office in Washington under the title *War of the Rebellion!*

Robert E. Lee, who might have become known as a traitor, is seldom thought of except as an American patriot, and there was more than a little significance in the way he referred to the South in his good-by to the Army of Northern Virginia: "With an unceasing admiration of your constancy and devotion to your Country and a grateful remembrance of your kind and generous consideration for myself, I bid you all an affectionate farewell."

CHAPTER FIVE

Bullets and Ballots: A Unique Test of Patriotism

★ In looking for a northern campus that would be typical of the times and that would provide a fixed point from which to view the Civil War as well as wars that have followed, one could probably do no better than to settle upon Colby College in Waterville, Maine. It was and is not a Yale or Harvard, yet it has never been so small as to be inconspicuous. As was the case with so many colleges, Colby was chartered by a religious denomination, Baptists, early in the nineteenth century, and it was given over initially to "literary and theological" studies that over the years became the liberal arts curriculum. Its students were idealistic; inspired by a visit of William Lloyd Garrison, they founded an antislavery society. But they were also at times youthfully crass; the president of the college once scolded them in this manner: "After all the pains we have taken to refine and elevate your feelings, some of you have a taste so low and boorish, that you can be pleased with noises which resemble the yells of a savage or the braying of an ass." They seem to have been not too different from college students today.

Colby was to have strong associations with the Civil War, producing the antislavery martyr Elijah Parish Lovejoy and also Ben Butler. When the news of Fort Sumter arrived on the campus, youthful ebullience erupted into a demonstration of patriotism that was being duplicated all over the North. Years later one alumnus reminded a classmate: "You remember better than I that spring day in 1861, when we heard the maddening news of the first attack on the flag. And you remember how you and Hall hunted up somewhere an old drum, mustered Dekes and Zetas and neutrals of all classes, and led the motley crowd through the frantically excited town." The boys, he recalled, listened to a speech by a local politician, but it was not patriotic enough, "not pitched on a key at all corresponding to the blazing enthusiasm and sacred rage of the youths before him."

That very afternoon, drill was started on the campus, and soon the young men were going off to war. A little more than a year later, Zemro Smith, who had been scheduled to graduate in the class of 1862, was writing back to friends at Colby that he was a "high private" receiving thirteen dollars a month and that "I should like to graduate . . . but now I feel that I could not be doing my duty without volunteering. My country demands my aid—to this country & its institutions, I owe all that I am or ever hope to be; and situated as I am I feel that I am a coward and a knave if I do not volunteer. Emery, I can give my blood to cement the Union—to strengthen the government, but I never will see her call for aid—never, never, see the government destroyed."

If the words sound ingenuous, they were no more so than those being written and spoken by thousands of young men whose records on the battlefield proved that they meant exactly what they had been saying.

Nathaniel B. Coleman, another young man from Colby College, became a company commander in the 20th Maine, a regiment that was destined to become famous because of its defense of Little Round Top at Gettysburg. The lieutenant colonel of the regiment was Joshua Chamberlain, from nearby Bowdoin College, and many of the captains and lieutenants were also college men. They constituted the Civil War equivalent of the R.O.T.C., and there was an amusing instance of how regular and civilian soldiers get integrated in time of war. The colonel of the regiment was a hard-as-nails West Pointer named Adelbert Ames (his toughness would be proved by the fact that he lived to be the last Union general officer aboveground), and Ames wanted to whip his volunteer regiment into shape, but he hammered it a little too hard. The result was that the line officers presented him with a "paper of reprimand" that they all signed. Things were on the edge of being explosive for a while, but there was a conciliatory meeting, and the civilian officers managed to cure the colonel of some of his bad habits, such as swearing at them, while he on the other hand stood up for needed measures of discipline. The result was an extremely effective fighting force, and the men of the 20th Maine must have thought that Ames had contributed, because in late 1863 when the regiment received a new flag, the old one having been shot to pieces at Gettysburg and other places, they sent the by-then almost sacred symbol of the old flag to Adelbert Ames, who had gone on to other duties and a brigadier generalship. The "paper of reprimand" incident was described in a letter Captain Coleman sent home to a Colby friend on November 10, 1862, and it was fairly typical of the way in which civilians and soldiers work upon each other beneficially when they are compelled to work together.

In the same letter Coleman described one of the dramatic moments of American military history—the farewell of General George B. McClellan, whom Lincoln had just dismissed from command because he had not moved fast enough after Antietam or anywhere else. The farewell was a weepy occasion because of the great affection for McClellan on the part of both officers and men. Coleman wrote: "We have just received the parting review of Gen. McClellan . . . Little 'Mac,' whom we were accustomed to meet with a cheerful countenance and a light manner, wore a look of mingled sorrow & anger which made an impression upon all, and called forth cheer after cheer from the long lines as he passed from hill to hill through the vast army. He rode a little in advance of his numerous aides and body-guard, with his hat off kindly saluting as he passed every detachment. He spent a few hours after review at Gen. Porter's Head Qrs. and sent an invitation to all the commissioned officers of the corps to visit him. There were a very large number present and it is said the scene was quite affecting. I did not go because my extra duties as Officer of the Day prevented. McClellan is everywhere greeted with universal & enthusiastic applause. The roar of cannon and the swell of cheering thousands which mark his passage through the army remind us of what we have read of receptions of famous chieftans of olden times. McClellan may be superceded in command, but never can he be superceded in the affections of his soldiers."

But this story was to be continued, with quite a different outcome than might have been expected. The men of the 20th Maine went on to get their baptism of blood and fire at Fredericksburg. And then at Gettysburg, under the command of Colonel Joshua Chamberlain, they became heroes by saving Little Round Top and the left of the Union line in as vicious and deadly a little battle as has ever been recorded. After that came the Wilderness, Spotsylvania Court House, Cold Harbor, and all the brutal battlefields of Grant's drive southward in 1864. And autumn found them in the trenches in front of Petersburg, where the war had come to a temporary stalemate, getting ready to vote in the presidential election. The candidates were Lincoln and their former commander, the beloved McClellan. For many of the soldiers, this represented an emotional crisis and a severe test of patriotism.

It also represented a crisis for the nation. In August, when the Democratic convention had met, the war had not been going at all well. Grant had been taking enormous casualties and apparently getting nowhere; Lee, with only a third of his losses, was maneuvering successfully to blunt the force of the Union attack and divert it from Richmond. Many people in the North were discouraged, sickened by the seemingly useless slaughter. In August the Democrats had proposed a platform declaring that the war was a failure and ought to be brought to a negotiated end. This had not been accepted by their candidate, McClellan. In his letter accepting the nomination, he had practically repudiated the platform out of respect, as he implied, for his old comrades in the Army. Nevertheless, the issue was probably as plain as it was ever going to be in a national election. A vote for Lincoln was

54

clearly a vote for going on with the war. A vote for McClellan, whatever he might say, was a vote for the party that had wanted to end the war.

As late summer and early autumn wore on, the prospects began to look somewhat brighter with Sherman's victory at Atlanta and Sheridan's in the Shenandoah Valley. Zemro Smith, who in July, 1862, had written that he would "never, never, see the government destroyed," was being just as good as his word. In September he was writing, "Things look cheering to us, and you must not get discouraged in the rear. Give us 100,000 men here within two months and Richmond and Rebellion fall. Could you see our position as I see it, you would be forced to the same conclusions. We are accomplishing more sitting apparently idle before Petersburg, and have accomplished more the last 30 days than all the campaign before." Zemro Smith could see what Grant saw: that Lee's lines around Petersburg, the strategic key to Richmond, were being stretched thinner and thinner and before long they could be broken.

Nevertheless, the breaking would cost thousands of lives; that was well understood by Union soldiers who had been attacking Lee's fieldworks all the way from the Rapidan down to Petersburg, and who had seen whole regiments cut down almost to company strength by the fire that Confederates delivered from the protection of earthworks, entrenchments, or gun pits. In the case of Zemro Smith's regiment, the 1st Maine Heavy Artillery, the cutting-down had taken place in short order. On June 18, the artillery regiment, which had been converted to infantry only a month earlier and which therefore was not experienced, had made an upright running charge against a line of these works and had lost nearly six hundred of its nine hundred officers and men within a few minutes.

So in the 1864 presidential election there was a definite issue as to whether the North, both soldiers and civilians, wanted to continue with the war. For this election, eleven of the twenty-five Union states made provision for voting by servicemen who were absent from their hometowns or cities. Some states provided for absentee ballots that could be mailed home. Others conducted voting in the field, supervised either by civilian election officials or by commissioned officers, and this meant that the votes of certain military units would be tabulated separately from those of the civilian population. Thus there was provided a unique laboratory of soldier opinion bearing upon the continuance of a war—a laboratory that has never since been duplicated. Today all voting in the armed forces is accomplished by means of absentee ballots, which are dispersed to the various home communities and mixed in with the civilian vote, so there is no way of knowing what this rather large number of people has to say. (In November, 1968, the number voting in the armed services was almost as great as the number voting in Iowa and greater than that in 28 states.) But in 1864, a representative body of soldiers, including many in the Army of the Potomac, which had been taking a beating all summer, was to have its votes counted separately, and thus its wishes would be made known. The soldiers were going to record a decision as to whether they wanted to continue sending their own lines against Confederate earthworks, where it was as certain as could be that many of the voters would be killed.

And the result was going to say something about the possibilities of patriotism—also about the nature and character of American armies in general.

Had this particular election taken place in 1861, when patriotically supercharged volunteers were rushing to fill the ranks faster than the recruiting offices could accept them, there would have been little doubt about the outcome. But by autumn of 1864, the "pure" volunteer, that is, one who enlisted completely of his own free will, was getting scarce. True, some of the original volunteers still remained. But their ranks were thinning. Much of the force was composed of men who had enlisted under special inducements and to avoid being drafted. So in the spectrum of patriotism it might have seemed that all degrees of loyalty were present, from the potential bounty jumper (one who enlisted to get a bounty and then deserted) to those who were truly dedicated. As an example of the latter, one veteran had written to the adjutant general of his state in 1863 offering to pay the general for his trouble if he would only help him get back into the Army; it seems he had lost one arm at Bull Run, and the examining physicians were being unreasonable.

It was very hard to tell how many were in the service because of real patriotism such as this and how many were there because they had been pushed in by a threatened draft. And this would continue to be true in all major wars. In a large and prolonged war there is no way of judging the exact number of men who in one way or another have been pressed into service, except to estimate that it is very great.

This was one of the big unknown factors in the soldier vote of 1864. The outcome of the election was almost as anxiously awaited by the South as by the North. When the votes were counted, Captain Coleman—he who had said that McClellan would never be superseded in the affections of the soldiers—must have been surprised to discover that the 20th Maine had cast only thirteen votes for McClellan, but 138 for Lincoln, that the corps had voted for Lincoln two to one, and that the Army of the Potomac as a whole had given Lincoln a decisive victory.

When the result was announced, a wave of cheering ran for miles along the trenches at Petersburg. At one point where the lines were close together, a Confederate soldier called across and wanted to know what had happened. A Yankee answered, "Old Abe has cleaned all your fellers out up North." There was a long pause and then the southerner said that he had cheered when he heard that McClellan was nominated, but he didn't feel much like cheering now.

In the North, knowledge of how the soldiers had voted did much to stiffen the spine of the civilian population. As for the Union soldiers, they felt that they had won a victory, and it was, indeed, a great moral triumph considering that some were voting for their own extinction. Joshua Chamberlain, former commander of the 20th Maine and by now a brigadier general, wrote that the soldiers "felt that they were part of the very people whose honor and life they were to maintain; they recognized that they were entitled to participate so far as they were able, in the thought and conscience and will of that supreme 'people' whose

agents and instruments they were in the field of arms. This recognition was emphasized by the fact that the men in the field
were authorized to vote in the general election of President of
the United States, and so to participate directly in the administration of the government and the determination of public policy.
The result of this vote showed how much stronger was their allegiance to principle than even their attachment to McClellan,
whose personal popularity in the Army was something marvel-
ous. The men voted overwhelmingly for Lincoln. They were unwilling that their long fight should be set down as a failure, even
though thus far it seemed so. The fact that this war was in its
reach of meaning and consequent effect so much more than what
are commonly called 'civil wars,'—this being a war to test and finally determine the character of the interior constitution and real
organic life of this great people,—brought into the field an
amount of thoughtfulness and moral reflection not usual in armies. The Roman army could make emperors of generals, but
thoughtful minds and generous hearts were wanting to save
Rome from the on-coming, invisible doom."

A private in the 20th Maine echoed something that Chamberlain had said: he wrote that the soldiers had been unwilling to
vote "that our campaigns had all been failures, and that our comrades had all died in vain." There would be still another echo of
that thought in a little vignette of a May, 1970, meeting, where a
resolution urging withdrawal of United States troops from Cambodia was under discussion. A young soldier, recovering from
wounds received in Vietnam, stood up and told the assembly that
if they approved such a resolution, it meant that everything he
had done over there was meaningless, and what faith in the
country he had left would be destroyed.

We may wonder how much of this sentiment—that of having
made an investment and being unwilling to declare it worthless
—might have been present in the presidential election of 1968,
had the issue of continuing the Vietnam war been forthrightly
presented to the soldiers at that time. We will never know the
answer, for a couple of reasons. First, the issue was not clearly
presented—and this is normal in our political process today;

party platforms fail in their purpose if they present divisive issues; the idea is to blur or fuzz real intentions so that the party's
candidates will be acceptable to as many people as possible.
After election the platform is forgotten anyway. And second, of
course, the soldiers' votes were dispersed through absentee ballots.

So we are left with the election of 1864, in which the issue *was*
fairly clear and in which many soldier votes *were* tabulated separately, as the only test case from which we can draw conclusions.
This case proves a fact and strongly suggests a theory.

The fact is that men on the firing line will not necessarily elect
to go home and save their skins if they have a well-understood
and -accepted cause to fight for. The theory is that as more and
more of a force is conscripted or enlisted under the pressure of
conscription, constant communication between the men and
their families or friends at home tends to produce a growing
homogeneity; that after a period of time, the opinions people
have in civilian life are substantially the same as those of the men
in the field and vice versa; and that if the war has support at
home the drafted man or draft-induced volunteer is just as patriotic as anyone else.

If this theory is accepted, it follows that in a democracy such
as the United States, a draft-supported force cannot be used as
an instrument of foreign policy without absolute assurance that
the body politic is behind the effort; otherwise both civilians and
soldiers grow discouraged, the enemy is encouraged, the nation
is divided, and there is a crisis of confidence in the government.

Vietnam seems to have borne this out. The charge is sometimes made that this war represented an imperialistic effort on
the part of the United States. That of course is nonsense if it is
intended to mean acquisition of territory, material gain, and direct control of other people's social and economic lives for the
purpose of profit. But with respect to our own people, and considering the disregard by our leaders for the necessity of popular
support in going into Vietnam, it must be said that this war was
imperiously begun; also that the armed forces have been used as
though they were an insensate instrument—a collection of pieces

59

on a global chessboard to be moved here and there without re-gard to their own opinions or those of their friends and families. A thoroughly trained and hardened professional force might pos-sibly be used in this manner. But as will be suggested by a later chapter, such a force—big enough to do all that is required under current foreign policies—can only be raised and maintained at enormous expense and with other disadvantages.

In this country, defense has always been considered a duty of citizenship. George Washington said, "When we assumed the sol-dier we did not lay aside the citizen." And Richard Nixon has stated, "I believe that every man in uniform is a citizen first and a serviceman second, and that we must resist any attempt to iso-late or separate the defenders from the defended."

The citizenly nature of American armed forces has again been demonstrated by their voting record in recent years, and since voting is a basic expression of patriotism, a brief examination of that record will not be out of place here.

Right after the Civil War, most of the soldier voting laws were repealed. Many states feared that these laws would result in mili-tary control of communities near Army posts. During World War I, however, many of the voting laws were reenacted. But in 1918, with almost two million service people overseas, there was little or no service vote; Congress had failed to pass laws that would facilitate casting ballots outside the continental limits of the United States. Again in 1942, although a federal voting law had been passed, voting in the armed forces was so difficult that fewer than 1 per cent cast their ballots. F.D.R. thought this was a disgrace and called for corrective measures. Congress and the various states responded with the necessary legislation, and in the 1944 elections almost a third of the nine million persons of voting age did vote—not bad for a group of people who were then locked in combat with the Axis forces. Because of legislative failure the vote slumped in the Korean War. But then in 1955, Congress enacted the Federal Voting Assistance Act, which, with the cooperation of the states, not only made it easier for the serv-ice people and others overseas to vote, but provided ways of in-suring that they had the necessary information. The results have been impressive. With respect to presidential elections, participation increased steadily to 1964, when 51 per cent of those eligible voted. In 1968 the armed forces were deeply engaged in the Vietnam conflict, in comparison with the relatively peaceful year of 1964, but even so, 46 per cent of those eligible voted. In the same election, 63 per cent of the eligible civilians voted, but under conditions that were somewhat more favorable; they did not have to worry about being pinned down by enemy fire on election day or being sent on a combat mission. However, it should be noted that the Marine Corps, which does not like to be outdone in any activity, cast 75 per cent of its eligible vote, which far exceeded the civilian score.

This is a good record, especially when it is remembered that so many of our people in the armed forces are under twenty-one when they enlist or are inducted and many cast their first votes while in uniform. The voting record speaks well for the concern our service men and women have for the Republic. And it emphasizes again that they cannot be used simply as a collection of tools but are an indivisible part of the people as a whole.

CHAPTER SIX

Patriotism in Song, Story, and Fraternity

★   The music, literature, oratory, symbolism, history, and folk-lore of the Civil War greatly enriched the tapestry of patriotic thought and emotion in America. It was natural that this should be so. This was a very large war; more Americans lost their lives in the Civil War than died in World War II—by some estimates more than in the two great world wars combined. And there was nothing remote about it, as the case with all subsequent wars has been; it was fought right here in this country, leaving its scars upon many a town and field and its firsthand memories with many families.

Thus, it affected our concept of patriotism in many ways in both the North and the South. Although the two sections would eventually unite in their allegiance to the national government (succeeding wars in which they fought side by side would have much to do with the reconciliation), there would always be a Confederate flag and there would always be a South as a more or less separate country in the hearts of its people and in the imagination of the nation as a whole; in fact, on the field of song and story, if a score were reckoned up, it would undoubtedly be discovered that the South had won the war. This brings to mind a true story told by a dear departed friend, Boswell U. Davenport,

63

or Bud as he was known from his initials B. U. D. and his kindly, entirely Christian disposition. Bud was riding on a sight-seeing bus through an area in the South containing several Civil War battlefields, and he became aware that the driver-commentator was describing as Union defeats battles that Bud knew to have been Union victories. Bud was a Virginian himself, but after a while the wonderful uprightness of his character got the better of the patriotic pleasure he was taking from these announcements, and after the driver had described another battlefield as the scene of a particularly disastrous Federal loss, Bud said to him in his gentle way, "Now really, didn't the Yankees actually win that one?" And the driver growled, "No, sir, not while *I'm* drivin' this bus!"

For many years after the war Union veterans were not inclined to forgive and forget either, and for some time it was the official line of their principal association, the Grand Army of the Republic, that the South had committed a treasonable, criminal act, which should not be glossed over by false sentimentality. But as the years went by, this feeling gradually waned, and Blue-and-Gray get-togethers became more and more common. At what must have been the last of these reunions of any size, held at Gettysburg in 1938 on the seventy-fifth anniversary of the battle and attended by about 1,800 of the 8,000 or so veterans of both sides still living, very little remained of the animosity that on three hot July days three quarters of a century before had made that field such a scene of bloodshed and agony. This gradual reconciliation between the two bodies of veterans on occasions of this sort that drew them together under the same flag was something unique to American patriotism; where would one look for a parallel? It is difficult, for example, to imagine the Roundhead and Cavalier veterans meeting to celebrate the seventy-fifth anniversary of the battle of Marston Moor, or a reunion between the opposed veterans of the Spanish Civil War of the 1930's.

Yet the old spirit never entirely died out. The author vividly remembers listening to a network broadcast of the 1938 reunion at Gettysburg. A smoothly professional announcer was interviewing a Union veteran at the point where he had fought in repelling Pickett's charge. The old fellow, apparently pointing to a spot ahead of them, was saying, "And when they got right up to there, they turned. . . ." The announcer was not quite content with this and tried to pump something a little more dramatic out of the aged veteran, not realizing that he was dealing with the equivalent of one of those unexploded Civil War shells that unwary souvenir hunters dig up, so he asked, "Now, sir, what do you mean by saying they *turned?*" And the old fellow suddenly yelled, "Why they run like hell!" Hell was a word you did not say on the networks in those days, so the announcer, who was a polished operator with a fast lip, tried to shush, divert, or talk louder than the old man, but he continued yelling, ". . . and anybody that says they didn't is a god da-a-amed liar!" going on to treat the network to some of the choicest profanity that has been uttered since the day of Pickett's charge itself.

At about that time, one of the greatest issues confronting the American people was whether Vivian Leigh would be acceptable to play Scarlett in the movie version of *Gone With the Wind*. The popularity of this book and movie was an indication of how the cause of the South, perhaps all the more romantic because it had been lost, had become part of the tradition of American patriotism. As for songs composed or popularized in the Civil War, many of them took on a sort of patriotic immortality. "Dixie" and "The Bonnie Blue Flag" would never lose their power to quicken the pulse. "The Battle Hymn of the Republic," although its anti-slavery religiosity would cease to be understood, persisted in its mystic and majestic appeal; it was sung by the choir in St. Paul's Cathedral, London, at the funeral of Winston Churchill, who had been voted an honorary citizen of the United States in 1963. In the early years of this century, many songs of the Union were still popular in the North; for example, there are few who have grown up in this region who have not heard:

> Yes we'll rally round the flag, boys, we'll rally once again
> Shouting the battle cry of freedom.

The Civil War also gave us the music that in its solemn way as played at military funerals has the greatest patriotic meaning of

all, inasmuch as it so often denotes a life given for the country—
"Taps." It was composed in 1862 by General Dan Butterfield,
who, in place of the rather harsh-sounding regulation "Lights
Out," wanted a call that would convey the mood of putting out
the lights and lying down to rest in the silence of the night.

The literature of the Civil War is too vast to enter into here,
either to appraise its patriotic content or for any other reason.
However, mention must be made of two literary legacies from
the war. One, of course, is the Gettysburg Address. The other is a
fictional story that is as timely today as it was when it was published in 1863: Edward Everett Hale's *The Man Without a
Country*. This is just about as sentimental a tale as was ever composed in the supersentimental midcentury era, and it ought to be
as easy to smile at as any of the other highly decorated confec-
tions of that age are. Yet even today it is impossible to read this
story without being deeply moved, and without thinking about
one's own relationship to America. In fact, any young man who is
considering a self-imposed exile or who is, even, only dissatisfied
with the way things are going in the Republic, might read it with
profit. For the benefit of those who have never read or who have
forgotten the story, it should be said that it concerns one Philip
Nolan, a young United States Army officer who is court-martialed for complicity in the alleged treasonous plot of Aaron Burr
to separate certain western states from the Union. When the
president of the court asks him if he wishes to say anything to
show his faithfulness to the United States, Nolan cries out in a fit
of frenzy, "D——n the United States! I wish I may never hear of
the United States again!" The court grants this wish as a sen-
tence, and from that moment, September 23, 1807, until the day
he dies, May 11, 1863, Philip Nolan never does hear of the
United States again. This is his only punishment, and it is accomplished by keeping him continually on ships of the Navy, transferring him from one to another so that he is always on a cruise
or in harbor far from American shores. On the vessels he is not
confined, he eats in the officers' mess, has his own quarters, and
wears his Army uniform complete except as to buttons, which are
plain; the regulation buttons have been removed because they

bear the letters "US," which he is not supposed to see. Following a standing operating procedure passed on from one ship's complement to another, no one ever mentions anything having to do with the United States to Nolan (although otherwise everyone is companionable and cordial), and all references to his native country are carefully removed from books and newspapers. Once a special problem arises. Nolan has an atlas from which the United States has been cut out but that shows Texas as part of Mexico. When word comes that Texas has entered the Union in 1845, the officers on the ship where Nolan is then quartered discuss whether they should remove Texas from his map. They decide against it, because to do this would be virtually to reveal to Nolan what had happened. Over the years Nolan's longing for his native land grows acute. Once he tells a youth on board, "Remember, boy, that behind all these men you have to do with, behind officers and government, and people even, there is the Country Herself, your Country, and that you belong to her as you belong to your own mother." But this is a rare confidence. The matter is almost never discussed; over the years Nolan's suffering is borne in silence. The most pathetic scene of all occurs when Nolan is dying and one of the ship's officers enters his stateroom at the ship's doctor's request and finds that Nolan has made a sort of shrine around his bed, with the Stars and Stripes, a picture of Washington, and a great map of the United States, which he has drawn from memory and marked with the quaint old names of fifty years previously: "Indiana Territory," "Mississippi Territory," and the like. He knows that there are now thirty-four states in the Union, because he has been watching the stars being added to the ship's flag from year to year, but he does not know their names or locations. He says that he has prayed night and morning for fifty-five years for "the President of the United States and all others in authority" according to the Episcopal collect. The officer breaks down and tells Nolan the history of the United States for the past half century, condensing it as best he can in a talk with a dying man and drawing in the states on the map. Nolan dies happy, leaving a request that he be buried at sea but that a stone be erected at one of the Army posts where he served, bearing the inscription: THE MAN WITHOUT A COUNTRY. IN MEMORY OF PHILIP NOLAN, LIEUTENANT IN THE ARMY OF THE UNITED STATES. *He loved his country as no other man has loved her; but no man deserved less at her hands."*

The story is a tearjerker in the best tradition of the sentimental age in which it was written, and yet as an allegory of patriotism it has seldom been surpassed, for there were then, and there are today, millions of Americans for whom banishment from this country would be almost the worst fate imaginable, and there are also many thousands of young men in self-imposed exile, some of whom must be feeling the pangs that afflicted poor Philip Nolan.

One detail of the story has Nolan's body found with something pressed close to his lips. It is his father's badge of the Society of the Cincinnati. This society, formed immediately after the War of Independence by officers who had served in that conflict, was the prototype of the veterans', hereditary, and other organizations that ever since have had much to do with the promotion of patriotism in America. In 1783 the new Society of the Cincinnati was looked on by citizens with a great deal of suspicion. Was this some sort of a cabal, they asked, to introduce an elite class of rulers? When people were reassured that the purpose was patriotic, they could still ask why the whole country was not to be considered a patriotic society—what was there about the Cincinnatians that gave them a patent on patriotism or made them its guardians? (A fundamental question that has had to do with such societies ever since.) But, generally, this sort of association was destined to be very popular and very much a part of the patriotic landscape in America.

Following the Civil War, another society of Union officers and their eldest male descendants came into being—the Military Order of the Loyal Legion, which still maintains its headquarters and an excellent Civil War library and museum in Philadelphia. In 1866 the Grand Army of the Republic, for which all veterans were eligible, was formed and lasted almost a century, until its last member died in 1953, being throughout the latter decades of the nineteenth century and the first of the twentieth a considerable patriotic and political power. In the last half of the nineteenth century many hereditary societies also were born or blossomed into new prominence, the best known being the Daughters of the American Revolution. Unlike the G.A.R.—which wanted all the members it could get so that it could exercise as much political leverage as possible in securing pensions, soldiers' homes, and other benefits—the hereditary societies, with their accent on select genealogy, tended toward smallness and the appeal that their exclusiveness entailed. For example, the Daughters of the American Revolution, founded in 1890, would have about 188,000 members by 1970, whereas the Society of Mayflower Descendants, reaching further back into history and founded seven years later, would have 14,000, and the Daughters of the Barons of Runnymede, founded in 1921 (and in terms of democratic-patriotic lineage a very hard organization to top, it would seem) would have only 650 members by 1970.

These were the two main types of patriotic societies in the nineteenth century—the veterans' and the hereditary—and there were forty or fifty of them before the century ended.

The G.A.R., with more than 400,000 members in 1890, naturally had the greatest influence. To illustrate: The G.A.R. adopted a badge that at a distance of ten feet could hardly be distinguished from the Congressional Medal of Honor. Did the government order the G.A.R. to cease and desist? No, it changed the Medal of Honor. In addition to their political power, members of the G.A.R. had an important patriotic influence in their home communities, particularly in the schools. There are millions of people alive today who doubtless can remember the times when, just before Memorial Day, a G.A.R. veteran came to the school to give a talk. The G.A.R. introduced Memorial Day in the North and also saw to it that other patriotic days were properly celebrated. The members also marked graves of soldiers, insisted on veneration of the flag, erected monuments to the war dead, and did many other things productive of a national spirit. In 1917 a former senator, speaking to the National Security League on the eve of World War I, said, "Until these old veterans began to totter and die, you did not need a Security League; you had patriotism at every fireside."

It was in the 1880's and 1890's that the patriotic societies began to take on the conservative tendencies that have distinguished them ever since. This was a time of greatly increased immigration from southern and eastern Europe—a radical change from the Anglo-Saxon, Scandinavian, Germanic, and other "almost-like-American" immigrants who had been arriving previously—and also a time of much social, labor, and political unrest. There was a new kind of talk: of anarchism, socialism, nihilism, and the like. The reaction of the G.A.R. was almost predictable. As Wallace E. Davies has pointed out, the former Union soldiers identified any resistance to the government as secession, and they undertook to "put down the rebellion" all over again. Some G.A.R. posts even volunteered their services to combat labor riots. At the same time, people representing the current establishment rallied around all patriotic societies; the very names of these societies, identified with traditions of the past, were reassuring and their ideas were even more so. Both the veterans' and the hereditary societies wanted to do something to combat radicalism and something to "Americanize" the new immigrants, and they realized that the best place to start was in the schools. Therefore they began working with history textbooks, introducing flag salutes and other patriotic exercises, awarding prizes and medals for essays on America, and taking other measures to see that students were sound in the faith by the time they graduated from grade or high school. What they did to the history textbooks often made true historians groan. Nevertheless, this sort of thing went on well into the twentieth century, and efforts to gain more objectivity were often misinterpreted. Typically, in 1918 there appeared a book called *Teaching the Child Patriotism,* written by Kate Upson Clarke. She recommended strong doses of such classics as "Horatius at the Bridge" and "How They Brought the Good News From Ghent to Aix" and stories of Nathan Hale, Israel Putnam, John Paul Jones, Stephen Decatur, Grant and Sherman, the orations of Wendell Phillips and Edward Everett, and other material "calculated to stir the spirit of true patriotism in the hearts of noble children." As for the new trend of thought, Kate Clarke had this to say: "We have lately been told by one of our foremost educators that 'the best schools are expressly renouncing the questionable duty of teaching patriotism by means of history.' To some of us who have brought up children, this startling statement came like a bomb."

By 1918 the decline of legendary American hero-patriots was already well begun, and we have had very few since, perhaps to our great disadvantage.

CHAPTER SEVEN

Nationalism, Imperialism, and Voices of Dissent

★ The idea of nationhood is so unthinkingly accepted today that the relative newness of the nation as a social unit in world history is forgotten—also its lack of complete public support in the years before the Civil War in this country. For a long time after the founding of the United States, there was a tendency on the part of its citizens to think of it as a confederation or, as the name implies, simply a group of united states. Had the original concept of nationhood been stronger, perhaps it would have been called Columbia or something of the sort.

It was the Civil War that welded the states into a real nation, and the federal government made this point very strongly in a couple of ways. One was national conscription, which enabled the President for the first time in our history to reach over the heads of the governors and lay hands on any able-bodied man of military age, anywhere he might be in the states. And the other was the federal income tax, which made the citizen's financial resources, as well as his life, subject to call on demand from the head of the nation. These two measures put the national government in the position of being regarded as a monster, not a friend, whenever people decided that they did not like what it was doing—a position that it has occupied ever since and that has made it increasingly difficult for the nation-state to be the object of continuous loyalty. The increased emphasis on America as a nation also brought into consideration its relationship with other nations of the world, and—in the nature of patriotism as it exists in America—it became more and more necessary to make moral and intellectual judgments on whether the national government was doing what was right for the country in its dealings with other countries.

There were a few intellectuals who called attention to the dangers of a highly nationalistic form of patriotism. Nationalism, they pointed out, led to war; and war was rapidly ceasing to make any sense if, indeed, it ever had. One of the most lucid voices was that of Henry George, who called attention to the enormous amount of real wealth that had been destroyed in the Civil War, to the economic inequities of the war that had made the poor poorer and the rich richer, to the increased peril of future wars now that there was knowledge of petroleum technology and such new explosives as nitroglycerine, and to the heightened vulnerability of civilized society, which had become vastly more complex, delicate, and interdependent in the last half of the nineteenth century.

But while leading writers and intellectuals might speak out in this manner, there was little organized pacifism in the half century that followed the Civil War. Before 1861, campaigns aimed at the worldwide abolition of war had been fairly conspicuous among the several reform movements that distinguished the first part of the century. But the peace workers, being humane people, had been caught up in the antislavery aspect of the Civil War and swept along in the general enthusiasm for the conflict that pervaded the North. The moral passion that is an essential ingredient of American patriotism in time of war was at high flame in the years 1861–65, and the afterglow lingered as a justification for what people could think of, if they wanted to, as a "good" war. The G.A.R. undoubtedly represented another influence that restrained antiwar sentiment; this organization was somewhat militaristic, as veterans' societies nearly always have been (although undoubtedly they would prefer being described as "in favor of military preparedness"), and in the 1890's the G.A.R. was even campaigning for military instruction in the public schools. Another factor of restraint upon the pacifists may have been the very enormity of the losses that had been suffered in the Civil War; there were just so many veterans lying in hospitals, so many widows, so many parents deprived of sons, that it would have been intolerable to advance the thought that all of this sacrifice might not have been necessary. But there were revulsions against military training in schools, one at Bowdoin College, where in 1874 members of the freshman, sophomore, and junior classes—in a sort of preview of today's anti-R.O.T.C. activities—refused to turn out for drill. The man who had to deal with this rebellion was the war hero General Joshua Chamberlain, then president of the college. Chamberlain sent the recreants all home, followed by a letter to their parents informing them that the boys would have to comply with the rules of the college or be kicked out. The students returned under these terms, but the courage and decisiveness that had served Chamberlain so well and earned him the Medal of Honor at Little Round Top did not serve him so well here. The governing boards soon afterward voted to make military drill optional, in 1879 the faculty voted to abolish it altogether, and three years later the governing boards discontinued the whole program.

The question as to whether the United States wished to become a militaristic and imperialistic nation was brought to a head by the war with Spain in 1898 and the events that immediately followed it. This war had a great deal of popular support; one evidence of this was the fact that it was fought entirely by volunteers as reinforcement for the small force of regulars—no draft was necessary. For this support, the public of that day has had to bear considerable blame in works of history. A version of the war that has had great currency is that it was an entirely shameful affair involving public hysteria whipped up by yellow journalism, a spineless President who was unable to resist demands for war, and a cheap victory over a weak opponent who was willing to accede to our demands anyway. Much of this may be true; certainly the Spanish-American War reflected very little credit upon the United States. But the hitherto accepted version has never emphasized enough the dissent that actually existed, nor, with respect to those who did favor the war, has it been completely in accord with a traditional characteristic of the American people: their tendency to have, or to think they have, a strong moral justification for engaging in warfare.

It therefore comes as a reassurance to note Frank Freidel's view that historians have now rejected some of these earlier assumptions and have recognized that humanitarianism was a strong factor in impelling the people of the United States to go to war over Cuba. It was a matter Americans had been thinking about, off and on, for many years. Fighting between the Spanish rulers in Cuba and native insurrectionists had first engaged their attention in the period 1868–78, and there had been talk of United States intervention at that time. Guerrilla warfare had broken out again in 1895 and had grown increasingly bloody and cruel; the Spaniards adopted military measures that produced widespread starvation and suffering. Epidemics raged, with yellow fever creeping into the southern United States. There was increasing sympathy for the Cubans in this country and growing diplomatic pressure on Spain. In February, 1898, the battleship *Maine* blew up in Havana harbor with great loss of life, and although it was never proved that the Spaniards had had anything to do with the explosion, many Americans suspected they had, and the event heightened emotions that already had a solid base of moral indignation; the newspapers had been running continuous stories of Spanish cruelty in Cuba, and, as William James remarked, people had been seeing the word WAR three inches high for three months in headlines. President McKinley, with the firm backing of Congress, decided that war was the only answer if the Cubans were to be relieved. War was declared on April 25, 1898, and ended the following August.

However, short as the war was, there was much objection to it, principally in New England. Speaker of the House Tom Reed, of Maine, was decidedly against it. Professor Charles Eliot Norton of Harvard urged students not to enlist for a conflict that he said was a throwback to barbarism that was going to increase, not decrease, the sufferings of the Cubans. The English writer and student of America Goldwin Smith wrote, "To an onlooker it appeared that even when the war had commenced there remained opposed to it a section of American citizens, large and respectable enough to furnish an indication of the real interest and destiny of the country not less trustworthy than that furnished by the war party. But the advocates of peace are always muzzled. 'The country, right or wrong,' becomes the accepted creed; and anyone who gives pacific counsel, though his patriotism may be unquestionable, gives it at his peril."

The war was over before dissension could build up a head of steam. The real controversy came as an aftermath of the war, and its result must reflect credit upon a generation of Americans, now nearly extinct, whose patriotism took the form of opposing a course that they believed was not in the best interests of the United States.

As a result of the quick victory over Spain, the United States, besides occupying Cuba, found itself with Puerto Rico, Guam, and the Philippines on its hands. Soon afterward it acquired Hawaii and Wake Island, and it held other small islands in the Pacific. There was much talk of establishing an American empire. This brought on a violent debate over "expansion," as it was called by its generally Republican proponents, and "imperialism" or "militarism," as it was called by opposing Democrats. The debate began in the summer of 1898 and reached its climax in the presidential election of 1900, in which "expansion/imperialism" was a great issue. Much of the argument concerned the Philippines, which Spain had ceded to the United States under protest for twenty million dollars. When the treaty of peace with Spain was presented to the Senate for ratification, there was strong opposition to the part of it which provided for U.S. annexation of the Philippines; we had no authority, opponents said, under the Constitution or anything else, to establish our rule over the inhabitants of other lands who could not be granted citizenship. The treaty was ratified, but the larger argument went on.

To understand how barefaced the advocacy of imperialism was, we need only listen to the oratory of Senator Albert J. Beveridge, which was apparently something to hear. ("Ye could waltz to it," Mr. Dooley said.) In one of his speeches in the Senate chamber, Beveridge said of expansion, "Mr. President, this question . . . is elemental. It is racial. God has not been preparing the English-speaking and Teutonic peoples for a thousand years for nothing but vain and idle self-contemplation and self-admiration. No! He has made us the master organizers of the world to establish system where chaos reigns. He has given us the spirit of progress to overwhelm the forces of reaction throughout the earth. He has made us adepts in government that we may administer government among savage and senile peoples. Were it not for such a force as this the world would relapse into barbarism and night. And of all our race He has marked the American people as His chosen nation to finally lead in the regeneration of the world. This is the divine mission of America, and it holds for us all the profit, all the glory, all the happiness possible to man. We are trustees of the world's progress, guardians of its righteous peace. The judgment of the Master is upon us! 'Ye have been faithful over a few things; I will make you ruler over many things.' "

Charles Denby, a member of McKinley's commission to study the Philippines, was more specific when he wrote, "We are coming to our own. We are stretching out our hands for what nature meant should be ours. We are taking our proper rank among the nations of the world. We are after markets, the greatest markets now existing in the world. Along with these markets will go our beneficent institutions; and humanity will bless us."

How arrogant, how offensive these statements seem today! And yet how many of the thoughts, particularly those of Beveridge, have a familiar ring, as though we had heard them only recently, and how much does the echo suggest that the old notion of America somehow having been God-gifted with a state of enlightenment that it is duty-bound to convey to the rest of the world has not yet entirely vanished.

The imperialism being advocated around the turn of the century was the old-fashioned sort: dominion mainly for profit. The extension of our influence to other parts of the world as it exists today can hardly be called imperialism in that sense, but there are those who might argue that we have been practicing imperialism of a different kind: that of ideology, with protection instead of profit as the aim.

In that light, there are often interesting parallels between objections raised then and now. One reason that was advanced for not taking over the Philippines was that we would be violating the principle of consent of the governed in imposing our will and way of life on people who might not necessarily want it. The probable tendency of this course to increase the power of the President was also noted. Goldwin Smith warned, "If you have an empire, you will have an emperor." William Jennings Bryan and others opposed imperialism on the grounds that it would require a large standing army and compulsory military service, which would be a constant source of irritation and danger to the Republic. Senator George F. Hoar was against it on ethical and constitutional grounds; if the nation took such a course he would liken it to "some prosperous thriving youth who reverses suddenly all the maxims and rules of living in which he has been educated and says to himself, 'I am too big for the Golden Rule. I have outgrown the Ten Commandments. I no longer need the straight waistcoat of the moral law. Like Jeshuron, I will wax fat and kick.' "

Morrison Swift wrote that "hard and selfish men, and hard and selfish policies, will control our imperialist relations. . . . There is no intention of mildness, humanity and justice in the forces that are now gaining ascendancy in American life," and he protested against the way in which imperialism was being foisted on the American public contrary to its will in "the greatest fourth-dimensional marvel of time." The expansionist Republicans did win the 1900 election, but there were many factors that caused the imperialist idea to turn sour. For one thing, Americans had not liked England's conduct of the Boer War and did not want to feel that they would soon be oppressing some foreign race in a like manner. When Rudyard Kipling addressed a poem to Americans, beginning each stanza with "Take up the white man's burden," the verses were jeered as much as they were cheered. As for the prosperous markets, they did not seem to develop. Instead, America had troublesome people-problems on its hands. The Filipinos had been conducting a revolt against the Spaniards, and they simply continued it against the Americans. Before long sixty thousand American soldiers were thrashing around in the jungles and hamlets of the Philippines; this bloody guerrilla war lasted well into 1902, and before it was over there was talk that would be familiar sixty-eight years later—protests against being "bogged down" and "mired" in a far-off Oriental country.

There were dreadful atrocities on both sides, with retaliation leading to steadily increasing cruelties. American soldiers burned villages, shot civilians. A few were court-martialed. More lost their lives than had been killed in the war with Spain, and it was estimated that 200,000 Filipinos died. Further, this guerrilla war was costing all kinds of money—nearly nine times the amount we had paid Spain for the islands—and how could *that* be explained?

The dissenters made the most of the horrors of the Philippine insurrection, and although they had lost the debate on the Philippine treaty and had also seen the election of 1900 go to the expansionist party, it might be said that theirs was the final victory, for materialistic imperialism had a very short life in the United States and never again would there be a demand for overseas possessions on any like scale. In fact, when there was an opportunity, following World War I, to acquire such possessions while colonial pie in the guise of former German dependencies was being cut, the United States would have none of it. And the Philippines were destined to have their independence.

The outcome was a tribute to a patriotism of protest that still adhered to the old vision of the United States as a people of high political morality whose important mission was to perfect their own society—not to rule others.

CHAPTER EIGHT

Patriotism Shows Its Darker Side

★ The world's most famous advocate of nonviolence at the turn of the century was undoubtedly the great Russian writer Count Leo Nikolaevich Tolstoy. He was an important influence on American pacifists; among his admirers and disciples were Jane Addams, William Jennings Bryan, and, oddly enough, Clarence Darrow, who would confront Bryan in the famous "monkey trial" in 1925.

In 1894 Tolstoy wrote a long essay entitled *Christianity and Patriotism*. The two, he thought, were antipodal. "It is a terrible thing to say," he wrote, "but there is not, and there never has been, a combined act of violence by one set of people upon another set of people which has not been perpetrated in the name of patriotism."

The essay was a powerful polemic against aggressive governments, war, nationalism, alliances, and all the forces that Tolstoy saw rising in Europe and threatening a massive conflict. It included one passage that could be taken as a chilling prophecy of what was to happen to his and neighboring countries twenty years later:

He spoke of the unlucky victims of war, "the everlastingly deceived, foolish working people—the people who with their blistered hands have built all those ships, and fortresses, and arsenals, and barracks, and cannon, and steamers, and harbours, and bridges, and all those palaces, halls, and platforms, and triumphal arches, and have printed all the newspapers, and pamphlets, and procured and brought all the pheasants and ortolans, and oysters, and wines eaten and drunk by all those men who are fed, educated, and kept by them, and who, deceiving them, are preparing the most fearful calamities for them; it is always the same good-natured foolish people who, showing their healthy white teeth as they smile, gape like children, naïvely delighted at the dressed-up admirals and presidents, at the flags waving above them, and at the fireworks, and the playing bands; though before they have time to look about them, there will be neither admirals, nor presidents, nor flags, nor bands, but only the desolate wet plain, cold, hunger, misery—in front of them the slaughtering enemy, behind them the relentless government, blood, wounds, agonies, rotting corpses, and a senseless, useless death."

Without the American people being aware of the black prospect ahead, Europe had become a powder keg of nationalism, imperialism, and militarism. And when it exploded in August, 1914, Americans were bewildered. They knew very little about Europe and had small means of finding out; our newspapers and press associations were largely based in London, with few newspaper correspondents on the Continent. And after the British Navy cut the German cable, a measure it took very promptly, the United States was almost entirely dependent for its information on the Allied Powers, which naturally made the most of their control of communications to establish highly effective propaganda machinery. Thus they were able to convey the most adverse impressions of the Germans imaginable and to convince most of the American public that the war was entirely the result of German militaristic aggression. And the domestic press was uncritical, to say the least. Many present-day Americans can remember newspaper cartoons of that time that showed the "Huns" with babies impaled on their bayonets and engaged in other atrocities.

Some years after World War I was over, in the 1930's, there

was a widespread feeling in America that our participation had been a mistake—a stronger feeling to that effect than has ever since been registered against any other war up through mid-1970, according to public opinion polls. And certainly in 1914 the United States had no intention of participating in the conflict. Why, then, was it drawn in?

The reasons might be divided into facts of the moment that were inescapably present and that had an urgency and importance that the generation of the 1930's could not quite remember —and more subjective thoughts, emotions, and dispositions that were equally incapable of being reconstructed. As to the facts, the conditions and events leading up to America's entry into the war are too well known to require more than a brief summary: trade and travel involvements by American firms and citizens, Britain blockading Germany, retaliation by Germany through submarine warfare, American ships sunk and lives lost, the British liner *Lusitania* torpedoed in May, 1915, with a loss of 124 American men, women, and children, warnings by the United States, warnings disregarded, and Wilson asking a willing Congress for a declaration of war on April 2, 1917. Neutral as America might wish to be, it was part of the world community, and it could no more withdraw into complete isolation than a family could shut itself up in its house and stay there because of a fight in the neighborhood. As to the more subjective factors, one very important step in the process of entanglement was the stirring up of fear and moral indignation by propaganda originating both in the nation and outside. Americans had known propaganda before, of course—that of the Hearst press in the Spanish-American War and of other presses in other wars. But now they were well into the twentieth century, and communications skill and facilities were improving; movies, for example, were a new and powerful force. Nothing before had ever compared with the weight, volume, and professionalism of the communications that flooded the country in and prior to World War I. In a way that could no longer be underrated or mistaken, the mass media were beginning to demonstrate their responsibility, or lack of it, with relation to American patriotism, which in the democratic tradition depends so greatly upon critical intelligence as a guide to conscience and to reason.

World War I and the years leading up to it also saw the advent of what might be called organized patriotism; the technique of the "drive" was brought near to perfection in efforts to sell war bonds through appearances of glamorous figures, to spur defense production, and to do other things. One of the most successful was the "preparedness" campaign. Long before there was any serious intention of entering the conflict, the advocates of preparedness began to harp on America's vulnerability, the woefully weak state of her armed forces, and the necessity to be militarily strong in order to preserve the neutrality and independence of the United States. General Leonard Wood, who organized voluntary citizens' training camps in the summer of 1913, was one of the chief proponents of preparedness, as was the ex-colonel of Rough Riders, Theodore Roosevelt, then growing old but still full of martial vigor.

As the danger of war increased, so did the power of the movement, which gained contributions from rich industrialists and the support of nearly all patriotic societies. One of the key organizations was the National Security League, which had among its avowed aims the promotion of military training, a larger Navy, industrial preparedness, government efficiency, and an "Americanization" campaign in government, schools, business, and industry. In support of these aims the public was bombarded with books, pamphlets, films, lectures. There were preparedness parades in large cities; the one in New York was so tremendous that it took all day and part of the evening to pass a given point. In January, 1917, a Congress of Constructive Patriotism was held under the auspices of the National Security League in New York; it included representatives from close to a hundred patriotic, fraternal, learned, women's, professional, sports, and other kinds of societies. Speakers were distinguished Americans from business, the academic community, the clergy, and the professions. The nation was warned to get ready, and a keynote was struck by Theodore Roosevelt: "The things that will destroy America are prosperity-at-any-price, peace-at-any-price, safety-first instead of duty-first, the love of soft living and the get-rich-quick theory of life." Long before this, of course, preparedness had become a political issue—one the Republicans had hoped to capitalize on in the 1916 election, only to see Wilson preempt it in a campaign for a larger Army and Navy.

But there were people—equally patriotic—who had other ideas. There were honest, out-and-out pacifists who said that the way to have peace was simply to stay out of war and who asserted that the United States was in no danger whatever from Germany, even though Leonard Wood was picking artillery positions along the East coast at places he declared were possible points of invasion. These people had distinguished leaders, including Robert La Follette, William Jennings Bryan, and Henry Ford, sponsor of a "Peace Ship" that carried a group of evangelistic pacifiers to Europe only to have war break out on board among the evangels.

And there were the socialists, who had gained considerable strength in the preceding decade (they had polled nearly a million votes in 1912) and who opposed the war on the ground that it was like all capitalistic wars—just another way of victimizing the working class. Toward both the socialists and the pacifists, there was a terrible intolerance, made easier to express because of harsh espionage and sedition acts passed by the Congress after the war had begun. Under these acts people who interfered with the draft or encouraged disloyalty could be imprisoned up to twenty years or fined up to ten thousand dollars; there were also heavy penalties for anyone who obstructed the sale of war bonds, discouraged recruiting, or uttered abusive language about the flag, the government, the Constitution, or even the United States uniform. More than fifteen hundred persons were arrested. Many radical union members were roughly treated by mobs. It was another instance of the religionlike intolerance of patriotism, of how, particularly in time of war under the rule of "military necessity," the American people are willing to forgo the normal processes of democracy, to submit to a totalitarian control over their lives, and to see the Constitution itself disregarded if civil liberties are even suspected of getting in the way of the war effort.

Another example of this intolerance was primarily racial in tone. Much of the public turned against the several million people of German descent in this country and even against German books and music, forgetful of the solid contributions German immigrants had been making to the United States for 150 years and more. There was some excuse for this. The country was finding itself in a new situation. It was engaged in a war with the Central Powers of Europe, and at the same time it included substantial numbers of people who had either been born in the nations we were fighting or whose parents had been born there. How would these potentially inimical groups react? No one really knew.

The outcome was a lesson in American patriotism of which insufficient note was made for guidance in the years ahead. There proved to be, of course, a few enemy agents hiding among the aliens. But from the settled population there was little trouble because of racial or national allegiances; the great majority either supported the war effort or refrained from interfering with it. In a true sense, most of them were patriotic Americans, and it is not difficult to understand why.

Going back to Morton Grodzins's thesis that in a democracy loyalty to the nation rests upon a pyramid of the individual's loyalties to groups of people and idea-systems that satisfy his life-needs, it is clear that the foreign-born and their descendants have readily formed this structure of loyalties in America. Further, they have usually experienced themselves and have often transferred to their children an impression that life is better here than it was in the countries they came from; they have seen, in effect, a before-and-after demonstration. Soon the only links with the former homeland that remain are the common tongue, among those who can still speak it, letters from a few relatives, a nostalgic clinging to old customs now and then, and a normal amount of racial pride. But primarily they are Americans and frequently they are better patriots than many members of old families.

This was a lesson that should have impressed itself upon America in World War I. That it did not was demonstrated by our treatment of Japanese-Americans following Pearl Harbor, when public and political outcry caused more than a hundred thousand of them, citizens as well as aliens, to be taken from their homes, farms, and places of business and lodged in relocation camps on the basis of race and race alone.

When war breaks out, what most people think of as being in the best interests of the country can be summarized in one word: winning. As a result, there occurs a remarkable transformation in the intellectual atmosphere, and this astonished the academic community in the years leading up to World War I almost as much as it did twenty-five years later. For many years, except for the carnival that had been the Spanish-American adventure, Americans had been unaware of what war meant. Only a few old men could remember the Civil War; only a few had much knowledge of the war of 1870 in Europe. It was thought that war had become an anachronism—that it had gone out of date because it had become too horrible, destructive, wasteful, and generally senseless. People were thinking about domestic problems: how to get rid of the slums, how to control the depredations of big business, and so on. Intellectuals were inclined to sneer at patriotism in its nationalistic sense. But once the sound of thunder just over the horizon was heard, the mood changed as does the color of a day under a darkening storm. The change was commented on by Shailer Mathews in a lecture delivered at the University of North Carolina in 1918. He reflected that "in times of peace many a good patriot has discounted national loyalty. He has elevated criticism into a supreme duty. As we look back across the years of tragedy through which the world is now passing, we hardly recognize the political attitudes of half a generation ago. Viewed through the atmosphere of a conflict which strains the resources of our nation, the political literature filled with hypercriticism in which we once rejoiced argues a mood of mind as foreign to these days as if it belonged to the men of Mars. In that far distant world at peace American intellectuals prided themselves on being superior to national enthusiasm."

As an instance of what Mathews was talking about, it will be illuminating to return, even if briefly, to a campus we visited in the Civil War and have regarded as typical of the college community through the years, that of Colby. Here we find that the impact of World War I was to a great degree a repetition of that produced by the Civil War. Again there was an emotional outburst provoked by outrages real or imagined on the part of the enemy, again participation in a unified national effort, this time to "make the world safe for democracy," again a rush to enlist, again military training on campus, with professors of mathematics, German, French, chemistry, and so on teaching such related military subjects as navigation, military German and French, chemical warfare, and the like. This training was instituted by student demand as well as by government edict, and the *Colby Alumnus* said, "It is now a college changed overnight into an armed camp." These were the campus militants of 1917.

CHAPTER NINE

Foreign and Internal Foes

★   One curiosity of patriotism, the fact that its most widely accepted style or form may be captured by one school of thought only to be lost to another, has previously been remarked upon in these pages. By the end of World War I, patriotism in America, once identified with the rebels of 1775, was the more or less unchallenged property of those who believed in the existing form of government, free enterprise, and the political, social, and economic status quo in general.

Therefore the reverberations of the Russian Revolution shook this country in the years right after World War I in a way that has been all but forgotten. Domestically, it was a period of strikes and civil unrest. The fear of anarchists, socialists, and other radicals that had alarmed the nation in the late nineteenth century sprang up again in renewed strength. In the newspaper cartoons, hideous bearded figures holding lighted bombs replaced the German Huns as bogeymen.

This marked the beginning of a change that was to have profound consequences in American patriotism. Hitherto, if enemies appeared they could usually be clearly identified, geographically, nationally, racially, and every other way. Now the enemy began to take the form of different ideas, a different system of government, and it could be here, there, or anywhere. It could be in the next town or the next house or even in a book. What made the matter more difficult was that it was often hard to tell an idea that was aimed at the good of the country from one that might be aimed at its destruction. In plain truth, it was getting harder and harder to exercise the conscience and judgment required in a good patriot. Harder for the individual citizen, harder for those in government.

One consequence, of course, was that people now looked to the federal government for protection against foes within as well as those without, and so fear of subversion had the effect of forging another patriotic tie between citizen and the nation-state.

As one of the country's chief defenders against "un-American" influences, the American Legion took up where the G.A.R. left off. The Legion was born in Paris in 1919 at a caucus attended by representatives of units in the American Expeditionary Force. "The Father of the American Legion" appropriately enough was Theodore Roosevelt, Jr., who was just as virile a patriot as his famous father had been. The younger Roosevelt not only fought in the A.E.F. but he was destined to die in the midst of the Normandy invasion as an assistant division commander in World War II and to be posthumously awarded the Congressional Medal of Honor. Shortly after playing his leading role in founding the Legion, Theodore, Jr., declared that the greatest protection America could have against the Bolsheviki, radical unionists, and red socialists was this society composed of ex-servicemen, which had as one of its published aims the promotion of patriotism and the combating of ideologies "which recognize neither the honor nor the dignity of the individual." In addition to its highly successful efforts to secure benefits for veterans and its work for child and youth welfare, the Legion has pursued an extensive "Americanism" program through several channels, including civic training, oratorical contests, school awards, citizenship classes for aliens, and the distribution of literature on American traditions and ideals. The Legion was instrumental in formulating a flag code and in passage of a federal flag law in 1942. It has been a proponent of military training and preparedness. In foreign relations, it has supported the United Nations (although pointing to the weakness of the charter and warning that "the persistent misuse of the veto power by Soviet Russia is destroying the ability of the United Nations to prevent war") and has favored NATO and other defense alliances. The tone of its philosophy has been strongly anticommunistic. Although hardly the favorite of liberal thinkers, in matters of patriotism the American Legion, with its 2,700,000 members and more than sixteen thousand posts, is probably more representative of the great masses of people in this country than is any other society or association.

The American Legion, the Veterans of Foreign Wars, and other veterans' associations, along with the hereditary societies, carried on very largely in the manner of their late nineteenth century predecessors, although they tended to become even more conservative under the pressure of disturbing social and economic forces. Relatively new among the patriotic societies— and soon to outnumber the older types—were the foundations, councils, committees, and like organizations that often display in their names virtuous words such as "Freedom," "American," "Constitutional," "Democratic," and that are formed for fairly specific purposes, some well endowed by wealthy contributors, several aimed at combating communism or anti-Americanism in a target area they often define as extremely large.

Such efforts became particularly prevalent in the years following 1929, after the economic collapse had shaken the nation to its very foundations. Our definition of patriotism throughout this discussion has been: love of country and readiness to act in its best interests as indicated by individual conscience and judgment. And this takes in much more territory than the field of war. In times of domestic crisis a feeling of patriotism also emerges. It was so in the early thirties. We had emblems such as the N.R.A. eagle—a brave bird clutching in one claw a cogwheel and in the other three bolts of lighting, symbols of the industrial and technological might by which the enemy of Depression was to be overcome. We had parades. We had a Leader to look to. We had to think about what was best for the country. In that sense the apparent failure of the competitive free enterprise system challenged several aspects of patriotic thought as it previously had been accepted. Many old words were taking on new meanings. For example, in the eighteenth century, when the patriots were the rebels, they were also the liberals; at that time the liberal was one who stood for freedom of the individual against interference by the state, and private enterprise was part of that freedom. But by the end of the Great Depression the most commonly accepted meaning had changed. The liberal had become the individual who wanted government to intervene and use its resources to protect the underprivileged, the ill, the old, and others in need of help—or rather to use the resources of those it taxed to do these and other things. (The liberality had much to do with redistributing other people's money.) At the same time, the good old-fashioned American virtues of self-sufficiency and resistance to government encroachment—the virtues of liberalism in 1776—found refuge in the camp of the "conservatives."

However, insofar as patriotism may be thought of as the predominant body of thought as to what is advantageous for the country, it was by no means as certain in the 1930's as it was in the 1920's that patriotism was the property of the conservatives, or those who stood for the status quo. There was division. A new and large column was branching off and marching under the banner of the N.R.A. eagle.

Another miracle of semantics that took place in the 1930's had to do with the word "socialism." In 1942 people were asked in a nationwide poll whether they thought socialism would be a good or bad thing for the country, and only one out of four said good. But by then, as the saying goes, they had had it. The federal government was owning and operating electric power systems, lending money, insuring loans, subsidizing agriculture and other enterprises, securing workers against the hazards of old age and unemployment, regulating business in dozens of ways, and otherwise participating in the economy. Although Americans were left with the illusion that this continued to be a country of free enterprise, the old system of unbridled competition had disappeared forever and had been replaced by a mixed economy in which there were many cushions against the harshness and hardships of the old dog-eat-dog days and many characteristics of the condition that only a minority of respondents in the 1942 poll said would be good for the country: socialism.

This ambivalence of the public mind was a phenomenon that, although it probably was well known to the more perceptive observers of American life, was never scientifically established until the opinion polls went into operation in the early or middle thirties. Since then these polls have recorded such an infinity of information that one who delves into it fully for the first time is amazed, or even appalled. He is also susceptible to horrible misconceptions (and it is with full knowledge of this peril that the author proceeds). Apparently, one of the reasons for the trickiness of polls is that a question asked to some extent determines an answer given. The question thus provides a limited view, so that looking at the world through poll results is like peeping at it through many keyholes, with a distinct possibility of gaining impressions similar to those the blind men formed of the elephant. What is most valuable, therefore, is the interpretation of the professional polltaker, the political-analyst-pollster, or some other properly disciplined person who sits down among a swarm of these statistics and draws conclusions based on broad information and experience. Such an analysis has resulted in the book *The Political Beliefs of Americans* by Lloyd A. Free and Hadley Cantril, which is based on surveys carried out in the fall of 1964 but also considers many others.

Much of this study deals with the phenomenon already mentioned: that of ambivalence. (A slightly stronger word will be seen to be applicable shortly.) The gist of its finding is that when Americans are questioned as to their basic beliefs concerning how far the federal government should participate in our lives with interference in state and local matters, regulation of business, social welfare, and so on, and how far the individual should be responsible for taking care of himself, only 16 per cent can be classed as liberal. The majority is conservative and middle of the road. Ideologically conservative, that is.

But when principles are considered as being put into practice —when people are questioned as to whether they think the federal government should act to meet public needs such as education, Medicare, housing, urban improvement, employment, and relief of poverty, 65 per cent are classed as liberal, 21 per cent middle of the road, and only 14 per cent as conservative. *Operationally* conservative, that is.

Free and Cantril call this discrepancy "almost schizoid." The present generation of youth might point to it as additional evidence of the "hypocrisy" of American society to which they are continually referring. However, it has some optimistic aspects that the youthful reformer might keep in mind. It can hopefully be interpreted to mean that Americans have certain ideological ideals, but they are not bound to them—they are not so doctrinaire and therefore not so inflexible and vulnerable to change as people living under a communistic or other system that is strongly oriented to ideology. Also, it can be argued that they are humanistic, and when human needs and ideology conflict, there is available a large capacity for adjustment and adaptation, which under proper conditions of leadership can take place with remarkable speed.

Through a little keyhole-peeping it is also possible at least to guess that in the relationship between citizens and government, purely economic considerations are not the most important of people's concerns. Polls that Gallup conducted in the period 1946–49 indicated that the various freedoms—of speech, press, religion, elections, and personal freedom in general—heavily outweighed economic values in the minds of most people as the principal advantages of living under the American form of government, with "free enterprise" getting a surprisingly light mention. However, a word of caution is in order here. One of the Gallup polls referred to asked this question: "If you had to choose between these two types of government, which one would you choose: a government whose main purpose is to provide the people with economic security—that is, the possibility of a steady income; or a government whose main purpose is to insure free elections, freedom of speech, press and religion?" In the United States 83 per cent chose freedom and 12 per cent economic security. But when a similar question was asked in Germany, then (in

May, 1948) not as prosperous as it is today, 60 per cent chose economic security and 31 per cent chose freedom. How such a question would have been answered in the United States in the hungry days of the Depression no one can say, but it is perfectly evident that the majority of Americans went along willingly enough with drastic changes in the economic system, and it may be suspected with reason that they have continued to be less concerned about the make-up of the system than they are with how well it works to satisfy their physical needs.

For a time at least, federal intervention during the Depression greatly strengthened the allegiance of many citizens to the national government. The fact that people were suffering and their communities, states, employers, private charities, and other institutions could do nothing for them, yet the federal government did act and did show itself responsive to human needs even to the point of introducing a peaceful revolution, did much to focus American patriotism on a Washington, D.C., where "government" and "country" had come to have more of the same identity than they had had for many years.

But such a relationship is a fragile one at best, and to illustrate its fragility, it is only necessary to leave the period of the 1930's for a moment and take a brief flight forward from the chronological course of our narrative. After the excitement of World War II and the patriotic wartime fervor of which Washington was partially the object, as the fifties and sixties wore on, and as the national government in support of its foreign adventures began to demand from its citizens more than it gave back to them, it was natural to expect that allegiance oriented toward Washington would fade. The change may have been indicated by two Gallup polls, one taken in 1941 right after the Depression and the other in 1968 at the height of draft quotas and high taxes. These polls showed that in 1941 the power of the federal government was of little concern compared with the power of big union leaders or large corporations. But in 1968 "big government" was named as a greater threat to the nation than either "big labor" or "big business." The ideological slant of these questions provides us with a necessary caution, but even so the change may be significant.

There can be little question that the Vietnam war has alienated much of our youth from the national government, and sometimes a human incident can illustrate this better than a poll. During the Cambodian uproar when many students were visiting
Washington, the draft director, Curtis W. Tarr, had many of
them into his office, and he became convinced that they represented the majority of the students in being turned against the
administration and the war because of the Cambodian intervention. But what he said he could not forget was one boy who sat
on the couch in his office and told him, "I'm afraid of the government."

A sense of fear that concerned the more liberal in the general
population was also brought on in the late sixties by reports that
the intelligence agencies of the federal government were assem-
bling a vast system of computerized and microfilmed information
on citizens who for one reason or another were "persons of interest" even though many had committed no crime. The thinking
behind this system did not seem sinister at the moment. Concern
about assassins, people who hijack airliners, people who bomb or
threaten to bomb (there were more than four thousand bombings
in the United States during 1969 and the first four months of
1970), and other mischief-minded individuals had prompted the
government to improve its surveillance methods in the interests
of public safety. For every action there is an opposite reaction, as
the physics book says, and this reaction provided another example of how violent people begin to draw about themselves and
everyone else a tighter net of possible repression. All this had
been given its first impetus by the assassination of President Kennedy and the report of the Warren Commission that followed it.
The report strongly favored more investigation of potential trou-
blemakers, "broader and more selective criteria" for use in recognizing such people, more cooperation among federal agencies
in this effort, and a fully automated data processing system for
making information quickly available. Since the commission was
headed by a chief justice of the Supreme Court, it could be assumed that the dangers to personal liberties had been carefully
weighed and found to be the least of the evils involved. Also, as

of 1970, there seemed to be no great alarm in Congress or among the public in general. Nevertheless, there are those who point out that the collection and "instant retrieval" of information on this scale, with criminals and noncriminals all mixed in together, is unauthorized and possibly unconstitutional—also that it is the mechanism of a police state, which can be used as easily for malign as for benign purposes. It is also perfectly apparent that in exercising the "broader and more selective criteria," the federal agencies must inevitably begin to pass upon questions of loyalty and disloyalty, or patriotism and nonpatriotism. All in all, it is another development that carries with it distinct possibilities of arousing suspicions among the citizenry and weakening bonds of unqualified allegiance to the national government.

It is somewhat astonishing for those of us who survived the Depression and the New Deal to reflect that Social Security, once considered such a radical measure, may actually be one of the most conservative forces today in terms of preserving the status quo. With the federal government serving as the custodian of funds for the after-sixty-five livelihood of millions of citizens, it is small wonder that those within hailing distance of that age do not wish to see that government overthrown.

Thus, beginning in the 1930's, the national government in one respect at least seized and put into escrow a great deal of popular support. How much further it can go in taking over the economic aspect of our lives without beginning to crowd too hard the ideological considerations that are undoubtedly present though elastic in the public mind, and how much further before beginning to infringe upon the personal freedoms that Americans seem to value is a question as yet unanswered.

If there is any one aspect of patriotism in America that impresses itself upon the mind repeatedly, it is the instability of the accepted body of beliefs that surround it, both in domestic considerations of what is in the best interests of the country and in concern about foreign affairs. One of the most striking aspects of the 1930's was the stubborn isolationism that, strong and deep-seated though it was, vanished in a day (December 7, 1941), to be replaced by a spirit of internationalism that was almost equally strong. To be a patriot in the thirties was in most cases to be an isolationist, and isolationism does not seem to have been associated with any particular class; in fact it was so predominant that it took in all classes perforce. It included the intellectuals and the dumbbells, rich and poor, liberals and conservatives, military men and pacifists. Herbert Hoover was an isolationist. So was Norman Thomas. Henry Ford, whose ill-fated World War I Peace Ship may have soured him on internationalism, was for isolationism. So was the American Legion. The early thirties in particular was a time of intense pacifism and of great popularity for novels and movies such as *All Quiet on the Western Front,* which featured the horrors of war. The memory of World War I was still bitter. According to the public opinion polls, all the wars in this century have been considered (after they were over) to have been a mistake by the majority, with one exception, World War II. And the war considered to have been a mistake by the largest majority, up until mid-1970 at least, was World War I.

Early in the 1930's college campuses seethed with antiwar sentiment. Until recently the author, who was attending Colby College at that time, had been under the uncomfortable impression that many of us signed something at Colby that pledged us never to go to war, and then of course we had gone, or been taken, a few years later. What was my relief, therefore, and improved expectation of getting to heaven, to hear otherwise from Alumni Secretary Sid Farr, who consulted the *Colby Echo* of April 19, 1933, and reported that this was not an oath but simply a vote or poll. He wrote, "In that issue, there appears an article concerning a balloting of Colby men regarding their attitude toward participating in war. Apparently this was an outgrowth of the Oxford balloting in England where the student body voted not to support the King and country in the event of war. At Colby it is recorded that slightly over 50% of the male students voted. . . . The breakdown is as follows: 15% voted that they would not participate in a war, period; 61% voted that they would only participate in a war if the mainland of the United States were actually invaded by foreign forces; 24% indicated that they would participate in any war which was approved by the President and declared by Congress." In an *Echo* of 1935 Sid also found a story about a "peace strike" of modest proportions: it seems that on one April morning the students did not attend their eleven o'clock classes and gathered instead in the chapel as a demonstration for the peace movement.

From these echoes of the past it can be seen that there would have been no support whatever on this campus in the mid-thirties for an undeclared war such as that in Vietnam and little support even for a declared war such as World War II.

The Oxford balloting referred to had to do with a resolution not to fight for king and country in the event of war, which was placed before the students of the Oxford Union in 1933 and which carried by a decisive vote. Winston Churchill, who considered this a shameful affair, said that it could be laughed off in England, but he had no doubt that it influenced calculations in Germany and Italy, where the idea that England was weak and decadent was given additional credence. Undoubtedly the leaders of the Axis powers had some such idea about the United States, but they were to receive a nasty surprise from the rapidity with which the nation rallied and responded to their challenge a few years later.

In 1935 the country was so determined to keep out of war that Congress passed the most sweeping neutrality legislation in our history. Yet as the totalitarian threat in Europe increased, and after the shooting broke out over there, everything began to look different. Typically, as we found ourselves in trade and travel complications similar to those of the years 1914–17, the people began to believe that World War I had not been quite such a mistake as they had supposed. Favor for preparedness and for military training rose sharply. Fears for America's safety increased with the fall of France. We approached World War II in an odd, dreamlike mood, with most people opposed to entering the war and yet strongly in favor of getting ready and believing that we would have to join the conflict eventually.

There was a prelude to the conflict in the Spanish Civil War, which broke out in the summer of 1936. American radicals, liberals, socialists, intellectuals, and pseudointellectuals saw in this a death struggle between what they took to be democracy (represented by the Loyalists, who were aided by the Soviet Union) and fascism (represented by the rebels under Franco, who was supported by Hitler and Mussolini). There were a great many mass meetings, much angry writing of letters to editors and articles for the liberal press, and some fighting by young Americans who went to Spain to volunteer.

But as far as any involvement of the United States in the affairs of Europe was concerned, isolationist opinion was tenacious right up to the end. A bill to extend the peacetime draft, which had been authorized by Congress in 1940, passed the House of Representatives by only one vote, less than four months before Pearl Harbor.

One of the ideas of the neutralists that in retrospect seems simply amazing was the proposal to amend the Constitution so that a national referendum would be necessary before the United States could go to war, except in case of invasion. Gallup polled the people and found them in favor of this idea 3 to 1 in 1935 and 2 to 1 three years later. Meanwhile, the proposal had been introduced into the House Committee on the Judiciary, and early in 1938 it narrowly missed (the vote was 209 to 188) being brought out of committee and onto the floor of the House for action. The measure was opposed by F.D.R., by his former presidential opponent Landon, and by other responsible leaders on the grounds that it would completely tie the President's hands in his conduct of foreign affairs. They were tied tightly enough already, the Neutrality Act having been broadened subsequent to 1935.

Yet although the country wanted to keep out of the war and was doing everything possible through legislation to avoid the conflict, people could not help becoming indignant about the fate of the nations being overrun in Europe, nor could they fail to become concerned about the future of France and England. These countries, it was recognized, were the main barriers between the totalitarian way of life and American democracy.

It is a characteristic of Americans that wherever two of them are gathered together who have a common worry, they immediately form a Committee of Concerned Citizens for Doing This or That, and it soon becomes a tremendous organization with the names of a hundred prominent civic leaders, movie stars, retired generals, and other illustrious people displayed on its official letterhead. (This phenomenon has already been noted as the third type of patriotic society that appeared to join the veterans' and hereditary associations about the time of World War I.) The years immediately prior to World War II saw an epic battle among organizations of this kind. On one side were the pacifist groups such as the Women's International League for Peace and Freedom, founded many years previously by Jane Addams, and such isolationist organizations as the America First Committee, originated by a young man who had been in antiinterventionist demonstration work at Yale but given its real muscle by wealthy midwest industrialists, famous senators, Charles Lindbergh, and other celebrities. On the opposite side was the Committee to Defend America by Aiding the Allies, but since aiding the allies by measures short of war was not enough to suit many people as the situation grew more alarming, a Fight for Freedom Committee was formed to urge actual entry into the conflict. These and other organizations laid down salvos, volleys, and barrages of supposedly opinion-influencing expressions: full-page advertisements in newspapers; letters to Congress and the public; news releases; radio talks, skits, transcriptions; demonstrations, posters; parades; show business spectaculars; meetings; rallies; pamphlets; books; lectures; personal visits to the White House, congressional offices, and the State Department by prominent people; and so on. Every channel of communication then known to mankind was used to try to convince people that they ought to get into the war or stay out of it or do something in between. Whether or not all this activity had much effect in changing public opinion is impossible to judge. It may have changed the minds of some people, such as congressmen, who *thought* it was changing public opinion. Undoubtedly it did much to clarify issues and bring all points of view to the foreground, and as a general public debate it was very much in the interests of democratic process. But it is more likely that events themselves were the most important factors in altering the mood of the public.

The story of our transition from peace to war is also in large part the story of Franklin D. Roosevelt and his skillfully managed opposition to the Axis powers. "Roosevelt haters" (there must still be many alive) might say that he manipulated us into the war. There are others who would cite his performance as an outstanding example of perceptive leadership, with F.D.R. always ahead of the public but never too far ahead. *The New York Times,* in an editorial on the twenty-fifth anniversary of his death, gave this verdict: "In retrospect, if allowed but one word to describe President Roosevelt's four terms of office, it would be *responsive.* Although unable to move easily about the nation because of his crippling infirmity, Roosevelt was somehow able to grasp the mood and desires of the country; and he both led and tugged the branches of the Federal Government in response to the people's needs."

A review of Gallup Poll results through the years 1939–41 does much to bear out the opinion that F.D.R. kept his finger closely on the public pulse with regard to the war, although how much of what happened was F.D.R. responding to the people and how much was the people responding to F.D.R. in the traditional manner of the American public in times of crisis is hard to say. The measures he took to reduce our neutrality and aid the Allies seem to have had the support of the majority most of the time. But the polls showed that as late as the end of March, 1941, the American people were 8 to 1 against entering the war. And even F.D.R. did not dare to order troops into overseas combat against the will of the people.

No one knows how much longer we might have stayed out of World War II had it not been for the Japanese attack on December 7, 1941. This was a fulminate comparable to the firing on Fort Sumter. In an extremely frank and revealing passage of his war memoirs, Winston Churchill said that after he received the news of Pearl Harbor, he went to bed and "slept the sleep of the saved and thankful." He recalled at the time something Sir Edward Grey, Britain's foreign secretary in World War I, had told him: that the United States is like a big boiler, and once a fire is lighted under it there is no limit to its power.

For World War II, the story of what happened on our typical college campus is roughly parallel to that of World War I and the Civil War. Some 1,350 Colby men and women, including, it is certain, most of the men who had voted against such a war, served with little doubt about the rightness of their cause and little regret later on. Overseas, many saw things that will always make it very difficult for them to believe that we can do without competent defense forces or trust ourselves to the tender mercies of dictatorial powers. On the April day in 1945 when the news of Roosevelt's death reached us in Germany, the men of my division were just getting their first look at the notorious concentration camps, at the hundreds of emaciated corpses stacked up like cordwood, the piles of ashes and charred bones of bodies that had been burned, and the few left living who were more dead than alive. A sergeant declared, "We haven't always known what we were fighting *for* but now I guess we know what we've been fighting *against*." A shaken and saddened private said, "I've heard about things like this but never really believed them before. I didn't think human beings could be like that. After seeing it, I couldn't feel any worse. The only consolation is that whoever did it are not part of the human race."

This was a common reaction at the time—the opinion that something impossibly inhuman had taken place, something that must be characteristic of a dark, hidden insanity or bestiality in the German race but that never could be done by Americans. At the time Andersonville was too far behind us and My Lai too far ahead.

Once combat was joined and even while it was still some months away, the American people rose to remarkable heights of patriotism. Early in 1941, when polled by Gallup on the subject of defense production, workers said it was not proceeding fast enough, and a majority was willing to work more hours without an increase in pay in order to speed it up. After Pearl Harbor the public was found to be ahead of Congress in favoring total mobilization and other war measures. People expressed themselves as being overwhelmingly satisfied with the handling of the military draft, and a large majority was willing to register for civilian defense work and take directions from the government as to where they would work. In 1945 we had a gross national product of only about $215 billion, as against $1,000 billion now, but nearly 40 per cent of the GNP was going into the war effort, and the war expense was 83 per cent of the federal budget.

We provided armament and equipment not only for our own forces but for those of Britain and Russia—so many planes that if hundreds were shot down it would make little difference to the outcome, so many ships that if dozens were sunk there would soon be more to replace them. Based on the excellent planning and preparation our military people had done in the years of peace, a small Army, Navy, and Air Corps was expanded into a mighty force of sixteen million people. This industrial and military power, added to that of our allies, overwhelmed our opponents. This was an awesome America.

It would not be quite true to say that the nation did all this without breathing hard, but under economic controls civilian life went on after a fashion. There were deprivations, but they were shared. And there was a spirit that would have been very pleasant had it not been involved with the tragedies of war. Executives who speeded the war effort were not members of the "military-industrial complex," they were folk heroes. So were the university scientists who devised new ways to do the enemy in. Groups of factory workers who exceeded their quotas were acclaimed. Generals were lionized; one would shortly afterward be made President and another Secretary of State.

The contrast with the state of affairs that has arisen out of the conflict in Southeast Asia is painful, but we ought to examine it and look for the reasons why, in the annals of American patriotism, World War II is a case history so superior to that of today.

Undoubtedly the reason outweighing all others is the fact that the United States was physically attacked in World War II. The effect of this, added to the emotions built up in this country over a period of many months by the brutality of totalitarian aggression, produced a unanimity of purpose that was shared by government and people and extended solidly to the men on the fighting front. Almost anyone who was involved in the war could sense this and would not need the results of a study or a survey to be convinced of it. Nevertheless, extensive studies were made, and while they revealed negative attitudes in the soldiers' minds, such as the idea that we were back in the same old European mess or fighting to preserve big business and the British Empire, the men tended overwhelmingly to agree with these thoughts: that we were in it whether we wanted to be or not and had to fight to survive; that we were not trying to take other people's territory but simply fighting to keep what we had. And a majority also agreed that we were fighting so that the peoples of the world could have democratic liberties (a refrain of the old "Make the world safe for democracy," which indicated that it may not have been such a bad phrase after all).

A cross section of Army enlisted men in various parts of the world were asked in June, 1945, whether they ever got the feeling that the war was not worth fighting. Gradations of response were allowed for ("never" . . . "only once in a great while" . . . "sometimes" . . . "very often"). The percentage of men who answered "never" tended to decrease the closer the men were to the scene of combat or the more they had been involved in actual fighting, and especially among those who were being medically discharged, there were grave reservations about the cost in human lives and suffering for a war that in the long view might have been prevented and that was obviously not going to prevent future wars. (Most of the soldiers thought that there would be another war within twenty-five years or so, and even in that era of relatively good feeling toward our ally the Soviet Union, distrust of Russia was strong.) Still, from 40 per cent to 54 per cent, depending on their closeness to combat, answered with the unequivocal "never," and in looking at the whole range of response, it was clear that the majority considered fighting in World War II *worthwhile*. With respect to American patriotism that apparently is an important word.

CHAPTER TEN

On the Road to Vietnam

★ Human memory throws a very small circle of illumination. We go from one year to another as a person walks through the darkness with a lighted candle, unable to see very far ahead or behind. And as for events that preceded our births, these are even beyond forgetfulness; they are recorded in books but only dimly understood when perused, as they often are, so laboriously.

Therefore, when many Americans, particularly those under twenty, first began thinking about the Vietnam war, they tended to regard it as new and isolated, the product of someone's stupidity, criminal negligence, or even malevolent design. However, a very brief review of history will show that the arrival of half a million soldiers in Vietnam, while it may have been the result of an unfortunate miscalculation, was a logical consequence of American foreign policy—also that those who made that policy were not unheedful of what the American people seemed to want and be willing to support at the time.

For a little more than a decade following World War I, the United States maintained an official policy toward the Soviet Union that was aloof, even hostile at times. In 1933, for the first time since the overthrow of the czar, our government recognized the U.S.S.R. and sent an ambassador to Moscow. Distrust of Russia was strong in the 1930's but not invariable; it depended on Russian actions. Thus, it deepened when Stalin and Hitler signed a nonaggression pact in 1939 and when Russia attacked Finland in November of that year, with most Americans cheering the remarkable Finnish resistance. There was a brief era of good feeling in the United States when Russia became our ally in World War II, but a Gallup Poll in the summer of 1944 revealed widespread skepticism as to the Soviets' postwar intentions. The author was one of those in the U.S. Third Army who met their Russian counterparts in Austria on the night of May 8–9, 1945, and can testify that the feelings of comradeship and good will were very great on that occasion; but after a few days of handshaking, hugging, vodka-drinking, reviews, dinners, and the exchange of medals, the iron curtain dropped with a clang. In the United States generally there was a kindly attitude toward Russians for a while; one of the favorite comments was that they were "the people most like Americans" and they would become satisfied and peaceful once they got more "consumer goods." But whether it was because they did not get enough Wheaties, soft drinks, and vacuum cleaners or for some other reason, the Russians continued to do things that upset us, such as blockading the Allied sector of Berlin, threatening Greece and Turkey, and bringing about a communistic take-over in Czechoslovakia.

A poll taken right after the Czech crisis indicated that public opinion had very strongly hardened against the Soviet Union. An overwhelming majority of those interviewed advocated some degree of firmness; more than two-fifths recommended either getting ready for or actually going to war. Another poll indicated that Americans supported the Berlin policy of the United States even if it meant fighting Russia.

In the postwar years and particularly after the Czech take-over, public opinion was also strongly averse to domestic communists, who were thought to be the least trustworthy group in America. It was believed by a majority that members of the Communist party in this country were primarily loyal to Russia, took orders from Moscow, and in the event of war with Russia would work against the United States. It was also emphatically believed that communism and Christianity couldn't mix.

There could have been two ways of thinking about Russia. One, that it was a nation that had been surrounded by hostile neighbors for years and that was seeking to establish a defense in depth across the land mass of Europe, where there was no protective barrier—no ocean or mountain range. The Russians had just suffered enormous losses from the German invasions, and many could remember how their soil had been invaded by anti-Soviet interventionists, including Americans, British, and Czechs in 1918. Another way of thinking was to consider Russia as the center of a conspiracy that took as its enemy the entire noncommunist world. It was this last mode of thought that occupied the minds of Americans almost to the exclusion of the first.

This, then, was the tone of suspicion and resolution on which the 1940's ended and the 1950's began. If we take as one of the elements of American patriotism a continuing judgment as to what is best for the country, it must be concluded that to be a patriot in this era meant more often than not to be anticommunist. The extremism of Senator Joseph McCarthy, which was so widely deplored and which resulted in McCarthy's censure by the Senate, was not inexplicable, nor should retrospective condemnation of this and other witch-hunting at the time be allowed to obscure the fact that many Americans were deeply concerned about communism and the threatening gestures being made by Russia. It might be said that this mood was generated by temporary emergencies, but it was also greatly strengthened by the lingering afterpain of the anguish we had just been through in World War II as a result, people were convinced, of letting aggressions go unhindered in the 1930's.

Also part of this mood was a great confidence in our military power, which had recently been so impressively demonstrated, and in both our civilian and military leadership in Washington. As a result of this trust and of the heightened concern about world problems, many powers that had seemed necessary to the President in time of war were allowed to stay in the White House after peace arrived. Under the National Security Act of

1947, the armed forces were unified and new arms of the Executive were created—agencies such as the National Security Council and the Central Intelligence Agency. Military leaders became more important in the inner councils. New functionaries took their places beside members of the cabinet: special assistants to the President, special counsels, special consultants. Together all of these people formed a sort of *imperium in imperio,* with only two among them elected by and directly responsible to the people: the President and the Vice President.

The cast of characters of this group would be constantly changing. Four times, new Presidents would assume the starring role—and because of the power that had accrued to them, their differing personalities would have momentous consequences. Many cabinet members and other department officials would change with succeeding administrations. Advisors, assistants, and counsels would serve for a time, influence important decisions, and then return to their law offices, university professorships, or other civilian occupations, praised or criticized only rarely for their contributions—certainly never called to account for them. Several foreign relations problems would be passed on from one regime to another. Yet for more than twenty years the basic foreign policy continued to be the same as that exemplified by the Presidency of Harry S Truman.

In the same year that saw the National Security Council system established, 1947, the Truman Doctrine was enunciated. It asserted a policy of supporting "free peoples who are resisting attempted subjugation by armed minorities or by outside pressures."

It was soon put into effect.

On June 24, 1950, President Truman was in Independence, Missouri, enjoying a quiet weekend with his family when he was informed that the North Koreans had invaded South Korea. The next day, flying back to Washington in the presidential plane, he had time for three hours of undisturbed thought—and some of these thoughts were later recorded in his memoirs. They are interesting because they seem quite typical of what nearly everyone, with the lessons of World War II still fresh in mind, was thinking at the time. On the plane Truman recalled the several instances of aggression by Hitler, Mussolini, and the Japanese in the 1930's and remembered how the failure to act had encouraged further aggressions. (This echoed an observation that was being made not only in high places but in neighborhood bars right after the war: if we had only lowered the boom on the bastards before they got started, there would have been nothing to it.) Now, Truman felt sure that unless the North Koreans were halted, we would have a repetition of recent history—more and more aggressions leading finally to World War III. This might be called the Munich syndrome (because Munich and Chamberlain's appeasement of Hitler there in 1938 had come to be a symbol of knuckling under to aggressors) were it not for the fact that "syndrome" suggests something abnormal, and this sort of thinking was completely normal in 1950.

And there were reasons for it. Harry Truman was not one to see spooks in the shadows, and he had plenty of evidence that the communists meant to make trouble. They had taken Czechoslovakia and Hungary from within, and they had tried to make inroads into Greece, Turkey, and Iran. Waking up almost too late, the United States had made successful countermoves, launching the Marshall Plan, announcing the Truman Doctrine, entering NATO, and deploying land and naval forces in support of this alliance. In 1948 the Russians had tried to grab Berlin—and had backed down when confronted by the United States airlift.

Truman's experts in foreign affairs had told him that this was going to be the pattern for years to come—the communists continually probing at a series of shifting geographical and political points, and the United States, if it wanted to protect the freedom of the Western world, which it had so recently rescued, embarking on a long-term, patient, vigilant application of counterforces at the places being tested.

Now the game had suddenly shifted to Asia. After taking China, the communists were going to make another little push into Korea. Maybe it looked easy to them; if so, they had not dealt before with Harry S Truman.

There was another consideration. The Korean challenge presented an important test of collective security under the United Nations. And the U.N. certainly deserved a try. On the basis of a U.N. Security Council resolution calling upon the North Koreans to cease their hostilities and withdraw to the 38th Parallel but without a declaration of war by Congress, Truman committed our armed forces to action on June 26. He consulted with congressional leaders on June 27, but by then instructions for intervention had already gone to General MacArthur, and the consultation was more for the purpose of informing the legislators than for seeking their approval and authorization. There was no problem. Both Congress and the public were generally acquiescent.

Meanwhile a new factor had entered the equation. In August of the previous year, 1949, an atomic explosion had taken place in Russia. When Truman was asked in a press conference in November, 1950, whether he was going to use the atomic bomb in Korea, he would not say *yes* and he would not say *no,* but the general sense of his verbalization was *no;* the prospect of nuclear war had become too terrible to contemplate.

And there we had the whole pattern that was to persist for many years: the dominant Executive, the Munich rationale turned toward the containment of communism, and the fear of nuclear war.

Polls taken in the first half of the 1950's showed that the policy of resisting Russian (or communist) aggression had a solid foundation of popular support. Majorities of 60 per cent to 70 per cent expressed the belief that stopping this aggression was more important than staying out of war.

Isolationists had dwindled to a small minority. Ever since Pearl Harbor the public had been strongly internationalist, and it would continue to be so through the 1960's. Polls repeatedly indicated that people were overwhelmingly in favor of taking an active part in world affairs. By the end of the 1950's, there was no longer much hope that the United Nations would be an effective peace-keeping agency, but the American public was still strong for internationalism. Questions answered affirmatively from a typical polling would have indicated a policy about like this: "Since the U.N. can't preserve world order we must, in addition to supporting the U.N., form defense alliances with other nations; we must do everything possible to build up our military strength and strengthen friendly countries in order to prevent the further spread of communism."

However, much of the public was to prove itself ambivalent in this matter. It was the opposite reaction of the American attitude toward socialism; in that case people had accepted the specifics as introduced in the social welfare measures of the New Deal while expressing opposition to the generality as conveyed by the word "socialism." Confronted with internationalism or interventionism, a large part of the public accepted the generality but rejected the specific, in this instance the war in Korea. It is hard to know what to say about this. It might unkindly be averred that Americans could approve a policy but did not have the guts for the bloody business of putting it into effect. But this would not be entirely just or true. On other occasions Americans have proved themselves more than equal to fighting long and bloody wars. A more generous theory is that the visceral stimuli of fear, anger, and apparent danger were lacking—that many people accepted the policy intellectually but were unable to support it emotionally. Others, of course, were simply unaware of our national goals, ideals, and reasons for involvement. Thus, we were dismayed when many Americans, captured by the enemy and "brainwashed," admitted that they had not the foggiest notion of why we were fighting in Korea.

Even among the best-informed young people (and then, as in Vietnam, the young had to bear the brunt of the war) there was much infirmity of purpose compared with the attitudes of World War II. Probably a good indication of this was the result of a large-scale survey of male college students in the spring of 1952. One of the questions asked was the same as a key question put to World War II soldiers in June, 1945—in effect, Did they ever get the feeling that the war was not worth fighting? It may be remembered that from 40 per cent to 54 per cent of the soldiers answered with a flat "never"—the 40 per cent representing the segment that had been in combat and the 54 per cent, men with no overseas service.

The situation, of course, was not completely comparable. But it is worth noting that only 19 per cent of the college students answered "never," and judging by the World War II survey, this figure would have been even smaller if the college men had been shot at a few times. It was recorded after this survey that the greater the student's conviction as to ideology (desirability of fighting for free peoples against totalitarianism), the more hawkish he was likely to be, but in total it was quite obvious that ideology did not count for enough.

Among the general public, support for the Korean War was initially fairly strong, although by no means unanimous. After two months of fighting, about two thirds of the public supported the war or, to put it more exactly, did not consider it a mistake when questioned by Gallup. However, once communist China had intervened and the full dimensions of the United States assignment were realized, support dropped rapidly and President Truman's popularity fell away. A perusal of Gallup polls for the year 1951 provides several parallels to the Vietnam war—enough at any rate, to make it possible with the benefit of hindsight to say that many of the attributes of a Vietnamese type of conflict as a malignant agent in the body politic were predicted. By the spring of 1951 at least half of the American people were regarding the Korean War as a mistake, while many were voicing the opinion that Congress ought to control the sending of troops overseas and expressing alarm about the rising cost of living. During the year President Truman's popularity fell to a dismal low; by Christmastime only 23 per cent of the public approved of the way he was handling the Presidency. Even for a man who had made the pollsters eat crow in 1948 with his unpredicted victory over Dewey, this was discouraging.

After Truman left office his popularity greatly increased (in the pattern of public opinion with regard to former Presidents) and he would come to be highly regarded for his conduct of the Presidency. But while in the White House he suffered a drastic loss of public support in the Korean War, providing an unhappy precedent for the experience of President Johnson in relation to Vietnam. When the Korean War was made an issue in the Eisenhower campaign in 1952, Truman considered it a low blow, and possibly it was; nevertheless the Korean "mistake" was a powerful factor in the election, and the generally accepted impression that Eisenhower "got us out of Korea" was a recognized adjunct to his popularity.

Coming to the Presidency from a military career, Eisenhower found that the National Security Council system, with its resemblance to a military staff, suited him perfectly. He greatly enlarged the system, which, in addition to the statutory members of the council, may consist of a considerable array of groups, committees, boards, and specialists comprising a highly coordinated substructure. Under Eisenhower the military forces were reshaped to emphasize nuclear weapons, and Secretary of State John Foster Dulles threatened the communists with "massive retaliation." But at the same time, Eisenhower attempted to use his world prestige in overtures to the Soviet Union aimed at enduring peace, and there were widespread hopes that relations between the two countries were improving when in May, 1960, just eleven days before a planned summit conference, the Soviet premier in high dudgeon announced that an American spy plane (the U-2) had been shot down over Russian territory and soon afterward used this incident to break off the conference.

Although the Eisenhower years were generally conservative in terms of foreign policy, his actions—such as those involved in defending Formosa and in sending troops to Lebanon—were entirely consistent with those of Truman. He was determined, as he stated in his first inaugural address, that "we shall never try to placate an aggressor by the false and wicked bargain of trading honor for security. Americans, indeed all free men, remember that—in the final choice—a soldier's pack is not so heavy a burden as a prisoner's chains. . . ." Also, under Eisenhower, noncombat aid to South Vietnam, which had begun in the Truman administration, was somewhat intensified.

When President Kennedy came into office, his inaugural address, delivered on a cold, windy, memorable day in January,

1961, left no doubt as to where he stood with relation to the policy of his predecessors. "Let the word go forth from this time and place, to friend and foe alike, that the torch has been passed to a new generation of Americans—born in this century, tempered by war, disciplined by a hard and bitter peace, proud of our ancient heritage—and unwilling to witness or permit the slow undoing of those human rights to which this nation has always been committed, and to which we are committed today at home and around the world. Let every nation know, whether it wishes us well or ill, that we shall pay any price, bear any burden, meet any hardship, support any friend, oppose any foe, to assure the survival and the success of liberty."

(How moving still is the remembered sound of these words—and what a poignancy now attends them!)

John F. Kennedy's initial tendency at least was to reduce the cluster of boards, committees, and other groups that had been attached to the National Security Council and to work more informally. Yet the dominance of the Presidency in foreign affairs continued. Under Kennedy the performance of the Executive group in such matters reached a notably low point and a remarkably high one.

The low point was represented by the Bay of Pigs incident in April, 1961, when about fourteen hundred anti-Castro exiles who had been trained with United States assistance attempted an invasion of Cuba but were quickly defeated and nearly all captured. This disclosed to the Congress and the American people how much control over important commitments they were losing. The only senator who was involved in the deliberations preceding the invasion was Senator J. William Fulbright, according to his book *The Arrogance of Power*, but this was an accident and the senator's adverse opinion had insufficient effect. Also, everyone was shocked when it later appeared that the affair had been mainly engineered by the Central Intelligence Agency, which is hardly a constitutional authority for arriving at a foreign policy and putting it into effect.

The high point, in which Kennedy and his group of associates performed superbly, took place in October of the following year, when Soviet missiles were discovered being installed in Cuba, and through shrewd diplomacy combined with a show of military strength, the President forced the withdrawal of the threatening weapons.

Under Kennedy, containment of world communism continued to be the main policy, but now that Russia and the United States were approaching a nuclear stalemate, Kennedy decided that massive retaliation was outmoded; it offered, as he said, nothing between a holocaust and a humiliating surrender. He therefore ordered a build-up of conventional forces more able to deliver a flexible or measured response. And it was here, in this provision for "brush fire wars" that the road headed straight for Vietnam. Yet Kennedy was apparently not on the point of sending combat forces to Vietnam. Important people in his administration were urging that the aggression be met with combined political, social, and military methods that would tend to make the South Vietnamese people loyal to their government and able to fight the Vietcong as guerrillas, rather than with conventionally uniformed and organized armed forces. There is evidence that Kennedy was receptive to such ideas and even originated many of them. Roger Hilsman, who as Assistant Secretary of State for the Far East was close to Kennedy in these matters, wrote in his book *To Move a Nation* that there were just over sixteen thousand American advisers in Vietnam in November, 1963, and that "President Kennedy made it abundantly clear to me on more than one occasion that what he most wanted to avoid was turning Vietnam into an American War . . . President Kennedy's policy, in sum, was to meet the guerrilla aggression within a counterguerrilla framework, with the implied corollary that if the Viet Cong could not be defeated within a counterguerrilla framework and the allegiance of the people of Vietnam could not be won, then the United States would accept the resulting situation and would be free to enter negotiations without fatal consequences to our position in the rest of Asia. But President Kennedy did not live, and no one can say with absolute certainty what he would or would not have done."

The fatal shot in Dallas on November 22, 1963, placed in

the White House a man with a strong and unique personality, one of the facets of which was a desire to get results. As described in Eric Goldman's *The Tragedy of Lyndon Johnson,* the President once declared, "When you have something to do, don't sit there. Do it, and do it fast," and Mrs. Johnson said, "Lyndon acts as if there is never going to be a tomorrow." Goldman also reports Mrs. Johnson as saying in mid-1965, "I just hope that foreign problems do not keep mounting. They do not represent Lyndon's kind of Presidency."

Perhaps they did not, and perhaps Lyndon Johnson could be accused of shooting from the hip in the case of Vietnam, and yet before the accusation is given full credit, it is well to remember the situation as it was then, not as it is remembered now.

There had been, it is true, a public revulsion against the Korean conflict, but who could say why? Maybe it was because MacArthur had gone too far, or not far enough. Maybe it was something else. But the reaction to the Korean War on the part of the American people did not seem to be indicative of their general international outlook, as expressed both in the public opinion polls and, much more importantly, in the actions of their authorized representatives in Congress. They were more concerned about international affairs than they were about those on the domestic front. The people had expressed themselves as being in favor of defense alliances, and defense alliances they now had, more than forty of them, approved and ratified by their senators.

Many of these alliances were with countries in the far Pacific. Security and mutual defense treaties had been signed with Australia, New Zealand, and the Philippines in 1951, with the Republic of Korea in 1953, with the Republic of China in 1954, and with a whole group of countries, the Southeast Asia Treaty Organization, in 1954. This (SEATO) treaty extended its protection to South Vietnam through protocol, and it would provide the basis for the Tonkin Gulf Resolution. A treaty with Japan had followed in 1960. Several polls subsequent to the Korean War had showed majorities in favor of helping other countries in Asia that might be attacked by the communists.

On the whole, it looked as though L.B.J. had clear direction as to what the country wanted him to do in Southeast Asia. Particularly reassuring was the support of the best-educated people. For years the polls had showed the college-educated to be consistently more internationalist in spirit and more inclined to intervention than the high school or grade school graduates, and this relative attitude applied to Southeast Asia. Also, internationalism had a slight liberal tinge, although, as was the case with isolationism in the thirties, it was so predominant that it tended to take in both liberals and conservatives thoroughly.

President Johnson may even have thought that old-fashioned patriotism could still flare up like red fire on the Fourth of July. When in August of 1964 it was reported that North Vietnamese vessels had launched torpedoes at U.S. destroyers in the Gulf of Tonkin, the President and the Congress reacted almost as if this were another Pearl Harbor or Fort Sumter. When the Vietcong bombed American billets in December and TV showed our dead and wounded being dragged from the blackened ruins, Johnson saw this as an attack upon the flag that could not be tolerated, and the massive intervention followed.

The deterioration of popular support for the Vietnam war and for President Johnson followed a pattern similar to that for Korea and for President Truman. For example, Gallup's interviewers were going about during and after the Korean War and during the Vietnam conflict asking people whether or not they believed sending troops to fight in the war had been a mistake. In the case of both wars, at the outset about six out of ten people said No, it had not been a mistake, and the toboggan slide started from there. Probably because the Vietnam war lasted longer, the toboggan went a little farther downhill.

Coincidentally Gallup Polls traced the decline of President Johnson's political fortunes. In 1964 his popularity had been comparable to the highest registered by Eisenhower or Kennedy. As for his prospects for reelection, early in 1966 polls showed that he had a lead over possible Republican contenders Nixon and Romney, but through 1967 the lead grew thinner with respect to Nixon and mostly disappeared against Romney. Senator Eugene

McCarthy's unexpectedly large vote in the New Hampshire primary was also an adverse sign. President Johnson's motives for withdrawing from the race may never be made entirely clear. Nevertheless, it is a warrantable assumption that the darkening of the political sky because of Vietnam was one of his important considerations.

One interesting, and possibly revealing, aspect of attitudes toward the war—from the standpoint of patriotic behavior—was the change on the part of the college-educated people and of the top layer of these, who might be designated as "intellectuals" at the risk of unfairly excluding a few who never made it to college but who still deserve the title. Irving Kristol has written, "No modern nation has ever constructed a foreign policy that was acceptable to its intellectuals. True, at moments of national peril or national exaltation, intellectuals will feel the same patriotic emotions as everyone else, and will subscribe as enthusiastically to the common cause. But these moments pass, the process of disengagement begins, and it usually does not take long for disengagement to eventuate in alienation. . . . It is reasonable to suppose that there is an instinctive bias at work here, favorable to government among the common people, unfavorable among the intellectuals."

Kristol pointed to the tendency of public opinion polls to bear out this observation, and he would have seen another instance in the deeper tabulations of Gallup Polls on the Vietnam war. At the outset the college-educated were backing the war more strongly than their less learned countrymen. (Apparently the highly audible antiwar protests of a few colleges have not been representative of the total college alumni population by a long shot.) In March, 1966, in answer to the standard Gallup question as to whether our troop involvement in the fighting had been a mistake, only about 22 per cent of the college people said it had been; they were more hawkish than the high school and grade school graduates. But the same question asked by Gallup in October, 1969, showed that there had been a flip-flop; now 64 per cent of the college graduates said Yes, the war had been a mistake, and now they were more dovish than the noncollege group.

One explanation might be that the better educated people simply had more information, and this thesis would be borne out by poll tabulations in general, in which the college-educated are classed under "don't know" or "no opinion" much less often than are people with less schooling. Free and Cantril in their *Political Beliefs of Americans* report a study that shows that among the college-educated, people who are well informed on foreign affairs are respectively twice and six times as numerous as they are among high school and grade school graduates.

However, whether or not they represent respectable "intellectual" opinion could still be questioned. People classed as college-educated by the polls may have been out of college for several decades or, under the rather broad criteria for this class, they may have gone to an institution that is oriented more toward a specific career than toward general learning, or to one that just isn't very good. A much sharper focus on the intellectual community was accomplished at the Survey Research Center of the University of Michigan and reported on by Philip E. Converse and Howard Schuman. This study grouped college-educated respondents in classes according to criteria that were taken to indicate the academic quality of the institutions they had attended. And the top classes, A and B, showed the flip-flop pattern (that of being hawkishly ahead of the noncollege population in 1964 but behind it in 1968) much more strongly than did the "lower-quality" classes C and D, while in those below D the reversal had not appeared by 1968. (There was another class, the "highest quality" of all, the postgraduate-educated, but they provided no grounds for comparison; they were more dovish than the general population to begin with.)

In this and other studies there is much to suggest that intellectual elevation does not make for the sort of ardent patriotism that follows the flag into battle without qualm or question. And whatever is made of this suggestion, it does seem in accord with our definition, which holds that patriotism in America involves the exercise of individual conscience and judgment. It is certainly the business of education to develop critical intelligence, and it is the habit of the American intellectual, with somewhat less justification than he has in matters of informed judgment, to consider himself the custodian of the nation's conscience. As far as the war in Vietnam was concerned, signs and soundings available in the late 1960's did not indicate any widespread belief among the masses of Americans that what the United States was doing or trying to do in that country was wrong in a moral sense. The assertion of "immorality" seemed to be most commonly associated with militant minorities in some of our institutions of higher learning.

On the other hand, there was no strong and general belief in the *rightness* of our cause either—the sort of conviction that in certain wars of the past has lighted and sustained the flames of patriotism. Moreover, actual experience with the concept of limited war was opening people's eyes to some special immoralities, if they could be called that, that had come to apply to America internally. There were, for example, the much-referred-to inequities of the draft. But a more serious inequity was the condition of having one part of the population (the members of the armed forces and their families) suffering the anguish of war while another and a greater part enjoyed the pursuits of prosperity and peace. It is one thing, perhaps morally justifiable, to sacrifice a few that many may live. But it is another if the many are living in affluence and ease—and in a state of profound apathy toward the sufferers. Coming home for the average Vietnam veteran in 1969 and 1970, even though he may have been wearing decorations or the scars of honorable wounds, was a thankless and disappointing experience; he was largely ignored by people who were going about their daily business and pleasure as though a war just as real to him and his family as World War II was to some of them, actually did not exist. For the parents of the dead, this general attitude, despite the many expressions of personal sympathy extended to them, has been an added and a most pathetic burden. Nor can it be said that there has been any widespread interest and indignation concerning the American prisoners in North Vietnam, who, according to most reports, have been inhumanely treated. There has proved to be something intensely dispiriting about the calculated measuring-out of blood that, people have now learned, is the limited war in actual practice, and many have come to believe there is something wrong with it—that if we are to be at war at all, we should all be at war.

The collapse of support for the Vietnam war on the part of so many Americans—not just the educated or the intellectual—put Lyndon B. Johnson into an unenviable box. He had to answer the question, "What are we doing in Vietnam, anyway?" Most people (including the educated) had forgotten the twists and turns of the trail by which we had traveled to get there. As for the generation of young people in college, coming fresh upon the scene with no background of World War II or the years right afterward, the conflict made no sense whatever.

It was all too far away. The whole thing had become an intellectual exercise—an abstraction—minus the emotion that in previous major wars has made even the intellectuals forget their scruples. When the Germans invaded Belgium in World War I, Clarence Darrow, who up to that moment had been a Tolstoyan pacifist, turned belligerent in a wink, making a remarkable comment to the effect that pacifism was a fine policy in peacetime, but it was no good in time of war. In talking about this distant conflict in Vietnam involving people whose names we could not pronounce although we might have sympathized with them had we known them, Lyndon Johnson could depend on no such wave of patriotic emotion to assist him.

Nor was the President able to explain the war in rational terms —a difficulty to be expected, since war is seldom a rational exercise. True, there were commitments, an established policy, an agreed-to global strategy. But people wanted the "why" of it in terms of now, not of ten years ago or of ten years into the future. And how, indeed, could this have been explained? Could it have been said that this was a war being fought to safeguard lines of supply and materials vital to our nation? One gets the impression that this is often what is meant when it is said that "our interests" are at stake. But it is impossible to go beyond the generality of such "interests" in any explanation, because when a President must ask men to die for The Economy he is obviously in trouble. Was there an answer in strategy—in denying the Chinese the rich territory of Indochina—in the "domino theory," in the idea that "if we fight 'em there, we won't have to fight 'em on the coast of California"? Possibly, but dying is a serious business, and the necessity for it needs to be based on something more than a hypothesis as to what *might* happen. Well, then, what about an appeal to "defend freedom and preserve peace?" (Words used in President Johnson's message to Congress asking for the Tonkin Gulf Resolution.) Phrases such as this, which might have meant a great deal in 1942, were somehow becoming meaningless; they had lost their power to motivate.

President Johnson retired from the scene. And by another twist of fate as it affects the destiny of the nation through changing personalities in the Executive office, this brought to the Presidency a man who had for many years been a foe of the communists and who had not hesitated to put his beliefs on record. For example, Mr. Nixon had written for the August, 1964, *Reader's Digest* an article entitled "Needed in Vietnam; the Will to Win," which was a clear and straightforward statement of his beliefs with regard to the conflict in Southeast Asia. In the article he expressed the conviction that South Vietnam was the key to the struggle against communism in Asia. Let this country fall, he pointed out, and the red tide would engulf Laos, Cambodia, Thailand, Malaysia, and Indonesia and come perilously close to Australia and the Philippines, while Japan with its great industrial resources would be forced to make an accommodation with Red China, and overnight the United States would cease to be a power in the Pacific. In the article he also compared those favoring an accord with the enemy with Neville Chamberlain at Munich, and he made another comparison with the case of General MacArthur in Korea. MacArthur, he pointed out, had wanted to win the war by striking communist sanctuaries across the Yalu River, and Mr. Nixon expressed the belief that MacArthur had been right. He then stated that we were fighting under the same sort of handicap in Vietnam, and military authorities did not believe we could win there while allowing the enemy the safety of their sanctuaries in North Vietnam. He urged that we win the war in Vietnam—otherwise, as our history had but recently shown, we would have to fight the aggressor somewhere else under less favorable circumstances.

If we believe that judgment as to what is in the best interests of the country is part of the American patriot's authorized equipment, then these views certainly were and are basic to one school of patriotism, and their degree of rightness or wrongness is probably one of the most important questions that Americans must decide and agree on. True, in 1964, they were expressed by Mr. Nixon as a private citizen. And it was also true that between 1964 and 1970 many conditions and attitudes would change. Nevertheless, it should not have come as a complete surprise that President Nixon decided to take a whack at the Cambodian sanctuaries in 1970 and that he continued to take a strong stand against the advance of the communists in Southeast Asia. A man's patriotic creed does not necessarily change just because he becomes President. What does change, to an astronomical degree, is the consequence.

In 1967 the Senate Committee on Foreign Relations began a series of meetings that had to do with the roles of the President and Congress in foreign affairs. The occasion was the introduction of a Senate resolution purporting to define a national commitment of the United States as an undertaking carrying in one form or another the endorsement of Congress. Thus the hearings were thought of as a beginning toward reasserting the Senate's constitutional right to "advise and consent" in the making of such commitments. But they went even beyond this purpose. They were, in the words of the committee chairman Senator J. William Fulbright, "an experiment in public education" in which the committee was acting as a forum through which experts and scholars could add to congressional and public understanding. In reading the report of these hearings, one gets the impression that even the committee members were amazed in reviewing the aggrandizement of presidential power that has taken place within the past thirty years. It was noted that in many cases the President had simply made "executive agreements" with the heads of foreign governments, thereby avoiding the necessity of Senate ratification, which the Constitution calls for in the case of a treaty.

The real eye openers, however, came in the discussions of what the President can do to implement a foreign policy with military force on his own initiative and authority. Many of these revelations were provided by Nicholas deB. Katzenbach, Under Secretary of State, representing the administration. The view expressed by Mr. Katzenbach was that the Founding Fathers had set no limits to either the power of the President or that of Congress but had sought to provide for control by a balance between the two, and after considerable verbal pursuit he was pinned down by Chairman Fulbright on a specific question relating to the Tonkin Gulf Resolution. The chairman asked, "Would the President, if there were no resolution, be with or without constitutional authority to send U.S. soldiers to South Vietnam in the numbers that are there today?" And Katzenbach answered, "It would be my view . . . Mr. Chairman, that he does have that authority."

Later, Senator Bourke B. Hickenlooper asked Katzenbach, "In connection with the thesis that the President has the right to order troops into a foreign country, for instance—and I will use a foreign country by way of an illustration—and commit them to battle, without resolution of the Congress or without authority of the Congress, does Congress have the right to pass a proper measure, a joint resolution or something else, to bring those troops out of that country contrary to the wishes of the President?" And Mr. Katzenbach answered, "I very much doubt that it has the power to do that," going on to say during an ensuing exchange, "I think you raise a much closer question if it refers to support of them under the Appropriations Act. On that I think as a practical matter it is perfectly obvious Congress can do this."

Toward the end of the hearings, one of the people appearing before the committee suggested that another way to deal with the President in this case would be to impeach him, but Senator Wayne Morse took immediate exception; impeachment, he said, under the Constitution could only be applied under a very limited set of facts bordering on treason.

The exchange of views as to the powerlessness of Congress was prophetic. When President Nixon ordered troops into Cambodia on April 30, 1970, Congress found that except for its grasp upon the purse strings, it was practically without recourse, and there was an explosion of protest on Capitol Hill that almost equaled that which wracked the country as a whole. In retrospect the Cambodian incursion (nobody, not even one of Mr. Nixon's opponents, likes to call it an invasion) was not a terribly serious widening of the war or encroachment upon international ethics—it was nothing to what the communists had been doing in that area of Southeast Asia for years. But in this country it was the trip-latch that loosed a flood of pent-up rage and frustration that had been accumulating for years and that now poured forth, inundating everything in its path. The President, the Pentagon, the R.O.T.C., the draft boards, corporations, universities—all were angrily attacked. Never before in America had there been such confusion, so much irrationality, so great a concern with symptoms and so little with disease, and no part of our society felt the weight of it quite so much as did the military.

CHAPTER ELEVEN

"Chuck Him Out, the Brute!"

★ General William Tecumseh Sherman, grim and grizzled as he seemed, was nevertheless something of a humorous raconteur. One of his favorite stories had to do with the great prewar chief of the army, General Winfield Scott, a massive man and a most impressive sight in full dress uniform. As Sherman told the story, one day Scott went to make a formal call on a family in Washington. He knocked, and the door was opened by a little boy who gazed up in open-mouthed awe at the great figure standing there in plumed hat, gleaming epaulettes, and brilliant sash. The little boy ran and told his mother someone was at the door. "Who is it?" she asked, and he answered "I dess it's Dod!"

DOD, which is now the commonly accepted acronym for Department of Defense, if it does not stand for a deified presence in Washington, at least signifies a vastly powerful one.

One of the more startling pages in William O. Douglas's recent book, *Points of Rebellion,* raises the question as to whether even a President would dare to hold a real showdown with the Pentagon, startling because Douglas should know better than most that the Pentagon in and of itself has no authority whatever under the Constitution. As for Congress versus the Pentagon, Marquis Childs observed in 1970 that members of Congress, however good their intentions, simply did not have the staff, the secret information, or the power to resist the Department of Defense with its annual budget of 70 billion to 80 billion dollars.

True, Congress has the ultimate power over the Pentagon—that of appropriations—and it is in a position to shut off the water if it desires to do so. But no congressman is going to vote against "national security," or to deny support to troops who are already in the field. And not every congressman is indifferent to getting some of the defense millions for the factories in his home region. Simply through its economic power, the Pentagon in the past quarter century or so has reached into nearly every community where there is major industrial activity; into many universities, which are recipients of its multi-million-dollar research grants; into labor unions; and into so many pay checks that everyone must pause and think for a moment before he can safely say that he is not and never has been part of the "military-industrial complex."

A large sector of our economy and a large proportion of many professions, such as that of electrical engineer, aeronautical engineer, physicist, and several others, became dependent on defense work for their livelihood. When a firm such as the Lockheed Aircraft Corporation announced that it was going under unless it got an additional $600 million on its defense contracts, it was not speaking altogether for the corporation but for a couple of thousand subcontractors all over the country, for a large part of the metropolitan community around Atlanta, and for other people dependent on it. Many here and elsewhere had moved their families hundreds of miles to settle near defense plants. Many had shaped their whole careers toward defense work. The degree to which the country had an economic tiger by the tail was indicated when it was estimated that defense cutbacks ordered in early 1970 were going to cost more than a million jobs.

There is also the question of to what extent defense has contributed to inflation. DOD has been quick to point out that defense costs as a share of the federal budget fell from 41 per cent in fiscal year 1970 to an estimated 35 per cent in 1971—the lowest share in twenty years; and also that they had been cut from a

9.5 per cent of the gross national product in 1968 to a planned 7 per cent in 1971—again the lowest percentage in twenty years. It is also fair to remember that even when defense costs in the late 1960's, including that of the Vietnam war, climbed to the vicinity of their highest World War II level, the total was still vastly lower than its 1945 counterpart as a share of the GNP.

But it was still high enough. Through the last half of the 1960's, defense costs plus veterans' benefits, which are a product of defense, were running to between 45 per cent and 50 per cent of the federal budget. And that represents a heavy burden when it is considered that the national budget must now provide for health, education, welfare, and other costs to a degree that was unheard of a few years ago. Technical warfare of the sort practiced in Vietnam proved itself to be horribly expensive, and it became more so under Pentagon contracts with floating lids. According to one report, cost overruns in 1969 had passed fifteen billion dollars and were still mounting at the end of the year.

Another effect of a large military establishment was seen in the large numbers of people withdrawn from the civilian work force to become more tax consumers than tax payers and able to contribute little toward the satisfaction of nonmilitary needs. By the end of the decade, this included the more than three million people in the armed forces, more than a million civilians employed by the military establishment, and millions more working in defense industries—all these added to the ten million or more who work in other departments of the federal, state, and local governments and whose numbers have been greatly increased by all the new programs that have been taken on in recent years.

There was serious inflation, even with a government-regulated economy, during World War II. There can be little doubt that today, in an unregulated economy, massive defense expenditures have contributed heavily to inflation.

Having now regarded **DOD** as a militaristic giant whose claws dug into every important sector of our economy and whose hobnailed boots have been grinding the faces of the poor, it is only fair to put ourselves in the military's boots and try to imagine how things look from inside the Pentagon. We hardly need to shed tears for DOD. But fairness does demand a look at both sides of the case—in fact, so does prudence, for this is not just a big corporation that will be replaced by another supplier if we do not buy its products, but an institution that has some relation to our personal safety. And adverse public opinion, particularly on the part of youth, had hurt the Department of Defense by the end of 1970 much more severely than most people imagine. If young people have ever really believed that they are helpless, that they cannot penetrate the vast and supposedly impersonal centers of the "power structure," then the effects of some of their activities on DOD might prove otherwise to them. This institution is made up of people who are no different from other people in wishing to believe they are doing work that is important and well regarded. It is this satisfaction of which they are being deprived, and the consequences could be most harmful to the country. It is one thing to bring the expenditures of the Defense Department down to some reasonable amount. It is another to tear down the men and women who make up the services. These include inferior people, as does any organization of any size. But anyone who has served with the best professionals must remember them with respect and even some affection. They are among the rather limited number of Americans who are not out to make money. They have their own mystique: a product of tradition, devotion to duty, adventure, comradeship, shared tragedies and triumphs, a sense of living for something larger than themselves.

They do like to have a little action now and then, and this is an unescapable consequence of being trained for war. However, the Pentagon does not start wars, even though it is always ready, as it should be, to participate in one. What happened following World War II was that the foreign policy on which the United States embarked was as much military as it was diplomatic, so it was proper, natural, and necessary to have the generals and admirals closely involved. But under the Constitution it is the civilian heads of our government who are responsible, and when these civilians decided that the United States was going to underwrite the security of free nations and then proceeded to make military assistance commitments all over the world, there was little that the Department of Defense could do but get ready to support these decisions.

It had to build up its strength; it had to make extra efforts in organizing, training, and combining with allied forces; and it had to develop tactics, techniques, and equipment for worldwide operations, including airborne and amphibious actions.

Further, in Korea and Vietnam our military people received instructions that no American force had ever received before; they could not pursue the enemy to his home base and destroy him; they could fight on one side of a fence but not on the other; in short, they could not win.

The antimilitary sentiment as a result of Vietnam injured the military establishment in many ways, most visibly in the R.O.T.C. program. It was widely reported that in the school year 1969–70 R.O.T.C. enrollments declined 25 per cent because of animosity on the campuses; there were about seventy attempts to burn or blow up R.O.T.C. buildings; and several highly regarded schools, including Yale, Harvard, Dartmouth, Princeton, Columbia, and Stanford, had decided to drop the program, bringing to more than twenty the number of colleges that had turned against it since 1966.

Quantitatively, R.O.T.C. is an important source of officers, generally the largest source for the Army and Air Force, but in this respect the damage seemed to be far from fatal. The dropouts took away only a relatively small percentage of the total R.O.T.C. membership, and there were other schools waiting to replace them. More worrisome was the loss of the elite colleges as related to the pride, prestige, and quality that are so important to leadership and effectiveness in the armed forces. Nothing could have emphasized more the loss in the minds of many young people of the honor and esteem with which the country has always regarded its military services, even if the regard has been intermittent. Moreover, the services are now going through a very difficult period, trying to adapt themselves to changing values and new roles in a future that no one can clearly discern. It is time for creative thinking of the highest order, for officers who will make waves if waves are necessary, and initiating this

133

sort of disturbance is many times more difficult for the 100 per cent career officer than it is for one who has somewhere else to go, if need be, for employment. From this standpoint, as well as in his ability to bring in fresh thinking from the outside, the high-grade R.O.T.C.-trained officer seems more important today than ever. But the current mood of society does not encourage him to serve in the armed forces, and something intangible but extremely important may be going by the board. As an example in one service only, the standards of Army quality are well taken care of by the U.S. Military Academy in the main, but what one single non-West-Pointer may contribute is illustrated by the record of George C. Marshall, a graduate of Virginia Military Institute. He was Army Chief of Staff and one of the chief architects of victory in World War II, Ambassador, Secretary of State identified with the Marshall Plan, Secretary of Defense, and winner of the Nobel Peace Prize. In the climate of 1970, one could only wonder how many young George Marshalls were deciding to devote their lives to their country through the military service.

Another aspect of this matter is that in the past, the caliber of R.O.T.C. officers has been such that a disproportionate number of them, after their service in the armed forces, have moved into leading positions of civilian responsibility: congressmen, ambassadors, governors, prominent business executives, and the like. And an "insider's" knowledge of the military establishment among civilian leaders cannot fail to be healthful in a democracy. After having been so deeply involved in our foreign affairs for so many years, what new direction will our military leaders seek in the future, what manner of continuing involvement will they be pressing for? It is just as well, now as always, for their civilian counterparts to be informed on such questions, and the alienation of leading colleges does not help that situation, either.

As another result of the Vietnam war, draft board offices have been raided and files dumped or damaged. In 1970 nearly three hundred offices had been attacked by the first of September. Some were destroyed by explosives. Thousands of young men fled from the country to escape military service. A whole draft-counseling industry sprang up, and these services of legal volun-

134

teers, church organizations, and other institutions helped many young men avoid the draft while adding their own implied condemnation of the military.

The Army was forced to take in many young men who were actively hostile to it. These reluctant soldiers published underground newspapers, refused military courtesies, slighted their duties, and otherwise impaired military discipline and morale. Severe racial problems compounded these difficulties.

Respect for the military profession declined sharply. Many wearing the uniform found it hard to live with this lowered esteem, which often took the form of shouted obscenities or other abuse in public. Moviemakers, who had once portrayed them as "good guys" almost without exception, now tried to outdo one another producing films in which military people were clowns, bumblers, sadists, and scoundrels.

Retention of qualified personnel in the armed services soon became a serious problem. With so much questioning of the military mission and so little appreciation by the public, service people began asking themselves if it was all worth it. Entailing as it does financial sacrifices as well as the possible loss of life or limb, the military career begins to seem much less attractive if pursuing it also means loss of respect and dignity.

In early 1970, for the first time in history, it was thought, a West Point graduate asked the Army to discharge him as a conscientious objector; his objection was specifically to the Vietnam war, and four other West Pointers issued a statement in support of his stand.

Distaste for the military was said to be descending even to the small boys in private military prep schools, where enrollments and applications were declining.

Even officers lodged deep within the labyrinth of the Pentagon were by no means immune. DOD is far from being unaware of, or insensitive to, public opinion. Every day, through clipping services, summaries of broadcasts, reviews of pertinent literature, reports from the halls of Congress, and other means, the officers are kept informed of what people are saying. And about every day in the spring and summer of 1970 they saw the military establishment criticized, attacked, opposed, and even vilified. By the end of May, the criticism had become so inordinate that even Senator Eugene J. McCarthy, the 1968 peace candidate, felt called upon to assert that the military was being unfairly blamed for disasters in Indochina that were largely the result of failures by the civilian leaders of the country.

Of course, as the real professional knows, his popularity waxes and wanes according to the danger civilians think they are in. The regulars who served in the pacifist days of the 1930's can well remember how they were regarded at that time. Even the drafted civilian-soldiers who were in uniform before and after Pearl Harbor can recall the sudden change of attitude when the bombs fell. Before that, they were little more than the objects of amused sympathy. Afterward, nothing was too good for them.

Appearance of the movie *Patton* in 1970 revived controversy over that remarkable figure of World War II and startled young people, who, through the medium of film, saw him in action for the first time. The movie opened with a shot of a giant American flag, which filled the entire width of the screen and which was evidently the backdrop to a stage upon which Patton was about to address an audience of soldiers occupying, as it seemed, the position of the movie audience. Patton, superbly played by George C. Scott, appeared in full dress uniform with all his medals, American and foreign, and made a speech that was obviously a modified version of the "fight talk" he used to give to the officers and noncoms of troops about to go into combat for the first time.

To an audience of 1970, most of whom were not alive in the days of World War II, the speech must have seemed completely wild and insanely militaristic. But the author remembers Patton himself making the original of the speech before the audience for which it was intended, with an altogether different backdrop. The scene was the muddy square of a little French town, with Patton standing on a packing crate clad in combat OD's and behind him a gray winter sky and the distant rumble of artillery from the front lines along the Saar. Surroundings like this make a considerable difference. So vividly did his words impress themselves upon me that some eight hours later, that evening, I was able to write them down with confidence of considerable accuracy—a feat of memory I have never accomplished before or since. The penciled words on their faded pages are before me now, and in reviewing them I find that the language is very rough and has to do mostly with advice on how to kill Germans and not get killed yourself, and with Patton's philosophy of combat, which, expressed in one word, was *attack*. Under the circumstances, I cannot imagine anyone I would rather have been listening to. Yet I have no doubt that if the General were alive and in action today, he would be branded as a murderer. In fact, his son, Brigadier General George S. Patton III, who seems to agree with his father that the purpose of soldiering is to kill as many of the enemy as possible as fast as possible, has been referred to by a well-known author as a distinctly brutalizing influence in Vietnam. It is the old story, as once written by Kipling:

> For it's Tommy this, an' Tommy that, an' "Chuck him out, the brute!"
> But it's "Savior of 'is country," when the guns begin to shoot.

However, the peacetime treatment of our military people prior to World War II was simply neglect for the most part, whereas in recent times they have become the object of strong animosity, in which there is a large element of irrationality. As an instance, when in 1969 a twenty-billion-dollar military procurement bill came up for discussion in Congress, a debate prolonged by obstructionists raged for nearly three months before the bill was passed. In summary, Senator Margaret Chase Smith, ranking Republican member of the Senate Armed Services Committee, had this to say: "The origins of the challenge to military spending in 1969 were to be found partly in a sense of frustration over an unpopular war, and partly through frustration on serious domestic problems such as housing, education, poverty, pollution and inflation.

"To these must be added a growing conviction, flowing from these frustrations, that America had somehow become overcommitted globally and, consequently, was spending more than was needed to protect what was deemed to be our vital interests. This last notion had a cart-before-the-horse aspect. If, in fact, the United States had become overcommitted throughout the world, the logical process would be a debate on the nature of our commitments with any reduction in arms to follow agreement on the assumption. To the contrary, some who were challenging military spending were trying to force a reduction in our commitments by denying sufficient force to back them up."

The cart-before-the-horse treatment has characterized many reactions to the war in Vietnam.

The consequences may be more grave than we imagine. Hostile attitudes toward the armed forces are among the chief worries of our military leaders. The serious nature of this matter was highlighted by a statement by General Earle G. Wheeler, then Chairman of the Joint Chiefs of Staff, in a copyrighted *U.S. News & World Report* interview published April 20, 1970:

"*Q. Where is all this likely to lead, if there isn't a change in these attitudes?*

"A. I would say it is going to lead to chaos—to disintegration of the services."

CHAPTER TWELVE

"Why Me?"

★ In the course of the War of Independence, George Washington formed a realistic opinion of patriotism as a force in war to be relied on unassisted by any other. He said he knew that patriotism existed and that it had done a lot of good toward fighting the British but that "whosoever builds upon it, as a sufficient Basis for conducting this Bloody war, will find themselves deceived in the end."

Patriotism in America has this definite characteristic: when men are told that soldiers are needed at the fighting front, each one asks himself very logically and sensibly, "Why me?"

This question of "Why me?" has been of paramount importance in all the wars that America has fought, and now that there are considerations of a drafted versus an all-volunteer force, it deserves to be reexamined in the light of our history.

The most conspicuous body of facts, figures, and judgments on this matter is the so-called Gates Commission Report. This came about because dissatisfaction with the draft had become a major issue by 1968, and in his campaign for the Presidency, Richard Nixon promised to do something about it. In March, 1969, shortly after he had entered the White House, President Nixon announced the creation of a fifteen-member commission headed by former Secretary of Defense Thomas S. Gates, which was directed to develop "a comprehensive plan for eliminating conscription and moving toward an all-volunteer armed force." The assignment was, as will be observed, not to examine into and report upon the practicability of such a force; it was to make recommendations for moving toward it, and it was accompanied by certain cautions from the President; we must, he warned, proceed carefully lest the national security be endangered.

In February, 1970, the commission released its unanimous findings in a tremendously detailed and documented report replete with charts and statistics. In it the prospects for an all-volunteer force were presented as extremely optimistic. The Selective Service Act was due to expire June 30, 1971. The commission expressed the belief that with the pay raises it was recommending and other improvements in personnel management, an all-volunteer force could be in existence by the following day. A standby draft was recommended for emergency use. In addition to questions of cost and other matters, the report discussed social, political, and military effects to be expected, raising the most common objections briefly and disposing of them with appropriate argument.

Reception of the report as expressed by columnists and other commentators was decidedly mixed. Some saw it as a superficial "hard sell" job, others as the answer to the military manpower problem. One branded it as a capitalistic scheme to hire the sons of poor workers to do our dying for us. Several said it was too optimistic. Many thought that the all-volunteer force would be a fine idea, but that the idea ought to be looked at more searchingly.

Reception by the Administration might be described as cautious. Without rejecting the report, the government made moves toward its implementation that were considerably short of those recommended. Nevertheless, the Gates Commission Report has achieved wide currency. It has appeared in the form of a paperback, and thousands of officially produced copies have been distributed to government agencies, libraries, and other depositories. Because it offers an answer to a question that is very central to patriotism in America—"Who does our fighting?"—it deserves comment here. Certainly the concept of an all-volunteer force is a desirable one in many ways. But how does it relate to the willingness of our people to supply manpower for a large, long-continuing military operation?

Even under the best of conditions—a state of general public favor for fighting a war—the lessons of our past are not encouraging, and this view places a somewhat different interpretation upon our military history than does the historical section of the Gates Commission Report, which, in its strong advocacy of the all-volunteer force, passed rather lightly over certain points that might have been further explained.

For example, the report says, "The United States has relied throughout its history on a voluntary armed force except during major wars and since 1948." Those are big exceptions, considering that the forces between major wars up to World War II were usually extremely small. Between the Civil and the Spanish-American wars, for example, the Army was down to less than twenty thousand at one point. As another example, just before preparation for World War II began, the Army consisted of only about 200,000 regulars and a National Guard of about the same size.

The report states that the War of Independence was fought "almost entirely by volunteers who were attracted by bounties," without indicating the difficulties that were encountered or the fact that a draft was imminent as the war ended. In the military operations of 1775–81, when purely patriotic volunteering failed to produce the number of troops needed, bounties of money and land were offered in order to stimulate enlistments. This was productive of many evils. The expense, for the financially weak states, was hard to bear. And often the bounties brought forward a poor quality of man. One of the worst examples was that of a state that hired deserters from General Burgoyne's British army in order to fill a quota. These men, who had already, in General Washington's words, "given a glaring proof of a treacherous disposition," deserted from his army just as fast as they had from Burgoyne's. Toward the end of the war a couple of states were instituting conscription, and Congress was recommending that all the others do the same, but the conflict ended before this became necessary.

After he had made his careful study of the War of Independence and all other American wars up through the Civil War, General Emory Upton, in his classic *Military Policy of the United States*, concluded: "While the patriotism of a people, taken collectively, is quite equal to keeping up a prolonged struggle for liberty, cost what it may, we find that the patriotism of the individual utterly fails to induce him to undergo, voluntarily, the hardships and dangers of war."

Of course Upton was speaking of the individual in general, which may sound contradictory but which is no more so than the thought he was trying to express: that a body of people wages war with a great deal more resolution than might be expected from the sum of its individual parts.

Upton also concluded:

—"That neither voluntary enlistments based on patriotism, nor the bounty, can be relied upon to supply men for the army during a prolonged war.

—"That the draft, connected or not connected with voluntary enlistments and bounties, is the only sure reliance of a government in time of war."

Nothing has happened to date that would warrant changing those assertions.

Apparently Congress came to much the same conclusions very early. In 1790 it rejected a proposal for a combination of universal militia service and a federal draft. But it passed a law in 1792 establishing a uniform militia in every state, and the states had the authority to call the militiamen into service; so did the federal government, for specific purposes stated in the Constitution. With certain exceptions, every able-bodied male eighteen to forty-five was enrolled in the militia. And so clearly was defense of the country understood to be a citizen's duty that each militiaman, under this law, had to provide his own arms and ammunition *at his own expense*.

Actually, the militia never amounted to much as a military

force. But the important thing about it was that it embodied the truly democratic principle that every able-bodied male citizen during a certain period of his life owed military service to his country, and it provided for a way of listing the names of these men and calling them into service when needed. Thus we had what amounted to a compulsory military service provision soon after the Constitution was adopted.

Concurrently, conscription in a more direct, or national, form was being born in Europe. The theory of equality introduced by the French Revolution led to universal military service and compulsory enlistment. With large conscripted armies Napoleon won his great victories and Prussia became a military power.

When the Civil War broke out in America, the truth of General Upton's conclusions soon made itself manifest. Both in the North and in the South voluntary enlisting failed as a means of producing the required manpower. But this does not come through very clearly from a reading of the Gates Report, which has this to say: "The Civil War, the greatest conflict ever waged on this continent, was largely fought by volunteers on both sides. When war was declared, the Union Army had fewer than 16,000 officers and men. Within the first two years, more than one million men answered the call to arms. Nevertheless, President Lincoln proposed a national draft in early 1863 to ensure that the necessary troops would be forthcoming. When it was enacted in March, the draft immediately aroused widespread resistance, which reached a bloody climax in the New York draft riots. The street fighting left more than 1,000 dead.

"Like the draft proposed during the war of 1812, the Civil War draft was not a 'pure' system of conscription. A draftee could provide a substitute or initially purchase an exemption for $300. Although conscription accounted for about 250,000 of the 2,667,000 men who served in the Union Army, only some 46,000 were actually drafted into personal service. Of the balance of those subject to the draft, almost 87,000 purchased an exemption and more than 116,000 provided substitutes. True draftees accounted for only 2.3 percent of the military manpower raised by the North."

The 87,000 men who, as the report notes, purchased exemptions, actually did not go to the war, although technically they were conscripted. Had they been deducted, the report might have said that the draft accounted for only 163,000 of the men who served in the Union Army. At any rate, the impression left by this section of the report is that the draft was not too important in the Civil War, that volunteering provided most of the troops, and that national conscription was put into effect in March, 1863, only as a sort of standby measure.

But a form of compulsion was in effect long before the spring of 1863, and it is safe to assert that the *threat* of the draft accounted for many more than 163,000 being in the Union Army, although how many more would be hard to say. The only year in which there was no military manpower problem was 1861; then Lincoln's call for volunteers resulted in so many enlistments that recruiting had to be stopped in the spring of 1862. That summer, however, the going got rough, and voluntary enlistments dwindled away. On July 2, 1862, Lincoln issued his famous call for "three hundred thousand more," but the response was so slow that something had to be done to spur patriots to come forward. Initially the spurring mechanism was that provided for by the old militia laws within the states. If a town did not come through with its quota of volunteers, it was threatened with a draft upon the militia. Everybody hated *that* idea, especially the politicians. If a political leader allowed a draft to take place in his area, he could expect very few votes for his slate of candidates in the next election. Consequently, large bounties were arranged for and offered by towns, cities, states, and the federal government.

For example, about a month after the July 2 call for volunteers, Lincoln followed up with an order for a draft of 300,000 militia, and this order also said that if any state should fail to provide its quota of the previously-called-for volunteers, the deficiency would have to be made up by another draft upon the militia. The draft was executed in very few places; instead Lincoln received "volunteers," many of them with their pockets well lined with money. Yet it is doubtful if the money would have brought them forward, had everyone not understood that there was a draft ready to be used as a stick in case the carrot did not work.

Even when the national conscription act was passed in 1863, the thinking behind it was that it also should encourage "voluntary" enlistments rather than raise men directly. Whenever the President sent out a call for troops, all men who were enrolled under the national conscription law became liable for the draft. But the call would be accompanied by quotas assigned to the various districts, and only if the people failed to come through with enough enlistments to fill the quota was the draft put into effect.

The nationally administered draft was even more of a horror to people than the state drafts because it represented a power that the federal government had never used before, that had always been resisted, and that many people felt it had no right to have. The poor had an added grievance because, as they pointed out, people with money could hire a substitute or pay commutation and get off: that rich men were allowed to fight the war with their money while poor men had to spill their blood. Essentially the accusation was not too different from the one that would be raised more than a hundred years later when the boy whose family was well-heeled enough to send him to college could be deferred, while the boy whose education had ended with high school had to go to Vietnam. In New York many of the men whose names were called for the Civil War were poor Irish immigrants who had just arrived in this country and who had no interest in the war; also they feared the Negroes as competitors in the labor market. There was a riot in New York the like of which has never been seen for murder, arson, atrocious assault, and loss of life. Typical of the irrational nature of all riots was one of the accomplishments of this one—the burning down of an orphanage for Negro children over the heads of its little occupants, who were forced to flee into the streets.

The story of the draft in the Civil War is not an edifying one, and as the Gates Commission Report notes, only 46,000 were drafted directly into service. But indirectly, used as a threat by the states and the federal government, the draft was a big factor.

In spite of everything people might tell themselves and each other as to who volunteered and who did not, it can be argued that the draft in one form or another was responsible for putting the majority of northern soldiers into uniform after the spring of 1862.

As for the Civil War officers who continued to serve in the regular establishment, the lessons of manpower procurement were graven deeply on the tablets of their minds. It is easy to imagine that generation of officers telling the next, "For God's sake, never start another big war unless you do it with unrestricted conscription," and this in effect was the plea that those in charge of the Civil War draft left behind addressed to their successors.

The Spanish-American War was over too quickly even to exhaust the first flush of volunteers; no draft was needed. But when World War I came along, a selective service act was passed immediately. There was little reliance on volunteering; in fact, recruiting of volunteers was soon suspended because it tended to throw the whole manpower program out of balance by allowing people to choose a service in which they might not be as useful as they would be somewhere else. It was the same story in World War II, and these two wars developed another use for the draft: to channel men into war-essential industries by denying them exemptions for work that was not considered essential. Of the 4.7 million who served in World War I, 2.8 million were drafted; but, as was the case with the Civil War, there is no way of measuring the total effect of the draft if its influence on voluntary enlistments is taken into account.

Gallup polls indicate that public approval for the idea of a draft, which was low in 1938 (about one third approving), increased rapidly during the war years until it stood at about three quarters approving in 1945, an attitude that continued at least up through 1966; also, during the war years an overwhelming majority of the general public thought that the draft was being handled fairly. True, not everyone was happy with it; many who were in the service in the months just before Pearl Harbor can remember seeing the word "OHIO" ("Over the Hill in October") chalked on barracks walls. And there were more than half a million draft violations, resulting in nearly thirteen thousand convictions in World War II. But considering that any form of conscription is unfair, and there is no way to make it fair, most Americans were remarkably well satisfied.

At the end of March, 1947, the draft law was allowed to expire, and of the draftless period of something more than a year that followed, the Gates Commission Report said, "The military soon expressed concern that it would not be able to obtain the necessary number of volunteers which might, in part, have reflected a 23 percent decrease in the Army's recruiting budget." But according to an editorial in the April, 1970, *Army* magazine, there was trouble not only with quantity but with quality: "The times were less affluent and the nation's mood much kinder to the military, but despite the recruiters' best efforts the armed forces were unable to maintain the relatively low strength levels authorized. The quality of the men was generally low—in an infantry battalion there might be only two or three high school graduates. Discipline was poor and the court-martial rate was high. The level of technical proficiency was low, even though the demand was very modest in comparison to today's requirements. It is significant that when selective service was resumed there was a marked improvement in almost all of the areas in which the services were deficient."

Renewed, the draft served us through the Korean War and ever since has been a permanent part of our military manpower procurement process.

For the Vietnam war the draft operated much as it always has; directly as a means of conscripting manpower and indirectly as a stimulus to enrollment in the active and reserve forces, including the R.O.T.C. and the National Guard. But how different has been the attitude, particularly that of youth, as compared with World Wars I and II! There is even an indication that the general public, which in the two previous wars mentioned was inclined to bear an animus toward "draft dodgers," might have become more inclined to be sympathetic. Louis Harris conducted a poll in December, 1969, in which people were asked whether the draft was wrong because it forced many young men to fight in a war they did not believe in. Among the respondents in total just about as many said *yes* as said *no,* with a majority of those under 29 saying that the draft was wrong on that basis. In another poll conducted by Harris at about that time, 46 per cent of the people interviewed disagreed with a statement that the anti-Vietnam protesters were "mostly young men who are trying to get out of the armed forces."

There really is no equitable way of impressing one man for military service while another is allowed to stay home, and so the inescapable unfairness of the draft, in the climate of a limited and unpopular war, made it seem to be an instrument of hateful tyranny to many young people.

In the two great World Wars the average person had little doubt about the rightness of going to war. But he was in some cases troubled as to how he would answer the question "Why me?" to his wife, his boss, and himself. The draft provided a very satisfactory answer. It has provided no such satisfaction to the draftees going to Vietnam, thousands of whom have lost their lives, and who might well have asked not only "Why me?" but "Why anyone?"

The lack of a satisfactory answer to the latter question had much to do with poisoning the attitudes of young people toward the federal government, the armed forces, industry, and universities that have been cooperating in the war effort. Their rage and frustration turned against anything connected with the war, regardless of its long-term merits—against the R.O.T.C., the draft board, whatever was nearest.

When President Nixon created the Gates Commission with instructions to develop a plan for moving toward an all-volunteer force, anyone with a knowledge of our military history might have considered the decision as highly significant. History seemed to say that an all-volunteer system would not support an army of any great size in a protracted war; therefore, it might have been reasoned, what people in government must be thinking about was a much smaller armed force than we had, commensurate, perhaps, with reduced foreign commitments and the realities of nuclear weapons. And there were, indeed, moves in that direction connected with the implementation of the internationally more conservative Nixon Doctrine. But the moves were extremely cautious. The Gates Commission estimated that to put the all-volunteer idea into effect for fiscal 1971 would require an increase in the military budget of $3.2 billion. The size of the armed force this would provide for was generally interpreted as 2.5 million. Other agencies of the government were said to be estimating much higher costs for the all-volunteer conversion. It was turning out to be a very difficult calculation, and what made it more so was the hostile and derisive attitude of young people toward military service. Ironically, this attitude was making the armed forces much less attractive and thereby was contributing to the continuance of what youth wanted to end—the draft.

The experience of other countries did not provide much guidance, for there was little basis of comparison. It was noted that Canada had an all-volunteer force, but the pay more nearly approximated civilian earnings and the force was less than 100,000 strong. England also had an all-volunteer force but had vastly decreased its world commitments and reduced its force to around 400,000. Neither country had a morale problem comparable to ours.

President Nixon began reducing the armed forces, but his initial reductions did not appear to be, and probably could not be, large. The total of military personnel projected for the fiscal year 1971 was 2.9 million, compared to 3.2 million in fiscal 1970. In meeting with a youth group in the Pentagon early in 1970, Secretary of Defense Melvin R. Laird was asked, "If the United States were to establish a volunteer army, what would be the minimum number of troops needed in the U.S. to carry out the functions of the Department of Defense adequately?"

He answered that he thought it would have to be down near the two million mark. "I do not believe that you can carry out and meet the present obligations which this country has under its present treaties at that particular level unless you are willing to spend a considerable amount of money in order to maintain a large, up-to-date, modern, well-equipped Reserve and National Guard here in the U.S. The cost—as you move down to a regular strength of around two million—the costs to maintain the Reserve and National Guard go up considerably."

In late summer of 1970 it was announced by the Department of Defense that any large emergency build-up of the armed forces in the future would be met with reservists and guardsmen rather than with draftees. But would these components be adequately manned without a draft? Its removal takes away an important incentive for "voluntarily" enrolling not only in the active duty forces but in the Guard and in the Reserve, including R.O.T.C.

It was not long after the Gates Commission Report appeared that Defense and other government officials adopted a cautious and significant change in phraseology. Instead of talking about an all-volunteer force, they began speaking in terms of working toward a "zero draft call." It was a more realistic phrase and one that did not hold up hopes that might be impossible of fulfillment.

The same caution was evident in President Nixon's message to Congress on April 23, 1970, in which he supported a move away from the draft and toward an all-volunteer force but suggested that Congress extend the existing induction authority beyond July 1, 1971, and proposed pay increases on a much less immediate basis than those recommended by the Gates Commission. He also urged reforms in the current draft system. The President said, "No one can predict with precision whether or not, or precisely when, we can end conscription. It depends, in part, on the necessity of maintaining required military force levels to meet our commitments in Vietnam and elsewhere. It also depends on the degree to which the combination of military pay increases and enhanced benefits will attract and hold enough volunteers to maintain the forces we need, the attitude of young people toward military service, and the availability of jobs in the labor market." He also said there is "another essential element . . . that is vital to the high morale of any armed force in a free society. It is the backing, support, and confidence of the people and the society the military serves. . . . At few times in our history has it been more needed than today."

On October 12, 1970, Secretary of Defense Laird directed the services to move toward a goal of "Zero Draft Calls by July 1, 1973." The attitude expressed by high civilian officials and military officers was one of hope and determination to do everything possible to achieve this goal, but no one was making any promises. It would depend, they said, on a number of things. Money for one. But money alone would not be enough. Army Chief of Staff William C. Westmoreland put it bluntly: "We cannot attract the kind of soldier we need into an organization denigrated by some, directly attacked by others and half-heartedly supported by many. This country cannot have it both ways."

Meanwhile, other people were trying to think of ways in which the draft might be sugar-coated and made more palatable.

One idea that gained wide currency in the summer of 1970 was that of a national service system that would allow a young man a three-way choice—he could take his chances on being drafted, volunteer for military service, or volunteer for civilian service in teaching, hospitals, social or law enforcement work, or something of that sort. A Gallup Poll reported it as being highly favored by the public. In a copyrighted interview with Dr. Curtis W. Tarr, Director of Selective Service, published in the July 6 *U.S. News & World Report,* this exchange took place:

"*Q. Do you favor any of the universal-service plans that some youths recommend?*

"A. There is a great interest in universal service—not universal military service, but universal service. I'm really surprised how much I hear from young people about the idea. Girls as well as boys say: 'The draft will never be fair unless you take everybody. Why doesn't the country utilize everybody in some program of alternate service?'

"*Q. Do you like that idea?*

"A. My reservation right now is that I think that in today's society the major domestic problems are not ones in which we have sufficient expertise to use large numbers of people.

"If the nation ever decides to use the talents of its young people in either a voluntary or mandatory program, it should be organized sufficiently so that the creative energies of young people really can be utilized.

"You had better have a job that needs to be done and one that

151

young people can do in an effective way. These people are disenchanted enough with the nation; there is no point in making it worse.

"*Q. Do you think universal service would be practical?*

"A. I do think that we are going to have to do something to rally among young people an affection for the nation, a concern for the future of our society, and a feeling of responsibility for having contributed.

"We are never going to bring this about in some kind of a program that seeks to do good things but does not accomplish them. So I have real reservations about universal service in the near future. But it may very well be that we'll come to the point where we can use great numbers of young people in the battle against environmental pollution, and tutoring in the inner city. Then either large, government, voluntary programs or universal service might be helpful."

The favor for a universal service program that Dr. Tarr and Gallup report, constitutes another amazing bit of evidence of the flexibility of the American people when considering human needs against ideological or even constitutional principles. In assigning Congress the power "to raise and support armies" and "to provide and maintain a navy" the Constitution, through a liberal interpretation, provides for conscription of men to serve in the armed forces; but it will take real imagination to construe the meaning that young men and women may be compelled to work at anything else. This smacks of totalitarianism and the Hitler Youth. In fact, such an arrangement could be taken to be the "involuntary servitude" that the Thirteenth Amendment to the Constitution expressly forbids except as a punishment for crime.

If a large emergency program to remedy some of the ills of our society is contemplated, the resources already in existence and available in the armed forces can hardly escape notice. The services now have valuable experience in constructing mass-produced modular housing units and in constructing and operating low-cost, efficient hospitals. Their vocational and technical training programs are unsurpassed. The U.S. Army Corps of Engineers has long been involved in public projects and might contribute in some way to improvement of the environment. In communication, transportation, data processing, many other activities, the services have acquired billions of dollars' worth of knowledge, equipment, and property. Before key people are disbanded and installations are closed down, it might be well to consider whether or not some of these costly resources might be made useful to society on an emergency basis, just as the aid of the armed forces has been useful before in times of flood, hurricane, and other disasters.

However, any sort of civilian service program seems quite unrelated to the main question, which is: How do we obtain large numbers of people to fight in military actions in which they may be wounded or possibly killed? It seems likely that if they are paid well enough, hundreds of thousands of young men will volunteer for the armed forces in order to learn a trade or technology or to travel or to gain some other benefit or occupation. But unfortunately, the role of the armed forces, when they are really needed, is to fight—a harsh, unpleasant business that the American people do well enough when they must do it, but for which they normally show no great appetite.

For example, on October 14, 1970, in a news briefing at the Pentagon, the Assistant Secretary of Defense for Manpower stated that only 4 per cent of the men needed for ground combat skills were choosing that type of service voluntarily—the other 96 per cent were being assigned. He also admitted that in Vietnam the draftees were "carrying a relatively heavy combat burden at the present time."

And that came fairly close to being the nub of the whole story. It was an aspect of American patriotism that was not particularly new. In fact, if George Washington could return, he would understand it perfectly. But he might well be appalled at the number of large, serious, interlocking problems the armed forces of today are compelled to face in undertaking to achieve an all-volunteer service—problems of public attitudes, of costs, of assigned missions, and of their ability to fulfill those missions.

The question in the center of all these problems, in all probability, is not so much one of a draft versus an all-volunteer force as it is one of the extent and nature of our foreign commitments. The extent, because this determines the size of the armed forces needed, which in turn seems to determine the point at which an all-volunteer force becomes practical. The nature, because—as wars of this century, including Vietnam, have indicated—for a military activity the public supports, a draft is accepted as a necessary evil and endured or even highly favored, but for an activity the public does not support the draft is relentlessly attacked. This order of getting at things is somewhat illogical, but that, apparently, is the way people behave.

The foreign policy of the 1960's was enforced and conducted as though this were not so.

CHAPTER THIRTEEN

The Ramparts We Watch

★   On August 2, 1966, in the course of an exchange of toasts with President Shazar of Israel, President Lyndon Johnson subscribed to a policy supporting "the security of both Israel and her neighbors" that had previously been enunciated by President Kennedy. Did the clink of wine glasses mark the affirmation of a national commitment? Apparently it did; it was a public assurance by a President of the United States. Had it been the announcement of an important new policy, it might have become a doctrine such as the Monroe Doctrine of 1823 warning foreign powers to stay out of the western hemisphere, the Truman Doctrine of 1947 saying we would support "free peoples" everywhere, and other presidential doctrines.

In the vast maze of obligations that is now our foreign policy, we have taken on commitments because of such presidential statements or letters; because of agreements with the heads of other governments made by our Executive; because of notes or declarations signed by our Secretary of State; because of joint communiqués made by our high officials with those of foreign governments; because of joint resolutions of Congress; because of treaties made in the constitutionally prescribed way by the President, "with the Advice and Consent of the Senate . . . provided two-thirds of the Senators present concur"; and because of other writings, signings, and sayings.

In an effort to restore clarity and control, in June, 1969, the Senate passed the resolution that it had begun to consider in 1967 and around which so many discussions of the famous hearings of the Senate Committee on Foreign Relations of that year had revolved. A relevant part of the resolution as passed was that "it is the sense of the Senate that a national commitment by the United States results only from affirmative action taken by the executive and legislative branches of the United States Government by means of a treaty, statute, or concurrent resolution of both Houses of Congress specifically providing for such commitment."

Under that restricted definition alone, our list of obligations as of August, 1970, included commitments involving us in the defense of the following countries:

Argentina	Dominican	Japan	Peru
Australia	Republic	Italy	Philippines
Belgium	Ecuador	Korea,	Portugal
Bolivia	El Salvador	Republic of	Thailand
Brazil	France	Luxembourg	Turkey
Canada	Germany,	Mexico	Uruguay
Chile	Federal	Netherlands	United
China,	Republic of	New Zealand	Kingdom
Republic of	Greece	Nicaragua	Venezuela
Colombia	Guatemala	Norway	Vietnam,
Costa Rica	Haiti	Panama	Republic of
Cuba	Honduras	Pakistan	
Denmark	Iceland	Paraguay	

It may be noted with some astonishment that we have a commitment to defend Cuba, a country hardly considered to be one of our friends. Cuba is on the list because it was part of the multilateral Inter-American Treaty of Reciprocal Assistance (the Rio Pact), signed in 1947 in the pre-Castro days. In January, 1962, the representatives of the American republics signed a resolution excluding from participation in the inter-American system "the present Government of Cuba, which has officially identified itself as a Marxist-Leninist government." In October of the same year our Congress passed a joint resolution that said that the United States is determined "to prevent by whatever means may be necessary, including the use of arms, the Marxist-Leninist regime in Cuba from extending, by force or the threat of force, its aggressive or subversive activities to any part of this hemisphere; to prevent in Cuba the creation or use of an externally supported military capability endangering the security of the United States; and to work with the Organization of American States and with freedom-loving Cubans to support the aspirations of the Cuban people for self-determination." The passing of this resolution followed reports of a heavy Soviet arms build-up in Cuba during the summer of 1962 and just preceded the Cuban missile crisis in October of that year.

Thus we have not only an explanation of how Cuba happens to be one of our "allies" but a close-to-home example of the ideological content of our foreign policy. It may prompt the question of whether we can ever reach an accommodation with giant communistic powers on the other side of the world if we feel it necessary to adopt a policy so stringent against a small and relatively weak neighbor only one hundred miles or so from our shores.

A few more notes of interest about our commitments:

The preceding list does not include Cambodia and Laos. The protection of the SEATO treaty under a protocol signed by the participating parties in 1954 was extended to them but was declined. The same protocol covered South Vietnam and has been considered to be part of the basis for our intervention there.

Under the rules of eligibility for our list (treaty, statute, or concurrent resolution) we also have a commitment to a region: the "Joint Resolution to Promote Peace and Stability in the Middle East" passed in March, 1957, under the Eisenhower Doctrine. Because of current interest in this region, a relevant passage is worth examining.

"Sec. 2. The President is authorized to undertake, in the general area of the Middle East, military assistance programs with any nation or group of nations of that area desiring assistance. Furthermore, the United States regards as vital to the national interest and world peace the preservation of the independence and integrity of the nations of the Middle East. To this end, if the President determines the necessity thereof, the United States is prepared to use armed forces to assist any such nation or groups of such nations requesting assistance against armed aggression from any country controlled by international communism: Provided, that such employment shall be consonant with the treaty obligations of the United States and with the Constitution of the United States."

This is flexible language. There is much of the same flexibility in the wording of all our commitments. However, there are different degrees of firmness. Those commitments pertaining to the European and South American countries and to Canada seem quite firm, as illustrated by relevant words of the NATO agreement: "The Parties agree that an armed attack against one or more of them in Europe or North America shall be considered an attack against them all; and consequently they agree that, if such an armed attack occurs, each of them . . . will assist the Party or Parties so attacked by taking forthwith, individually and in concert with the other Parties, such action as it deems necessary, including the use of armed force, to restore and maintain the security of the North Atlantic area."

Even this is qualified, as in "such action as it deems necessary," but it is not so qualified as treaties affecting countries of the Asian sphere. For example, the relevant provision of the SEATO treaty (United States, Australia, France, New Zealand, Pakistan, Philippines, Thailand, United Kingdom, South Vietnam) says that in the event of aggression each party will "act to meet the common danger in accordance with its constitutional processes."

Thus the network of our commitments, extensive though it may seem, is a fabric that can be reduced or stretched. The reason for the great latitude in wording is, of course, that it would not be possible or advisable for the United States to spell out exactly what it would do ten or fifteen years from now under circumstances that cannot be foreseen. Matching this lack of specific instructions in our written commitments, we have our Constitution saying on one hand that Congress shall have the power to raise, support, and make rules for the regulation of armies and navies and declare war, but that the President is the commander in chief of the armed forces. This seems to allow the interpretation that as long as any armed forces are in existence, the President of the United States can send them anywhere abroad that he wants to.

The foregoing has dealt with formal commitments approved by both the Congress and the President. But there is in addition the activity that the President can conduct on his own initiative; this has always existed, but never to such a degree as it exists today; it has grown into a subsurface operation with dimensions that apparently are clear to only a few people.

Without congressional declarations of war, past Executives have committed troops at least 150 times. But usually these actions have been well publicized. To cite a few of the more spectacular interventions, there was no secrecy involved or desired when President McKinley sent soldiers to China in 1900 to help put down the Boxer Rebellion, or when President Theodore Roosevelt later sent troops to Panama, Cuba, and the Dominican Republic, or when President Wilson ordered our armed forces to take Vera Cruz in 1914.

The obscurity that shrouds many such operations today is relatively new and appears to be the product of several factors. There is the "executive agreement," raised to power by F.D.R. and continued with ever-increasing efficacy, which requires no public or even congressional discussion. There is the cloak of secrecy assigned to nuclear matters in World War II, which somehow has been extended to nonnuclear operations as well. There is the growing employment of the military euphemism: we do not send officers and men, we send "military advisers" at the outset; sometimes we do not establish bases, we set up "training units," and so forth. Also, airmen and aircraft have come to have a curious meaning; they are not "combat troops" in the sense of infantrymen, although a flier who has had his plane riddled by fire from the ground might not agree with this concept. There are these and other ways of doing things without stirring up public opinion.

One result of all this is that a considerable strain is placed upon American patriotism. The patriot is sometimes *compelled* to accept the principle of "my country right or wrong" because he often simply does not have the information needed to exercise his own conscience and judgment. Nor, it is now asserted, do his representatives in Congress, in all cases.

In an article written for *The New York Times Magazine* of August 9, 1970, Senator Stuart Symington charged that important information is being kept not only from the public but from Congress in the conduct of many of our foreign affairs and their associated military operations. The value of Symington's opinion is heightened by the fact that he has occupied a unique series of posts for observation: as a Pentagon official, as a member of the Senate committees on Armed Services and Foreign Relations, and as chairman of a subcommittee of the latter investigating U.S. foreign commitments since early 1969. Symington asserts that some of our activities abroad are now much better known to our adversaries than they are to the American public and in some cases to Congress.

As an instance, he stated in his article that since 1964, at first under the euphemism of "armed reconnaissance," the United States had been conducting a clandestine air war in northern Laos; that while the Vietnam fighting was being reduced with much publicity, the Laotian war was being increased secretly; and that Congress had been given information that was woefully insufficient or even misleading.

In situations like these, there is always a temptation to ascribe sinister purposes to our leaders—but if such purposes exist, they have been characteristic of all recent Executives, which would be more bad luck than we have any reason to expect. What is undoubtedly closer to the truth is that these Executives, given the power to act, have been acting as they believe good patriots should. It is the manner in which their decisions have been arrived at and put into effect that constitutes the chief threat to the democratic process involving consent of the governed, and to patriotism, if we are at all concerned about the public backing that, under our system of government, is necessary to support foreign or any other kind of policy.

It is entirely possible, of course, that the management of a far-flung global network of commitments is beyond the capability of a democracy—that a form of society under which people are meant to govern themselves includes of necessity certain characteristics that make it virtually impossible for them to govern affairs in distant lands. The difficulty of having everyone informed on complex and remote situations, long and often divisive debate, slow decision-making, and the fact that foreign opponents always know what is being discussed and planned just as well as we do —these may be among the disadvantages of a democracy in the field of foreign affairs. Goldwin Smith's 1898 observation comes to mind: "If you have an empire, you will have an emperor." What the United States had seventy years later could not truthfully be called an empire in the sense of dominating other lands for direct gain; in fact, we were losing billions of dollars through our overseas efforts. But as between the apparatus of managing and policing an empire in 1898 and what the United States was doing in 1968, there was a resemblance and a suggestion that a similar observation may strike at the heart of the matter: "If you have something that is a good deal like an empire, you must have someone who is a good deal like an emperor."

But we are a democracy. And the contradiction is a difficulty that each Executive has had to face for the past quarter century.

Before the awakening that came with Vietnam, our Presidents had more than a little justification for believing that the American people would be behind them in anything they might care to do in the resistance of aggression and the containment of communism. Therefore, acting as though they had been given a mandate, they deployed the military forces they had been given to command. In support of both our formal treaties and our other overseas commitments, this deployment was widespread under Presidents Truman, Eisenhower, Kennedy, and Johnson, with Nixon beginning a withdrawal. In 1969, locations of major installations (there were many minor ones) included the following:

Azores	Formosa	Mariana Islands	Ryukyu Islands
Bermuda	Germany	Marshall Islands	Spain
British	Greece	Midway Islands	Thailand
West Indies	Greenland	Morocco	Turkey
Canada	Iceland	Netherlands	United Kingdom
Canal Zone	Italy	Newfoundland	Virgin Islands
Crete	Japan	Pakistan	Vietnam
Cuba	Korea	Philippines	
Ethiopia	Libya	Puerto Rico	

In mid-1970, as a result of his subcommittee investigation on foreign commitments, Senator Symington reported that we had more than a million men overseas in 384 facilities and 3,000 minor installations, with 300,000 more at sea.

As to his intentions for the use of this worldwide force, an Executive might wish that he could be regarded as we sometimes think of Russia or China—as unpredictable and "inscrutable." Even considering the cases to which Senator Symington has called our attention (in which, at least, the home folks have been baffled), this is not completely possible. With a vigilant press trumpeting information and speculation to the world, the President of the United States cannot achieve total mystification.

And yet even with this handicap, President Nixon has done remarkably well, not only in the surprise Cambodian incursion but in enunciating our general foreign policy. Typical is his report to Congress presented in February, 1970, and entitled "U.S. Foreign Policy for the 1970's." Representatives of Russia and China may buy copies at the Government Printing Office and read it without a great deal of specific enlightenment. They will find certain statements that will give them reason to beware, such as:

"The United States will keep all its treaty commitments."

"We shall provide a shield if a nuclear power threatens the freedom of a nation allied with us, or of a nation whose survival we consider vital to our security and the security of the region as a whole."

They should especially beware (as we all should) because the President has given evidence that he is capable of matching his deeds to his exact words. However, considering the generality of language in the document and the flexibility that exists in the wording of treaty commitments, the Nixon Doctrine can mean almost anything the President wants it to mean. The general tone is one of a much more conservative approach to foreign interventions on the one hand, and on the other an affirmation of the principles of collective security.

One valuable service the document performs is to describe in some detail the National Security Council as it works at present with its supporting committees and other groups and the various individuals who contribute to its deliberations. The system is designed, in the words of the President, "to make certain that clear policy choices reach the top, so that the various positions can be fully debated in the meeting of the Council."

This system for gathering and analyzing information, much of it secret, such as that contributed by the C.I.A., plus the moral weight of having the safety of the nation in its care, plus the ability to consider both foreign and defense matters in a unified procedure, makes the N.S.C. group an extremely powerful organization. There is nothing to compare with it in Congress: no such availability of information and no such unity, with, for example, foreign and military policies falling into two completely separate jurisdictions in the Senate—those of the Committee on Foreign Relations and the Committee on Armed Services. We should inquire, however, whether or not there is among the information that reaches the highest echelon of the N.S.C. system something that bears upon the resources of patriotism that are available to carry out any given decision. And this can be a tricky appraisal. We seem to have learned from Vietnam that the American people cannot be committed to a protracted foreign war in cold blood, even though they have approved in principle the foreign policy that led to the war. This is an emerging element of global strategy that poses one or two rather worrisome questions. For example, has the reaction to Vietnam been so adverse that the American people would not now support an action called for by NATO? And what about Thailand? Under the SEATO treaty we have a commitment to that country, which is not far from the present scene of conflict. Does anyone seriously think that our people would now support a full-scale action there? If not, must we undergo the humiliation of not keeping a promise? This might be easy enough to do under the word of the agreement, but not so easy under its spirit and the moral judgment that must surely follow our failure to live up to written obligations.

This is one of the great questions that American patriotism has now come face to face with: How far are we prepared to go, not with pious statements or shipments of supplies but with the bodies of our young men, in backing up the network of commitments we now have around the world?

Would the United States be better off with no treaties whatever, so that we might be free to act as the people wish to act, unbound by considerations of twenty years ago or twenty years in the future? What are the arguments for such a policy (which would still be a foreign policy) and what against?

This is the sort of question the Nixon Doctrine does not answer—and that is probably as it should be. Yet in the light of all the anguish America has been through as a result of our intervention in Southeast Asia, the absence of any nationwide debate on the wider and more fundamental issues of foreign policy raised by the Vietnam war is somewhat surprising. When the Nixon Doctrine was announced, the only public comment from Congress reported by the Associated Press was that of five senators. There was considerable comment by editors and columnists, with the favorable opinions far outweighing the unfavorable. An opinion widely shared was that the doctrine was sensible and in tune with both realities abroad and the mood of the American people. Several editors welcomed the emphasis on partnership with other nations rather than on a "world policeman" or go-it-alone policy, as well as the emphasis on strength to resist aggressors and willingness to negotiate. A minority called it too general or vague. There was little evidence of isolationist sentiment, either in this round of comment or in that which followed the proposal to withdraw twenty thousand troops from Korea, which came later on. A few thought the Nixon Doctrine was too interventionist. But there was nothing that could be called a controversy, and perhaps that, too, was as it should be.

Nevertheless, an uneasy sense remained that what we were proceeding with was a policy that could be expressed essentially as "more of the same, with caution." It had the flavor of an interim plan and prompted a speculation as to whether the Executive branch was in the process of sketching out a grander design. If so, it is to be hoped that the design will be grand enough to encompass the capacity of American patriotism to support it when the chips are down.

At the very least, we seem to have been left with a few questions that call for our wiser heads to take counsel with one another —questions as to the extent and nature of our foreign commitments, the process by which they are arrived at, the military strategy and tactics whereby we propose to back them up if necessary, and who has the authority to put these military actions into effect. After 20 years, it would be strange if the thinking which preceded the making of all our treaties is still valid. And we obviously need a psychologically sounder way of committing military forces than we have been employing in the years that have followed World War II. Early in these years, much power was surrendered by Congress to the Executive in the belief that we have to be ready for a "push button" war. Yet in none of our crises of recent years (with the possible exception of the Cuban missile affair—and that lasted almost two weeks) has there been so little time that deliberation was not possible.

The Founding Fathers, after their experiences with George III, had a great fear of kings, and one reason was that kings were always getting their people into wars, often regardless of the public good. So in the Constitution they divided the authority, making the President the initiator of foreign policy and the commander of the armed forces, but making it necessary for Congress to approve treaties, appropriate money for the armed forces, and declare war. (Jefferson apparently thought that they had loaded the scales on the side of Congress. He wrote: "We have already given in example one effectual check to the Dog of

War by transferring the power of letting him loose from the Executive to the Legislative body, from those who are to spend to those who are to pay.") They hoped that thereby we would never have a military dictatorship.

But (and the Fathers probably would not be surprised if they returned and observed this) the situation does not allow an easy solution. Can we be sure of staying out of wars we do not really want to get into by insisting on the constitutional balance of power? The best answer is to remember Tonkin Gulf. It may be argued that the Congress was misinformed. It may be argued that the resolution was overinterpreted. But the fact remains that Congress did not resist a massive commitment of troops. Recently President Johnson, on a social visit to Congress, gave his former colleagues a sly little dig during an interview with reporters. He said in effect that Yes, he was glad to be back here—that "this is where they are in touch with the people," and he added, "every two years."

Can the people themselves, by some means of surveillance, guarantee that they will not be involved in an unwise war? How many wrote to their congressmen, or to the President, to protest the Tonkin Gulf decision? How many wrote afterward to scold their representatives in Washington and tell them they would never vote for them again? It is a safe guess that not many did. According to public opinion surveys, fully a quarter of the American people did not even know in the spring of 1964 that there was any fighting going on in Vietnam, and only a quarter are adequately informed on foreign affairs at any time. To the average citizen, foreign policy is one of the many things that keep adding to his feelings of helplessness and frustration, such as the highly automatic automobile or dishwasher that he does not understand and cannot fix when it breaks down. He can arrive at only one correct conclusion: if it does not work he ought to buy another make.

In his book *The American People and Foreign Policy,* Gabriel A. Almond points to the difficulty of instilling in the general public through mass media or mass education anything beyond the most superficial knowledge of international problems. He thinks there is little to be expected from mass enlightenment—that much more might be accomplished by training specialists who would be available in large and important social groups such as unions and associations to provide information and guidance and to train and educate other key figures, by widening the curricula of certain schools and colleges and by taking other measures to introduce information and critical judgment into our society at key points of communication. Considering the importance we have assigned to such judgment in our definition of patriotism, some such scheme as this might well make an improvement in its quality.

But in looking around for new ways in which to bring the people into closer touch with foreign policy, it is easy to forget that we already have a mechanism, provided by the Constitution, and that is the Congress, if it can be restored to its former position of importance and power in foreign affairs. In fact, the Congress is the only means we have by which some assurance can be gained that the people, through their representatives in the national government, are behind the government's policy.

During the 1967 hearings on our foreign commitments before the Senate Committee on Foreign Relations, two of the most constructive statements were made by Representative Paul G. Findley and Senator Clifford P. Case. Findley regretted that the whole matter of Vietnam had not been "placed on the anvil of democracy here on Capitol Hill"; had it been, he thought, the people could have made their views known through their elected representatives, divergent views could have been synthesized in debate, the country would have expressed its national will and purpose—and the President would then have had a solid basis on which to proceed. Senator Case said: "I think one of the very strong reasons for the constitutional provision for a declaration of war by Congress is that it is in itself a step in the mobilization of the country to fight a war, and that that drawing together of the people behind a grave decision of this sort has to be accomplished in some fashion involving them in that decision. We cannot accept, even though we have given the President the power to destroy the world by pulling the atomic trigger, that these lesser questions are still not enormously important. They are even more important because they are the more likely to come up, and we must maintain in some fashion an involvement of Congress, because that means the involvement of the people in these decisions. Especially is this true when we are operating, as we are now, under a draft law which requires men to serve in the armed forces without their consent."

In any study of ways and means to strengthen the hand of Congress, it will be found that the President's dominance in foreign affairs is not unrelated to his administration of domestic programs. For more than thirty years, mayors, governors, and congressmen have been running and dumping every conceivable kind of problem on the floor of the White House, and Congress has been appropriating more and more money to solve them through federal action. In mid-1970 there were estimated to be more than a thousand such domestic programs being administered by nearly sixty federal departments and agencies at a cost of about $100 billion a year. One curious result is that "federal money" is now thought of as a sort of manna from heaven, not as money that the government gets from the taxpayers and then hands back to them minus a sizable bite for administering the transaction, and the rather fundamental truth that the federal government does not *have* any money has long ago been forgotten. Another result is that to get this "federal money," the congressman must often now go hat in hand to an agency of the administration. This does not put him in an enviable position if simultaneously he must add his weight to putting a restraint upon the President in a matter of foreign policy. It is not beyond imagining that he may even receive a telephone call from the head of the agency to whom he is looking for a dispensation, telling him that the President is "very much interested" in the passage or the nonpassage of a congressional measure having to do with international affairs or military spending.

Considered as a companion to the Nixon Doctrine, Nixon's New Federalism—a concept aimed at decentralizing government so that more and more functions can be carried out at state and community levels—may have a beneficial effect on the conduct of foreign as well as domestic affairs. But as might be expected from the difficulty of reversing a massive thirty-five-year-old trend, its results are hardly perceptible as yet.

As the 1970's began, the only signs of change in our network of foreign commitments were those of degree and method in the policy of supporting it; still not significantly altered was the network itself, which, however sound it might be intellectually, had failed at two important points, Korea and Vietnam, to enlist sufficiently the emotional support of the American people.

CHAPTER FOURTEEN

Valor in Vietnam

★ In World War II, and probably in other wars preceding it, patriotism was not much spoken of by American servicemen. Talking about it was not good form, to use an English phrase for which there seems to be no GI equivalent. This does not mean, however, that patriotism was not strongly present, as anyone who uttered a genuinely disloyal statement would have been likely to discover.

But the soldier, sailor, or airman in Vietnam has found himself in quite a different position from that of World War II. He soon lost the support of the people back home. By and large he could not have had the feeling that he was fighting for a worthwhile cause, which was the mainstay of his father and uncles while they battled the Germans and Japanese. Without this support and this inner conviction, how have men managed to fight, and fight bravely, many of them, in Vietnam?

Is this patriotism?

If so, it is of a higher order than we have any right to expect. In Vietnam important elements of patriotism that otherwise would have sustained the fighting men had been sheared away. What remained, however, was at least one of the building blocks out of which patriotism is probably constructed—in the language of social psychology, loyalty to "the primary group." In the armed services this is, of course, the squad, crew, platoon, company, battery, or other unit with which the individual is associated; it is the little community of people whose standards he wishes to live up to, whose approval he desires, who reward him with various satisfactions, and upon whose survival his own may depend.

The strength of this concept is borne out most dramatically by the following incident, which has been duplicated all too frequently in Vietnam.

Five American soldiers are moving through the jungle on an October day in 1965. A live enemy grenade flies out of the brush and into their midst. There is no time to pick it up and hurl it back, no time to get away. One of the soldiers throws himself on the grenade, muffles the full force of the explosion with his body, and by giving his own life, saves those around him.

His name is Milton L. Olive III.

He is eighteen.

He is black.

He is awarded the Medal of Honor posthumously.

An unusual act? It can certainly never be called common. But by the middle of May, 1970, Medals of Honor had been awarded to forty-six men who had absorbed the blasts of grenades, mines, or booby traps with their bodies in Vietnam or placed themselves between their comrades and an impending explosion. The deed was done so quickly in most cases that there could have been no time to think, nothing more than an impulse. And the psychologists who have told us that self-preservation is the No. 1 instinct might give this phenomenon some thought.

Forty-four of the men who offered this sacrifice in Vietnam died. Two were lucky. In early February, 1968, Thomas J. Kinsman, twenty-two at the time, virtually repeated Milton Olive's act in very similar circumstances but escaped with severe wounds. A year later, John L. Levitow, then twenty-three, was flying in a gunship at night when the aircraft was struck, oddly enough, by a mortar round. The explosion ripped a hole two feet in diameter in the right wing, while metal fragments made more than 3,500 holes in the fuselage, wounding all the men in the cargo compartment where Levitow was stationed. The blast also tore an activated flare from the hand of a crew member who had been just about to throw it out the door for illumination of the ground below, and the flare landed among some ammunition. Here is what followed, as chronicled in *Air Force Magazine:* "The flare was armed and the ejection fuze was burning. In ten seconds it would eject explosively from its casing and in another ten seconds would ignite and burn at 4,000 degrees Fahrenheit.

"Airman Levitow, though stunned by the concussion of the blast and suffering more than forty shrapnel wounds in his back and legs, had struggled to his feet and was giving immediate help to the man nearest him, who was bleeding profusely. As he was helping the other man away from the cargo door, Levitow spotted the smoking flare. Fully aware that when the ejection fuze went off, the flare components would separate with lethal velocity, he also knew that the ignited flare could explode the Minigun ammunition and burn through the floor of the aircraft, destroying vital control cables and causing the aircraft to crash.

"Levitow had no idea exactly how long the fuze had been burning, but he did know that a flare that has been shaken violently becomes unstable and can ignite or explode at any time. With complete disregard for his own safety, he made for the flare.

"By then the aircraft was partially out of control, and the flare was rolling wildly from side to side. Suffering from a loss of blood and a partial loss of feeling in his right leg, Airman Levitow struggled to reach the flare. He was unable to grasp it with his hands, so he unhesitatingly threw his body upon it. He hugged it close and dragged himself back to the cargo door. With his last remaining strength, he hurled the flare through the open door. At that instant the flare separated and ignited in the air."

The aircraft made it home safely, and after recovering from his wounds and flying another twenty combat missions, John Levitow returned to Connecticut, where he is now a civilian. Just before the Fourth of July he was involved in a large civic event that had as its aim the promotion of patriotism. The author spoke with him on the telephone and did not take the liberty of asking him why he had done what he had done with the flare, but was curious as to why he engaged in the patriotic activity. He said, "I don't feel that just having the Medal is enough."

Not enough! And he had come within a split second of burning himself to a cinder in the service of his country.

By May 14, 1970, 157 men had been awarded the Medal of Honor for valor in Vietnam, ninety-nine of them posthumously. Considering the numbers of men involved in the Vietnam war and the duration of the conflict, and judging from the nature of the acts described in the citations, this record compares more than favorably with that of other wars in this century against the same standards of bravery.

Almost half of those receiving the Medal of Honor for service in Vietnam were twenty-two years of age or under at the time of the action that earned the award.

But this degree of participation by youth in awards of the nation's highest tribute to patriotism is significant only in its statistical normalcy; the median age of men on active duty in mid-1968 was 22.7. The same condition applies to Negroes. Eighteen of the Medal of Honor men were black, which to the total of 157 recipients roughly represented the proportion of black to white people in the armed forces in Southeast Asia.

In the 157 awards all the services were represented, and apparently nearly all the racial stocks common in America. Places of birth included thirty-six states, the District of Columbia, Puerto Rico, Italy, and Hungary.

In brief, both in comparison with other modern wars and in the generality of characteristics among the recipients, the results suggest that the capacity for heroism and self-sacrifice as exemplified by the Medal of Honor awards is a fairly standard product of our people, and perhaps of all peoples. There is just no telling who will turn out to be a Medal of Honor man. One who received this award for service in Vietnam was a conscientious objector who had been allowed to serve as a medic.

Another was a university dropout. After he left college, he took a draft-deferred job, but the deferment expired and he had to go to Vietnam. One night just two months before his time was up, his platoon was attacked by Vietcong in estimated battalion strength, and this young man turned into a one-man army. He helped repair a 90 mm. recoilless rifle under fire and repeatedly discharged it pointblank into the oncoming enemy horde. He single-handedly broke up a couple of assaults with grenades, moving from position to position to help out where needed and inspiring others by his example. Exposed to heavy fire, he redistributed ammunition, cared for the wounded, and personally directed artillery and helicopter fires, placing them at times within a few yards of his position. As the result of his leadership and courage, his unit was saved and a large enemy force was virtually annihilated. When someone asked him why he had done all that, he replied, "It just seemed like it had to be done."

In the years from 1965 to 1970 there were many such tales of heroism in Vietnam, and the general public could hardly have been less interested. As for media treatment, except for the routine stories describing the Medal of Honor awards in Washington, there was very little coverage, and the ceremonies themselves became more and more subdued. No Ernie Pyles recorded the heroism of the GI in this war, and no Alvin Yorks, no Audie Murphys emerged from it.

In none of the major wars America has fought have the people in combat found themselves so isolated. Everyone who has served overseas in time of war knows how remote the United States seems—as far away as the moon. When there is added to this sense of remoteness a consciousness that the people back home are not behind the war effort and that many of them are simply apathetic and unconcerned, the fighting men are thrown upon their own resources. It is then that their loyalty must attach itself to the Americans who are immediately around them.

We have heard a great deal about this being the first war to be "brought into our living rooms" by television. The phrase can be questioned. Brave as they are and often as foolhardy as they seem to be, the TV correspondents cannot take their cameras, their sound equipment, and other paraphernalia to the spot where the most trying events of war happen, when they happen, and portray them in the way they happen. Nor, quite probably, can any other means of communication. As good a method as any is plain old-fashioned writing, and for any comparative study the method has great value, because men have been writing about their experiences in war for hundreds of years.

In an earlier chapter, excerpts of a few letters written by Colby College men in the Civil War were presented, and the reader may remember how they exuded patriotism of the most enthusiastic kind—a patriotism that was wholly dedicated to support of the national government, the Union. These letters were quite typical of that war and that generation. Returning to Colby as a sort of fixed reference point from which to view another war, there follow now letters from a Colby man in Vietnam that, there is reason to believe, are typical of the reactions of our young men to the war in that country. They were written by Robert C. ("Mike") Ransom, Jr., the eldest of the six sons of Robert and Louise Ransom of Bronxville, New York. Mike attended Colby for two and a half years, then went to work in a bank. He enlisted in the regular army after receiving his draft notice in August, 1966. After the required preliminary training, he attended Infantry Officer Candidate School at Fort Benning, Georgia. The O.C.S. is an institution of which very little is heard; it becomes important only when wars get large; then, with the service academies and R.O.T.C. falling far short of delivering the number of officers needed, O.C.S. goes into action. In World War II its graduates made up the great majority of ground and air force officers, and by 1968 it was contributing a substantial part of the officer corps in Vietnam.

At the Benning O.C.S. Mike Ransom went through an intense period of mental, emotional, and physical stress designed to fit him for responsibility in combat—up at five thirty on a typical day and going until eleven thirty at night, forced to cope with a hundred demanding details, and subjected to arduous physical, academic, and leadership training. One objective of O.C.S. is basically humane, although it seems to be just the opposite: it is to crack a man up, if he is the crackup type, before he finds himself responsible for other men's lives on the battlefield. This is a new and strange experience for today's youngster, but often he appears to welcome it. In the words of a student brigade commandant, "All of a sudden he's challenged right down to his bones— and he's delighted."

Mike could not be called a youngster exactly, but he was only twenty-two when he graduated from O.C.S. and was commissioned a second lieutenant of infantry on July 21, 1967. After a tour of duty in the states, he arrived in Vietnam on March 8, 1968. In a letter home he wrote of his first impressions. "From our billets we could hear machine gun and mortar fire from the perimeter two or three miles away. We could also see illuminating flares in the sky to light up the battlefield. Yes, I am scared. But I think it's more of the unknown than of bullets. I expect to learn a lot during the next year; I'm not sure what it'll be, but I'll learn a lot."

By March 27, Mike was officially assigned to an infantry company, and in a letter of that date he was describing activities in his area and his first reactions to the war. He reported that there was little contact with the enemy, that the principal danger was from mines and booby traps, which were accounting for 75 per cent of all casualties and that "nobody is particularly wild with patriotic feeling for the war." He was able to identify a couple of reasons for what enthusiasm there was; one was self-preservation, or shooting the enemy before he shot you, and the other was a desire for revenge when friends were blown apart by VC booby traps. He was also beginning to feel the remoteness. "While I am able to read Stars and Stripes and listen to AFVN radio newscasts, I still feel very cut off from the world outside of VN. I would love it dearly if you would subscribe to *Newsweek* for me. Also, what do you think of Bobby for President? What about Westmoreland's new job? What does everything mean?"

By April 3, he had been on his first combat mission, as a platoon leader, and he was again referring to the danger from mines and booby traps and the casualties they had inflicted upon other platoons of his company. "So far, my platoon, the 3rd, hasn't had any trouble, but these booby traps are so well hidden, that no matter how good you are, they'll get you.

"I heard Johnson's speech on AFVN Radio last night and think it to be the best one of his career. I am heartened by his bombing reduction and pray as does everyone else here that Hanoi will respond. What do you make of it? Also, how about his not running for President? I was beginning to think that the only way for this war to end was to have Johnson reelected in November. This I feel would cause Hanoi to back down to a show of American popular support for the war. Please comment."

In an undated letter written soon afterward, he again complimented President Johnson's speech for its "deescalation and non-candidacy," as he put it, and wrote: "It created in me a great sense of hope that this foolishness over here will end fairly shortly. There is not a man over here that wants to see this war go on any longer. This is not to say that anybody shrinks from doing a job. But everyone is as confused as I as to exactly what, if anything, we're accomplishing and wants the war over ASAP.

"I lost my first man last week. He was killed by accident by another man in the platoon. . . . Of course it really tears me up to lose a man, especially like that, but I must not show any emotion over it. I've got to press on, keep doing my job. Even among my men this is universal. They are saddened by the death of a buddy, but he is gone. The concern among the team (for that is what we are) is how it will affect the man who shot him. Will he fall to pieces over this and be unable to perform his function? This is what we are worried about first and foremost."

This same letter dwelt upon the difficulties of waging war among a population in which friends cannot be distinguished from foes. "The enemy in our area of operation is a farmer by day and VC by night. Every male is required to register at his provincial capitol. He is further required to carry an ID showing his picture, fingerprints, age, etc. But anyone with a VC background is supposedly denied an ID. Simple, you say? All we have to do is come to a village and police up everyone without an ID, right? Well, about 3 months ago we captured a VC printing plant that manufactured ID cards. . . . More than once we have captured or killed people with weapons whom we recognized as one of those smiling faces we had picked up and released earlier. It's maddening . . . but we can't do anything to them until we catch them with a weapon or actually shooting at us."

On April 22, one of Mike's men was killed by a mine explosion. "Both his feet were blown off, both legs were torn to shreds; his entire groin area was completely blown away. It was the most horrible sight I've ever seen. Fortunately he never knew what hit him. I tried to revive him with mouth-to-mouth resuscitation but it was hopeless to begin with." The explosion also wounded seven others, including Mike, and he was hospitalized briefly.

The incident left other than physical scars. "I am now filled with both respect and hate for the VC and the Vietnamese. Respect because the enemy knows that he can't stand up to us in a fire fight due to our superior training, equipment and our vast arsenal of weapons. Yet he is able. Via his mines and booby traps, he can whittle our ranks down piecemeal, until we cannot muster an effective fighting force."

Mike went on to write that in the month he had been with the company they had lost four men killed and thirty wounded, yet they had not seen a single verified VC or fired a round at one. His animosity toward the Vietnamese was growing because "they come around selling cokes and beer to us and then run back and tell the VC how many we are, where our positions are, and where the leaders position themselves. In the place where we got hit, we discovered 4 other mines, all of them placed in the spots where I, my platoon sergeant, and two squad leaders had been sitting." (This apparently was a bivouac area the platoon had occupied on the previous night and was returning to.)

On May 2, he wrote that his platoon was down to twenty from an authorized strength of forty-three, and since hitting the minefield he had been nervous all the time. Yet something—the lessons of Fort Benning, his loyalty to his men, or some other influence or combination of influences—had made a change in Mike. He was now writing: "Despite losing people and being scared all the time, I find being an Infantry Platoon leader an exhilarating, exciting, and, yes, rewarding job. I have ambitions to go higher, even in my short 2 years in the army, but I don't really want to because Platoon level is the last at which I can have close working contact with my men. I think I've developed a pretty good working relationship with my people, one in which they depend on me for leadership, but they know that I must be able to depend on them too."

On May 3, Mike was severely wounded by a mine. He was taken by helicopter to a surgical hospital, where he died eight days later.

Mike Ransom's letters are important for several reasons, and one of them is that they underline the very serious question of whether conventional armed forces have any business operating in a civil guerrilla war in an Asian, or possibly any other, country. The letters describe conditions that seem impossible, with the enemy blended indistinguishably into the civilian population, always present but unknown, always killing by means of mines and booby traps, and often guided to his victims by civilian informers. Mike expressed his anger toward this blend of people several times in his letters in the most vehement and bitter terms, which have not been quoted. And these, it should be remembered, were the reactions of a well-educated and well-brought-up young man who had been active in the youth group of his church. His experience makes more understandable, although no more forgivable, the action of a company in another regiment of Mike's division—the company that allegedly perpetrated the My Lai massacre in the same month in which Mike entered combat, March, 1968.

Another reason Mike's story is important is that it demonstrates how, in a far-off war that does not even really exist as far as most Americans are concerned, in the obscurity of a distant jungle, unthought of, forgotten, a man may still adhere to qualities of courage and loyalty to his fellow countrymen that are among the essentials of patriotism. It was in the darkness of night on May 3, 1968, when Mike led his squad off a landing zone to establish an ambush position in what was to prove his last action. A mine was waiting for them and it exploded, wounding several men, including the young lieutenant. A Bronze Star citation told what happened. "Although severely wounded, Lieutenant Ransom displayed outstanding professional competence as he constantly talked to his men and prevented panic. His actions prevented further injuries from additional mines in the area. He then reorganized his element into a tight defensive perimeter until they were able to receive assistance. Despite his wounds, Lieutenant Ransom refused medical attention until the other injured men of his squad had been treated." Another award of the Bronze Star, First Oak Leaf Cluster, commended Mike for "exceptional leadership qualities and a calm professionalism seldom found in an officer of his limited experience" during the whole period of his combat service in Vietnam.

In addition to the official words of commendation, Mike's parents received a letter from a nurse in the Second Surgical Hospital MA, which was in its own way to be cherished:

"Dear Mr. and Mrs. Ransom,

"It is with great difficulty that I write this letter expressing my deepest sympathy over the loss of your son, Robert, known as Mike to us. I have never written a letter like this before, but then in my six years of nursing I have never met so courageous an individual as your son.

"I was able to care for Mike daily and I want you to know that his sense of humor and will to live made my work much easier. Things he could no longer do for himself . . . like brushing his teeth . . . things that surely brought him discomfort . . . like turning him . . . brought only thank yous, humorous remarks, a gleaming smile, or a twinkle from his eyes.

"Mike fought hard, terribly hard, to overcome his body's wounded condition. But strong as he was, his body could only endure so much. Mike was never afraid and, although I'm sure he realized what was happening, he never, never lost his smile and his courage.

"I guess I really wanted you to know that Mike did not die alone, with no one caring. I cared, we all cared . . . we all share your sorrows. Be ever so proud of Mike!

Most Sincerely,
Connie Schlosser
Captain, ANC"

There is a P.S. from Vietnam that Mike had added to his last letter: "You might tell any friends you have in Washington to get off their fat asses, quit quibbling, and start talking about ways to end this foolishness over here."

On May 6, 1970, students at Mike's college, Colby, which had been the scene of so many patriotic activities in the past, voted by an overwhelming majority to go on strike in protest against further expansion of the war.

CHAPTER FIFTEEN

Pro Patria and Pro People

★ This chapter was begun on the evening of the Fourth of July, 1970. The Independence Day sun came up behind a gray mist that was shrouding the Connecticut shore, the weather was hot and humid, and by midmorning a thunderstorm was rumbling overhead. At 11 A.M. the author sat down to watch a televised exercise in Washington that was part of Honor America Day. The exercise linked patriotism and religion in that combination that seems to occur so naturally in America. The acceptable trinity of priest, rabbi, and minister was present. An astronaut who had read the Bible to us from space led a prayer here on earth. Kate Smith sang "God Bless America." A Pawnee Indian Eagle Scout led the audience in a pledge of allegiance. A girl who either was or had been a beauty contestant gave a patriotic reading entitled "I Speak for Democracy." From time to time a faint jeering was heard in the background, and the announcer told us that these were Yippies, standing in the reflecting pool. (The exercise was being held in front of the Lincoln Memorial.) The Yippies were being kept far in the distance by the police, and they appeared on the TV screen only as very small specks. Once, however, the camera did pick up a large sign being held up near the reflecting pool. It said, "Hour of Decision: God *or*

Country?" A good question. Billy Graham began speaking, and he seemed to be well on the way to answering this and other questions when there was a flash on the TV screen, a faint hiss, and the image of the evangelist disappeared. Lightning had struck a power line in the vicinity and imposed a blackout on this part of the state, so I did not get to see Fulton J. Sheen but was able to resume viewing Honor America Day in the evening when there was a show business extravaganza in Washington headed by Bob Hope.

There was much about Honor America Day that was vulnerable to, and did in fact attract, highbrow ridicule. But it was estimated that more than 250,000 people were present in the 90-degree heat, and millions more watched on television. That represented a lot of patriotism of a sort, and we need all we can get, of all kinds. Indeed, we had seen all kinds in the previous two months. Flags had been everywhere. It was widely reported that sales of flags had doubled over those in 1969. As for the little flag decals, they were said to have passed beyond fifty million in number. Several magazines came out with red-white-and-blue or star-spangled covers for their Independence Day issues. The best by all odds was that of the *Saturday Review*, showing Louis Armstrong and his trumpet against a large word JAZZ printed in patriotic colors. Besides being Honor America Day, the Fourth of July was also Mr. Armstrong's seventieth birthday, and it would be hard to think of anyone who has contributed more to the pleasure of life in America and therefore, perhaps, to our affection for the country as well as for him.

Also, during the previous few weeks, there had been more discussion of the flag and of patriotism than anyone could remember as having taken place in a like period of time.

One characteristic of the flag, as the eminent divine Shailer Mathews once remarked, is that it is a symbol so charged with emotion that people cannot look at and judge, even, whether or not the design is aesthetically good or bad. It seems also that the flag blinds the individual who is looking at it with a dazzling reflection of his own ideas; hence, during the few weeks previous to Independence Day, 1970, the flag had been the center of more fist fights than it had of constructive discussion. It used to be that when the flag went by, you got a lump in your throat; during this period you were likely to have got one on your head.

Perhaps, along with the bruises, a very desirable impression had been left: that Americans ought to be more tolerant of each other's patriotism. Not completely tolerant, of course, for that would destroy all basis of discussion; but a great deal more tolerant than was the case during this troubled time. One problem of patriotism in the 1970's is simply that of achieving the rational balance in human relationships that has always been the essence of a civilized society. There is much to suggest that there will be considerable danger ahead if the balance is not achieved.

A public opinion analyst recently estimated that between 60 per cent and 90 per cent of the people in this country had been "turned off" by demonstrating groups. This estimate may be high at its upper extreme, but the polls have shown that a substantial majority of Americans are strongly against those who disturb the peace with violent protest. And certain ingredients of this majority are most interesting. To mention just one: back in the late nineteenth century and even in the early twentieth century patriotic societies that were conducting "Americanization" programs were afraid that the immigrants would turn out to be anarchists, socialists, and other supposedly undesirable people if some such education were not provided for them. The Americanizers need not have worried quite so much. The immigrants and their descendants now include some of the most ardent patriots of the kind the G.A.R. wanted to produce, while many youngsters who are eligible to be Sons and Daughters of the American Revolution are rioting in the streets. The Americanization of these people came about through stronger forces than any the G.A.R. could muster: through achieving in this country financial comfort and security, varied kinds of freedom, and personal fulfillment. Meanwhile, many have seen their homelands fall under communist rule or its threat. Why would they not be concerned about America and willing to defend it as their homeland? It is believed that white ethnic groups now contribute substantially to the corps of hard-hat patriots. It is also pointed out that their reaction against young radicals is as much against a new life-style as it is against what they take to be the youngsters' lack of patriotism. These are Americans who made their way in this country according to the old rules. Many were poor and disadvantaged at one time, but they worked, saved, and overcame the disadvantages. No one gave them anything. No one made allowances if they broke the law. If they went to school they had to attend classes and pass exams. Many served in World War II and Korea without protest. Consequently, when they see the old rules of the game flouted, they are understandably enraged.

These newly minted Americans plus many of the older stock make up a sizable majority in this country that is growing increasingly irritated by violence. To a degree there is a similarity between the America of today and the Germany of the pre-Hitler years. We have inflation, rioting in the streets, a fear of communists, and people recognizable by costume, color, or race against whom there is prejudice. We have precedents indicating that when in real or fancied danger, our society will take whatever means it thinks it needs to preserve itself, while constitutional safeguards go out the window.

For example, we might remind ourselves again of the more than 100,000 persons of Japanese ancestry who were evacuated from California in the spring and summer of 1942 and sent to inland relocation camps. This was one of the worst violations of civil liberties in our history, and it was conducted on the basis not of individual guilt but of one, and only one, distinguishing characteristic, which in this instance happened to be race. Along with Japanese aliens, seventy thousand Japanese-American citizens were removed from their homes, farms, ranches, and places of business, including citizens with as little as one sixteenth of Japanese blood. This affair had its uglier aspects; it appeared that the Japanese immigrants had adapted themselves a little too well to the competitive enterprise system, and for this and other reasons there were people in California who had been wanting to get rid of them for a long while. Nevertheless, the main reason given was military necessity and national security, even though many of those incarcerated were trying in every way possible to prove their loyalty and most of the known or suspected enemy sympathizers had already been picked up by the authorities. Although originally inspired by group pressures on the West Coast, this action, according to a public opinion poll, was approved by Americans in substantial majority (93 per cent in the case of Japanese aliens, 59 per cent in the case of citizens). It was also approved by all the best people, including Earl Warren, then attorney general of California, members of Congress, the Supreme Court, Walter Lippmann, and other responsible individuals and groups. Doubtless many amends have since been made to the Japanese-Americans who were compelled to suffer this experience; but the point is that under the stress of emergency and a danger that seemed more real then than it does now, it happened. And if the war had gone badly for us, what happened might have been a hundred times worse.

In time of fear and danger, and with public clamor and support, it is easy enough to subject any group to repressive measures, up to and including barbed wire and a circle of machine guns. Nor is it necessary to go all the way to barbed wire to achieve serious repression. Every time violence replaces reason, there is a reaction that draws the net a little tighter. During 1969 and 1970, bills relating to campus disturbances were introduced in forty state legislatures, and on June 28, 1970, *The New York Times* reported that thirty-two states had passed laws aimed at preventing future disorders. The most common forms of legislation were those intended to take scholarship or grant funds away from students convicted of illegal demonstrations, to dismiss faculty members involved in protests, and to establish penalties for students destroying school property or interrupting normal class activity. While laws such as these may seem reasonable and justified under the circumstances of the moment, it requires no great stretch of the imagination to understand how some of them may call for an exercise of judgment on the part of state officials of the future that would result in the suppression of needed protest activity and of academic freedom in general.

Therefore, if we are not to find ourselves living in an America that is no longer the land of the free, it will be a duty of patriotism in the coming decades to achieve necessary changes in our society without violence and to understand better those who are advocating and working for change. There is much about patriotism that is mystical and incapable of being put into words; this is the slight raising of hair at the base of the scalp when the flag goes by or "The Star-Spangled Banner" is played, and this is the action of men who without thought or hesitation, in the manner of a Milton Olive or a John Levitow, throw themselves between danger and their friends or between the Republic and its foes. But the dictates of common sense alone would lead one to believe that patriotism is also highly pragmatic: that people fight to defend their country because they have a good country to defend and it is very much worth their while to do so; that for the individual, patriotism depends on deriving personal satisfactions from the life offered in the country that is home—more so, perhaps, than upon the lofty and purely disinterested devotion so often associated with patriotism; and that love of country is best stimulated by making a country more lovable.

At present there are two classes of people among whom such improvement is possible and urgently called for: the black and the young, most visibly represented by the black militants and the young radicals.

During the Cambodian uproar, the black militants largely turned their backs upon the protest movements, considering them a diversion from racial problems. It is true that blacks have less reason to be loyal to this country than any other group has; they have received fewer of its advantages. Yet they have been Americans longer than almost all other racial groups; in 1790, for example, they made up nearly a fifth of our population. Blacks fought at Bunker Hill and in all the wars our country has engaged in. And there is much to indicate that they feel this is their country as much as it is anyone's. At the risk of touching only superficially on their attitudes, it may be interesting to note and comment on a few of the polls that have dealt with black patriotism. In 1942, one survey asked people if they thought Negroes were being as patriotic as the white people in this country, and 63 per cent answered *yes*, which indicated what was true: that the black population was contributing effectively to the conduct of the war. On the other hand, as Joe Louis pointed out, life under Hitler was not a very good alternative to the troubles they were having in America. Still—in answer to a question in 1966, 87 per cent of the blacks across the country said they would personally feel this country is worth fighting for if it got into a big war.

Even more significant is the result of another study by Opinion Research Corporation, reported on in its April 15, 1969, *ORC Public Opinion Index: "Black separatism has become less attractive to the American people.* There is considerably less sympathy among the public today for the idea of new, separate black communities than was the case fifteen months ago. Much of this change has occurred among whites. A majority of whites were in favor of black separatism in November, 1967, but less than half go for it now. Only one in four blacks today would like to see Negroes have their own schools, businesses, political leaders, and other social institutions."

Concern about the patriotism of various races is nothing new in this country. Americans were worried about the Irish in the mid-nineteenth-century, about immigrants from southern and eastern Europe in the 1880's, about the Germans in World War I, and about the Japanese in World War II. And in every case the worries have been unfounded. But the black racial problem is different for several reasons, and the blacks are inheriting—in the decayed centers of the nation's cities—some of America's worst social ills. By the mid-1980's, according to a *Newsweek* estimate, more than a dozen of our large cities, among them Chicago, Philadelphia, St. Louis, Baltimore, Oakland, New Orleans, Atlanta, and Jacksonville, will have black majorities. As a consequence (if we are still a democracy by then), these cities probably will have black mayors and governments, and if we are speaking of creating a more lovable America, upon these people will fall the most severe test of patriotism any Americans have had to face on the domestic front. They will need all the help they can get.

What the blacks' troubles are, are fairly clear, or they ought to be, by this time. The difficulties with the young are much more puzzling. There are a great many cliché opinions, such as "all this trouble is caused by just a few kooks," and the word "hippie" is used indiscriminately to indicate any young person of unconventional appearance. But the results of responsible studies do not bear out the clichés.

As to the idea that discontent is not widespread, here are the opening three paragraphs of the June, 1969, *Gallup Opinion Index* reporting on interviews with more than a thousand students at fifty-five representative campuses across the nation, as well as special investigations at eight embattled campuses:

"Those who comfort themselves that the trouble on the college campuses of America is caused by only a 'handful of students' and that the majority is completely out of sympathy with the goals of the militant few would be disabused of this view if they were to talk to students across the nation, as 75 representatives of the Gallup Poll did.

"The opinions of a Rutgers University sophomore represent those of many students reached in this survey: 'The militants on campus may have gone too far, but society needs to wake up. Students are genuinely concerned with the way things are on campus and in the community and they want these things changed.'

"Attitudes vary from college to college and region to region on specific issues such as the ROTC, special courses and facilities for Negroes and college defense contracts, but at the heart of the discontent over these and other matters is the feeling that society as a whole is seriously ill and that changes are imperative."

Another large nationwide study was completed in 1969 by Roper Research Associates and published in *The Public Pulse* as "The Concerned Generation." Of the college seniors interviewed in this study, 40 per cent were pessimistic to some degree about the direction American society is taking, and war was not their only concern or even the largest of their concerns, the top four of which were as follows: race relations, poverty and slum conditions, crime and lawlessness, and avoiding future wars.

In January, 1970, *The Gallup Opinion Index* published the results of another large study, in which, among other questions, college students were asked, "Suppose you were President, what specific things would you like to do on the domestic front?" and "What specific things would you like to do on the international front?" On the domestic front the leading answers were: increase aid to poverty-stricken areas and persons; improve race relations, provide equal opportunity; attend to urban problems (clean up cities, slums, ghettos); improve, expand education; revise welfare programs; fight air and water pollution, practice conservation; control inflation, lower the cost of living; overhaul present tax system, make it fairer; clean up politics; devise ways to control crime and violence. On the international front they were: end the Vietnam war; promote relations with other nations, including communist nations; stop being "policeman of the world"; cut back on foreign aid; give economic but not military aid; promote arms treaties; reevaluate our foreign aid policy, foreign commitments; help underdeveloped countries; strengthen the U.N.; improve the image of the U.S. abroad.

The Gallup studies indicate that college students of today are a new breed in many ways. For example, "The important difference between college students of today and those of earlier years is their great desire for change, supported by the conviction that change can be brought about without waiting for years or decades."

Another difference noted by Gallup is a greatly increased involvement of college students in working among the poor or underprivileged and in doing other social work. A majority of students (51 per cent) say they have done this sort of work. So this generation seems not only aware of the nation's problems but willing to do something about them to a degree that was unheard of on the campuses of the past.

Along with many facts on other aspects of college life, Gallup makes a note for historians of the future that says that as of the year 1969, 6 per cent of the college men had beards, 28 per cent had long sideburns, and 13 per cent of all students dressed in a slovenly manner; that these are badges of an antiestablishment, nonconformist point of view; but 51 per cent of the students thought it is all just a fad, with one student predicting that five years from now everyone will have his head shaved.

This is the broad spectrum of the college population as revealed by opinion polling techniques. At the end of the spectrum, where the colors get red and hot, even more interesting aspects are revealed.

The Roper study previously mentioned notes that "a small but passionate minority," 9 per cent of college seniors nationwide, is "severely disenchanted" with American institutions and that these are brighter than average young people. It is undoubtedly in this small segment that two distinctly different types of the disenchanted exist: the hippies, who have simply turned their back on conventional society and gone off into a world of their own, and the young radicals, who are attempting to change society.

If the author may be permitted a few paragraphs of unscientific speculation, he would advance the notion that the hippie life is brought on to some degree by natural laziness and the charm of what at first appears to be a carefree life far removed from the grinding treadmill on which poor old Ma and Dad are clumping along—and that it is a life made possible to a large extent by the parents' dollars. But beyond this, there is apparently serious alienation and a search for alternatives to the scientific, technological, highly organized existence that distinguishes America today.

Also, undoubtedly the possibility of a type of war that is more horrible, more destructive, and more cataclysmic than any ever known before in history has had a profound effect upon the lifestyle of many young people. A Russian professor (as described by Tolstoy) once reported on a phenomenon he called "Malevanism," which appeared in the province of Kiev apparently some time in the late nineteenth century; it seems that a man named Malevanny convinced a number of people that the world was coming to an end, whereupon they all adopted a manner of life that sounds familiar: they gave up working; gave away their belongings; sold the necessities of life in order to obtain parasols, silk kerchiefs, and the like; dressed up in colorful clothing; were

possessed of a strange serenity that gave way at times to sentimentality or exaltation; they were emotional and talkative, with
tears of joy that came easily and as easily vanished; and "they
spent their time making holiday, visiting one another, walking
about. . . ."

Something akin to Malevanism is apparently going on among
many young people not only in America, but in other countries.
It is almost as though these people had given up on industry and
reason, the exercise of which, it may be argued, has produced the
scientific and technological horrors we face today. They have
even advanced the notion that the antidote to war may simply be
love; with much emphasis in their life-style on simple acts of
human communication.

At the moment, the hippies are not regarded as a group of any
importance on the domestic scene; they are not the activists;
they are not doing anything socially significant as it affects the
American people generally. However, with the curious international, interracial, interreligious reach of this phenomenon into
other countries, it may be wondered if it might not in some way
become globally important.

On any rational basis, we are not doing well in efforts to gain
international harmony. The prospects for a one-world government such as people dreamed of briefly after World War II do
not seem promising or likely unless such a government is forced
into being upon the smoking ruins of the present world and the
few survivors who may remain. There have been indications that
the American people would not be willing to give up their sovereignty, although they might be willing to relinquish the control
of an American military force to a United Nations peace-keeping
command. Historically, we have never given the one-world concept much real support. We refused to enter the League of Nations. We have often, in our conduct of foreign affairs, treated
the United Nations as an afterthought. Probably other nations
have similar mental reservations.

Yet factually and realistically it appears that if there is any
hope for us, it will not be found in being Americans or Chinese
or Russians or Protestants or Catholics or Jews or Mohammedans

or white or black or yellow or red—but in that we are people. In that case, patriotism would lose its fatal flaw of nationalism and come to mean simply loyalty to the human kind.

One is tempted to hope that some sort of change not wholly logical can take place and that war will disappear simply because it will become unfashionable, so that we may look at military manuals some day with the same amused curiosity that a 1905 Sears Roebuck catalogue now engenders.

Once in a while there is a glimpse of world community. When the astronauts of Apollo 13 were coming home in their crippled spaceship in the week of April 12, 1970, people in many countries were praying for them, and the Russian cosmonauts sent a message expressing their anxiety and their hope for a safe return to "Mother Earth."

But in the same week, 101 Americans died almost unnoticed in Vietnam—and who is to say that three men on a jungle trail at midnight, in danger and in fear of their lives, should not be as much the objects of worldwide prayers as three men in space? Or three ill and starving children in Africa, trembling on the brink of extinction? How can people of different nations develop with respect to one another the same awareness everyone had of the astronauts? It is a very great problem, considering that people of the same nation normally can barely communicate their concern across the street. For that reason no possible or unusual channel of communication should be overlooked, including that of styles or cultures peculiar to youth.

The hippie as a patriot is a very odd concept and, it must be admitted, an unlikely one. If the "Peace" theme that is part of his life-style could be made an international reality, no greater service to the country could be performed. On the other hand, if it exists merely as a childish euphoria in a widening part of our population, to the continued impairment of our defense capacity, the consequences could be ghastly. There is nothing in history to warrant the belief that peace can sweep effortlessly over the world like a summer breeze. And until more encouraging acceptance appears, we must conclude that there is still much hard thinking and hard work to do in the arena of political action. In connection with such action, on both the domestic and international fronts, another youth minority comes to our attention: that discussed by Kenneth Keniston in his book *Young Radicals.*

One of Dr. Keniston's basic assumptions is that the affluence of modern life, which frees the adolescent from the need to work, has created a longer stage between childhood and adulthood during which many individuals are able to achieve more intellectual and psychological development and more awareness of the world around them than was ever possible for youth before—and that this relatively new condition facilitates the growth and production of the unusual people he calls the young radicals. There are two primary characteristics of these people that make them especially interesting in the consideration of our concept that recognizes that individual conscience and judgment are integral qualities of patriotism in America. These are the traits of moral concern ("moral," of course, is understood not to have much to do with sex anymore) and intelligence, which, according to Keniston, the young radicals have to a remarkably high degree. Secondarily, they have qualities of passion, persistence, and involvement that are consistent with a long tradition of American activists and reformers.

These people, who make up what is often called the New Left, comprise that end of the youth population spectrum where dissatisfaction with our society deepens to its most intense hues and where something positive—not passive, as is the case with the simply alienated hippies—is being done about it. What is being done varies tremendously. The New Left includes in itself a shading of positions ranging from a few who would achieve reform within the existing political structure to those who advocate disruption, insurrection, and revolutionary violence to achieve their ends.

The individuals in the group also vary a great deal, but after studying a number of them intensively through personal interviews in the summer of 1967, Dr. Keniston made several generalizations of which a few are noted here with the hope that characteristics he wrote pages about are not being too much oversimplified in paragraphs.

The young radicals, he says, are not anti-intellectual, but they are in many cases antiacademic because of a belief that the academic world is arid, involuted, and ineffectual in political and domestic affairs.

Although distrustful of constituted authority because of what they consider to be outdated policies and unkept promises, they are not rebels against such basic principles of the American democracy as free speech, equal opportunity, or justice or against personal values of their parents such as honesty, concern for people, and responsibility. It is our society's failure to put principles into practice that disturbs them.

Their lives are fluid, flexible, open to change and to people. They do not identify with tradition, leaders, or heroes. Immediate and personal human relations take precedence over those of formal organization. Getting a job done takes place over doctrine.

They are willing to fight for their beliefs, yet nonviolence is all-important to what they wish to accomplish. They are opposed to warfare, to compulsion in human affairs, to all forms of force in man's relationships.

They are subject to great weariness and disappointment, which is understandable. People who are undertaking to reform the military-industrial complex, end poverty and discrimination, give the individual more importance, reverse American foreign policy, and do other things of this magnitude are bound to get discouraged at times. Also, some of the disadvantaged persons they try to help are sometimes hostile, apathetic, or unreliable.

Dr. Keniston obviously developed a great sympathy for these young people, and this last aspect worried him somewhat, as indicated by the following comment (please keep in mind that he wrote the book in 1967 or early 1968): "If a growing number of activists, frustrated by political ineffectuality or a mounting war in Southeast Asia, withdraw from active social concern into a narrowly academic quest for professional competence, then a considerable reservoir of the most talented young Americans will have been lost to society and the world."

Events that have taken place since this was written should have encouraged college students of all shades of dissenting opinion. Young people made an unsuccessful but dramatic effort in the campaign of Senator Eugene McCarthy for President in 1968. Undoubtedly their protests awakened the general public to the debate on the Vietnam war and contributed importantly to a policy leading to withdrawal of our troops. And the wounds they have inflicted upon such massive institutions as the American military and educational establishments should leave little question about their destructive power at least.

There are questions to be raised, however, about tactics and strategy. There is considerable evidence, as already mentioned, that the bombing, burning, and other violence of the far-far-left have turned a large part of the American public against *all* youth movements. Also, the extremism of many young people, often bordering on the ridiculous, their lack of humor and sense of proportion, their use of vulgarity and invective, may be not only bad manners but bad tactics.

Sooner or later, youthful protesters will have to weigh the value of making dissent highly visible through activities that shock and alarm against the fact that they are alienating large numbers of people who actually feel in sympathy with their aims. To illustrate: in one survey relating to the Vietnam war, it was found that six out of ten respondents who thought the war was a mistake were also against the antiwar demonstrators.

As for strategy, the young reformers do not appear to have any. There are few constructive plans and little vision of the future. Notably lacking in their performances has been the skillful use of the pamphlet, that great tool of reform that, left behind in the hand of a prospective convert, supplements the effect of emotion with the solid persuasion of reason. It is apparently only another cliché opinion to call the young radicals communists. While some undoubtedly are communists, there appears to be no substantial agreement among them on Marxism or any other system of thought that would outline a clear program for society. While this may reflect a more pragmatic and a more honest approach to our problems than ideologies that their elders publicly subscribe to but privately do not honor, more evidence of constructive thought would be at least reassuring.

Also, as Dr. Keniston suggests and as even the young activists would probably admit, they have been so busy activating that they have not had time to study and inform themselves fully on the exact state of society and the world, what historical forces have preceded them and are still to be reckoned with, and other aspects of available knowledge that should be useful to reformers.

Not everyone will regard the young radicals as sympathetically as Dr. Keniston has. Many will disagree with him heatedly. But if the element of criminal violence can be put aside, everyone must concede that the qualities of intelligence, dedication, willingness to work long hours, conscience, and a passion for humanity that he describes, taken together with youth, make a combination so rare that they are worth consideration as a national resource.

Nearly everyone will also agree that one of the influences of the young, even though they may not realize it, has come from their simply refusing to take for granted what many of their parents accepted as gospel. The preceding generation held to traditional patterns, generally swallowing the words and attitudes of their elders without questioning motives or underlying causes. But somehow today's youngsters have taken it upon themselves to challenge ideas that it would never have occurred to their mothers and fathers to doubt. This is a job that needs doing now and then. There are many long-established concepts that ought to be examined to see if they meet the test of today's problems; if they do, it will be good to have them confirmed; if they do not, they probably ought to be changed.

Among these concepts, there is nothing sacrosanct about patriotism. It not only should be challenged, it is being challenged by the young, and education appears to be one of the factors that is producing the challenge. Recent studies by Daniel Yankelovich, Incorporated, indicate that patriotism is considered very important by only 35 per cent of the college youth as compared with

60 per cent of noncollege youth (and that religion is regarded by the two groups in about the same relative way).

This finding, however, calls for a couple of comments. One is that should the country again find itself in actual danger, experience indicates that this attitude on the part of college youth would change drastically. For example, when in 1933 Winston Churchill was condemning the young men of The Oxford Union for resolving not to fight for king and country, he did not know that he would be praising them ten years later as being among the finest generation, in his opinion, that England had ever produced. The other comment has to do with the vagueness of definition that usually surrounds patriotism and the obvious possibility that when questioned many of the students equated it with nationalism; that, in fact, has been the cast and color of a very prominent school of patriotism for the past several years. And no well-informed, reasonable person, especially if given the benefit of a college education, can doubt that nationalistic patriotism (as well as denominational religion, for that matter) has often been a dangerously divisive force in the world. The Tolstoyan view to that effect cannot be disregarded (any more than can that of Albert Gallatin, who regarded patriotism as beneficial if kept within the bounds of our moral responsibilities to other nations) as the puzzle of the future is resolved.

The two main elements of the tangle with which today's youth must soon begin to struggle as responsible citizens are, of course, the domestic and the foreign, with important strands interwoven. For example, the cost of the war in Southeast Asia in 1969 was about $29 billion. Less than half of that amount was what the United States paid for the Marshall Plan, which had much to do with restoring war-torn Europe. As the 1970's began, there appeared to be several aspects of the current condition that called for an internal Marshall Plan to build new housing in the United States, abate poverty, control crime, fight pollution, improve education, restore public transportation, and do all the other things that needed doing. At the same time our generals and admirals, whom we were not much inclined to listen to anymore, were telling us that Russia was about to pass us in the deadly game of military technology and strength, particularly in naval power. And meanwhile, millions of Americans still believed that totalitarian force constitutes a dangerous threat to Western civilization. These views were currently unfashionable. The threat seemed remote. Most people were not particularly excited by reports of teachers and leaders being slaughtered in faraway Asian villages; it was only when U.S. planes were hijacked and burned by terrorists or innocent officials were kidnaped and murdered in neighboring countries that Americans got a real smell of such strong-arm tactics. But even the brief awakening of moral indignation attending these incidents tends to promote an understanding of what could happen following a large and shocking international aggression of the same nature. Then American opinions and emotions might become considerably more unanimous.

At any rate, of the two fronts, domestic and international, that call for the energies and brains of our young people now in college, it seems that foreign affairs have the greatest need for their attention. The complexities of international relations require such great knowledge and understanding and so much study that we must look almost entirely to our colleges and universities to develop the necessary minds; nowhere else are comparable resources to be found. The college community has recently had a great deal to say about our foreign policy. More and more faculty members are urging that their colleges "take a position." But attempting to use the college or university as a political instrument is not the same as using it to prepare its graduates to be effective on the political scene, and it may be wondered whether the more important and the proper role is not in preparing the thousands of educators, journalists, legislators, and other key people who will be influential in our international relations as well as the young people who will enter the foreign service. Senator J. William Fulbright, Chairman of the Senate Committee on Foreign Relations, has this to say: "Neither the government nor the universities are making the best possible use of their intellectual resources to deal with the problems of war and peace in the nuclear age." And "It is a curious thing that in an era when interdisciplinary studies are favored in universities, little has been done to apply the insights of individual and social psychology to the study of international relations."

One of the insights that might well be examined would have to do with the role of justification in our foreign relations—an aspect peculiarly important to the maintenance of a patriotic spirit in America. A word that recurs frequently in modern statements of foreign policy is "interests." We are here or we are there in the world because of our "interests." But sometimes the nature of these "interests" becomes difficult to explain, especially when a long military operation is involved and men must die for them.

It is then that the question, "Is it worth it?" arises—a question that, as we have seen, was put to young men concerning World War II and Korea with quite different results. It is also suggested that the test of worthwhileness goes far toward explaining the apparent contradiction between professed principles and actual practice that is sometimes noticed in America. In at least two periods of this century, those of the Great Depression and the Vietnam war, this test has come to be inexorably applied. In the Depression, it was not judged worthwhile to maintain the purity of free enterprise while people were suffering from unemployment and hunger. In the case of Vietnam it was not judged worthwhile to continue a massive expenditure of blood and treasure in a war that, up close, seemed unexplainable and unsuccessful, even though it was a logical result of long-agreed-upon policies.

Thus, it could be argued that a sense of, and a seeking for, worthwhileness have been part of the American character for a long time and are only being reasserted, with great force and urgency, by the present generation of youth. Also, it seems reasonable to conclude from our history that being "worth it" means being morally as well as rationally justifiable. Admittedly, in time of war, establishing the moral element of this foundation can be a tricky business. When the Russians were decorating our generals in May of 1945 with large ornate medals such as The Order of Liberation of the Fatherland, the Soviet officers had a little joke about another medal that was supposedly available: The Order of Chastity, Second Class. Combining morality and war is like dealing with degrees of chastity in a bordello. Nevertheless, we have subscribed to certain international moral judgments pertaining to war, some of which are coming home to roost, as the following incident shows.

In March, 1970, two American seamen hijacked a U.S. ship bound for Thailand with a load of explosives and napalm bombs and took it to Cambodia, where they were held in detention by the Cambodian government. When interviewed by a newspaperman, one of the men said he had been guided by the results of the Nuremberg trials—that he felt he would be guilty if he simply followed orders and participated in the delivery of thousands of bombs intended to be dropped on the people. Whether or not his motives were as noble as this statement might indicate, the hijacker had touched a sensitive nerve.

The principle of individual responsibility, holding that neither orders from a superior nor high governmental position is a valid defense for the individual who is charged with a war crime, is probably the best-remembered precedent established at Nuremberg, but the trials that took place there in 1945–46 had so many implications that the whole affair is worth reviewing.

Following the end of the war, an executive agreement concluded by Russia, Great Britain, France, and the United States provided for the establishment of an International Military Tribunal on which each country was to be represented in the trial of high German officials accused of war crimes. Incorporated in the agreement was the charter under which the tribunal was to operate and that was to serve as law in the trial. A pertinent section of this charter follows:

> The following acts, or any of them, are crimes coming within the jurisdiction of the Tribunal for which there shall be individual responsibility.
>
> (a) Crimes against peace: namely, planning, preparation, initiation or waging of a war of aggression, or a war in violation of international treaties, agreements or assurances, or participation in a common plan or conspiracy for the accomplishment of any of the foregoing.
>
> (b) War crimes: namely, violations of the laws or customs of war. Such violations shall include, but not be limited to, murder, ill-treatment or deportation to slave labor or for any other purpose of civilian population of or in occupied territory, murder or ill-treatment of pris-

oners of war or persons on the seas, killing of hostages, plunder of public or private property, wanton destruction of cities, towns or villages, or devastation not justified by military necessity.

(c) Crimes against humanity: namely, murder, extermination, enslavement, deportation, and other inhumane acts committed against any civilian population, before or during the war, or persecutions on political, racial or religious grounds in execution of or in connection with any crime within the jurisdiction of the Tribunal, whether or not in violation of the domestic law of the country where perpetrated.

Leaders, organizers, instigators, and accomplices participating in the formulation or execution of a common plan or conspiracy to commit any of the foregoing crimes are responsible for all acts performed by any persons in execution of such plan.

In the course of a trial that lasted ten months, twenty-one defendants faced the tribunal, Martin Bormann being tried *in absentia*. Three were acquitted. Seven received long prison terms. Twelve, including Bormann, were sentenced to death. One of these, Göring, committed suicide in his cell; the rest were hanged on October 16, 1946.

Following V-J Day, there were also war crime trials and executions of Japanese. One of the most pertinent cases, as summarized in timely fashion by James B. Reston, Jr., in *Saturday Review* had to do with an order given by General Yamashita to "suppress" guerrillas in the Philippines and the consequent wiping out of five villages by a company of Japanese troops who shot the civilian residents. Yamashita was executed along with a number of officers and men, although Reston pointed out that at the time of the shooting the General was not in communication with his troops.

When reports of the alleged massacre at My Lai began to occupy the attention of the public, the distressing implications of precedents set by these postwar trials twenty-five years previously became too obvious to require comment.

Less obvious but capable of being equally distressing are the implications of the Nuremberg charter in its designating as a crime the "planning, preparation, initiation or waging of a war of aggression." We have thought of our effort in Vietnam as a war not of, but against, aggression, and any fair-minded analysis would give that impression great support. However, it appears that the longer a war such as this goes on, the harder it becomes to explain it to the rest of the world, and this will probably always be the case when the soldiers of one country are fighting in another several thousand miles from home in the midst of a population in which friend cannot be told from foe. If future military operations could be conducted on the basis of dealing with national or other distinct entities, military morality would be greatly clarified, even though it may with some propriety be asserted that combining war and ethical behavior is an Alice-in-Wonderlandish concept to begin with.

Against this rather fundamental difficulty, and in spite of the self-flogging Americans were indulging in toward the end of the 1960's, the case for the United States in terms of unselfishness and high ideals over the preceding quarter century was not a bad one. But it certainly had become terribly confused, so confused that whether the fault was in communicating the facts or the facts themselves, only God knew. He and some of our dissident young people, who unhesitatingly ascribed the superior "morality" to the North Vietnamese and Vietcong in spite of frequent reports of terror and torture perpetrated by these people that would take considerable explaining, to a Nuremberg court or anyone else.

There continue to be different views on the Nuremberg trials. One school of thought holds that this was a great advance toward a world of law and order; another, that it was a punitive postwar lynching bee in which Americans seriously compromised their integrity by sitting on a tribunal of judgment with representatives of a Stalinist regime against which war crimes equal to some of Hitler's had been alleged but had gone unpunished or even uninvestigated.

Whatever the final judgment may be about that, certain international precedents for the guidance of human conduct have been established, or else we have hanged ten Germans whimsically. And perhaps it is just as well for America that these precedents now exist. Even if it is impossible to qualify for the Order of Political Morality, First Class, we ought to try at least for Second Class. The reason is not simply for the Sunday-school-ish sake of being good but for the health and well-being of American patriotism.

The whole history of our people indicates that public support for the national government varies according to the degree of conviction people have that its course is justified not only on rational but on moral grounds. When this conviction has been strongest we have been most united and therefore most effective. When it has been weakest we have been most divided.

The practical and political meaning in a somewhat different context (that of the conscientious objector) was enlarged upon in 1919 by Harlan Fiske Stone when he wrote:

> "The ultimate test of the course of action which the state should adopt will of course be the test of its own self-preservation; but with this limitation, at least in those countries where the political theory obtains that the ultimate end of the state is the highest good of its citizens, both morals and sound policy require that the state should not violate the conscience of the individual. All our history gives confirmation to the view that liberty of conscience has a moral and social value which makes it worthy of preservation at the hands of the state. So deep in its significance and vital, indeed, is it to the integrity of man's moral and spiritual nature that nothing short of the self-preservation of the state should warrant its violation; and it may well be questioned whether the state which preserves its life by a settled policy of violation of the conscience of the individual will not in fact ultimately lose it by the process."

If the conscience of one person is to be so regarded, then certainly that of millions of people merits commensurate respect. One who understood this was President John F. Kennedy, as evidenced by the conclusion of the speech he intended to make in Dallas on November 22, 1963:

> "We in this country, in this generation, are—by destiny rather than choice—the watchmen on the walls of world freedom. We ask, therefore that we may be worthy of our power and responsibility—that we may exercise our strength with wisdom and restraint—and that we may achieve in our time and for all time the ancient vision of peace

on earth, good will toward men. That must always be our goal—
and the righteousness of our cause must always underlie our strength.
For as was written long ago, 'Except the Lord keep the city, the watch-
man waketh but in vain.' "

Selected Bibliography and Notes

Adams, James Truslow, *The Epic of America.* New York, Blue Ribbon Books, Inc., 1931.

Almond, Gabriel A., *The American People and Foreign Policy.* New York, Harcourt, Brace and Company, Inc., 1950.

Barber, James D., *Citizen Politics: An Introduction to Political Behavior.* Chicago, Markham Publishing Co., 1969.

Beard, Charles A., and Beard, Mary R., *A Basic History of the United States.* New York, Doubleday, Doran & Company, 1944.

Bennett, Lerone, Jr., *Before the Mayflower: A History of the Negro in America, 1619–1966.* Chicago, Johnson Publishing Co., 1966.

Black, Hugo L., Associate Justice, U.S. Supreme Court. Opinion, June 15, 1970, *Elliott Ashton Welsh II v. United States,* No. 76, October Term, 1969.

Brock, Peter, *Pacifism in the United States, from the Colonial Era to the First World War.* Princeton, N.J., Princeton University Press, 1968.

Cantril, Hadley, ed., *Public Opinion 1935–1946.* Princeton, N.J., Princeton University Press, 1951.

Chase, Stuart, "American Values: A Generation of Change." *Public Opinion Quarterly,* Fall, 1965.

Clark, Tom C., Associate Justice, U.S. Supreme Court. Opinion, March 8, 1965, *United States v. Daniel Andrew Seeger,* No. 50, and associated cases Nos. 51 and 29, October Term, 1964.

Converse, Philip E., and Schuman, Howard, " 'Silent Majorities' and the Vietnam War." *Scientific American,* June, 1970.

Curti, Merle, *The Roots of American Loyalty.* New York, Columbia University Press, 1946.

Davies, Wallace E., *Patriotism on Parade: The Story of Veterans' and Hereditary Organizations in America, 1783–1900.* Cambridge, Mass., Harvard University Press, 1955.

DOD Pam 5–10, Office of Armed Forces Information and Education, Department of Defense. Washington, D.C., 1960.

Erskine, Hazel, compiler. Collection of nationwide poll figures . . . tabulated by age . . . from polling question archives maintained by *Public Opinion Quarterly* of Columbia University.
—— "The Polls: Is War a Mistake?" *Public Opinion Quarterly,* Spring, 1970.

Encyclopedia of Associations, 6th ed., Vol. I, *National Organizations of the United States.* Detroit, Gale Research Co., 1970.

Free, Lloyd A., and Cantril, Hadley, *The Political Beliefs of Americans.* New Brunswick, N.J., Rutgers University Press, 1967.

Freidel, Frank, "Dissent in the Spanish-American War and the Philippine Insurrection," in *Dissent in Three American Wars.* Cambridge, Mass., Harvard University Press, 1970.

Fulbright, J. William, *The Arrogance of Power.* New York, Random House, Inc., 1966.

Gellermann, William, *The American Legion As Educator.* New York, Teachers College, Columbia University, 1938.

Goldman, Eric F., *The Tragedy of Lyndon Johnson.* New York, Alfred A. Knopf, Inc., 1969.

Grodzins, Morton, *Americans Betrayed: Politics and the Japanese Evacuation.* Chicago, University of Chicago Press, 1949.
—— *The Loyal and the Disloyal.* Chicago, University of Chicago Press, 1956.

Hapgood, Norman, ed., *Professional Patriots.* New York, A. & C. Boni, 1927.

Harlan, John M., Associate Justice, U.S. Supreme Court. Opinion, June 15, 1970, *Elliott Ashton Welsh II v. United States,* No. 76, October Term, 1969.

Hilsman, Roger, *To Move a Nation: The Politics of Foreign Policy in the*

Administration of John F. Kennedy. Garden City, N.Y., Doubleday & Company, Inc., 1967.

Hughes, Emmet J., *The Ordeal of Power: A Political Memoir of the Eisenhower Years.* New York, Atheneum Publishers, 1963.

Issues. No. 3—Commitments of U.S. Power Abroad, Department of State. Washington, D.C., 1969.

Keniston, Kenneth, *Young Radicals.* New York, Harcourt, Brace & World, Inc., 1968.

Marriner, Ernest C., *The History of Colby College.* Waterville, Maine, Colby College Press, 1963.

Mathews, Shailer, *Patriotism and Religion.* New York, The Macmillan Company, 1918.

Merk, Frederick, "Dissent in the Mexican War," in *Dissent in Three American Wars.* Cambridge, Mass., Harvard University Press, 1970.

Millis, Walter, *Road to War: America, 1914–1917.* Boston and New York, Houghton Mifflin Company, 1935.

Morison, Samuel Eliot, "Dissent in the War of 1812," in *Dissent in Three American Wars.* Cambridge, Mass., Harvard University Press, 1970.

Murdock, Eugene C., *Patriotism Limited, 1862–1865.* Kent, Ohio, Kent State University Press, 1967.

Nixon, Richard, *U.S. Foreign Policy for the 1970's: A New Strategy for Peace.* Report to Congress, February 18, 1970. Washington, D.C., 1970.

Proceedings of the Congress of Constructive Patriotism, held under the auspices of the National Security League, Washington, D.C., January 25–27, 1917.

Pullen, John J., *The Twentieth Maine: A Volunteer Regiment in the Civil War.* Philadelphia, J. B. Lippincott Co., 1957.

Ransom, Lieutenant Robert C., Jr., *Letters from Vietnam.* Privately printed, 1968.

Smith, Goldwin, "The Moral of the Cuban War." *The Forum,* November, 1898.

Star, Shirley A., "The Orientation of Soldiers Toward the War," in *Studies in Social Psychology in World War II,* Vol. I, *The American Soldier,* Chapter 9. Princeton, N.J., Princeton University Press, 1949. The four-volume series of which this is a part was based on work of the Research Branch, Information and Education Division, U.S. Army, during World War II.

Stockstill, Louis R., "The All-Volunteer Force: Its Cloudy Pros and Cons." *Air Force Magazine,* June, 1970.

Stone, Harlan Fiske, "The Conscientious Objector." *Columbia University Quarterly,* October, 1919.

Sullivan, Mark, *Our Times: The United States, 1900–1925,* Vol. I, *The Turn of the Century, 1900–1904.* New York, Charles Scribner's Sons, 1926.

Tolstoy, L. N., *Christianity and Patriotism,* trans. by Constance Garnett, with an introduction by Edward Garnett. London, Jonathan Cape Limited, 1922.

Truman, Harry S, *Memoirs,* Vol. II. Garden City, N.Y., Doubleday & Company, Inc., 1956.

Upton, Emory, Brevet Major General, U.S.A., *The Military Policy of the United States.* Washington, D.C., Government Printing Office, 1904.

U.S. Commitments to Foreign Powers, a report of hearings before the Committee on Foreign Relations, United States Senate, 90th Congress, first session, August 16, 17, 21, 23, and September 19, 1967. Washington, D.C., 1967.

Wirth, Fremont P., *The Development of America.* Boston, American Book Company, 1942.

Woetzel, Robert K., *The Nuremberg Trials in International Law.* New York, Frederick A. Praeger, Inc., 1960.

In the Notes that follow, the preceding works are referred to by the last name of the author or first few words of the title if no author is indicated in the Bibliography, or by author's name and the title if more than one of his works is listed. In addition, the following abbreviations are used.

AIPO —American Institute of Public Opinion (The Gallup Poll), Princeton, N.J.
Brit —*Encyclopaedia Britannica,* Chicago, 1957.
CD —*Commanders Digest.* Publication of the Department of Defense, Washington, D.C.
CG —*The Congressional Globe.*
CR —*Congressional Record.*
DSAOS—Department of State *American Opinion Summary.*
GCR —Gates Commission Report. *The Report of the President's Commission on an All-Volunteer Armed Force.* Washington, D.C., 1970.
GOI —*Gallup Opinion Index,* publication of Gallup International, Inc.
Harris —Louis Harris and Associates, Inc. (The Harris Survey), New York.

210

NORC —National Opinion Research Center, University of Chicago.
NYT —*The New York Times.*
ORC —Opinion Research Corporation, Princeton, N.J.
POQ —*The Public Opinion Quarterly.*
Roper —Roper Research Associates, Mamaroneck, N.Y.
SRC —Survey Research Center, University of Michigan.
WP   —*The Washington Post.*
WS   —*The Evening Star* and *The Sunday Star,* Washington, D.C.
WWI —World War I.
WWII —World War II.

Annotation is limited to parts of the text that are not supported by readily located contemporary or historical records.

CHAPTER ONE: DIFFERENT KINDS OF LOVE

p.2   President put patriotism ahead of political survival: comment of Senator Jacob K. Javits, on "The Big News," WTOP-TV, June 16, 1970.

3   Polls signaling political peril: AIPO, April 11, 1970, on approval of handling Presidency; AIPO, March 14, 1970, on wanting troops withdrawn; Harris, June 4, 1970, on wanting withdrawal even if South Vietnam government collapsed; Harris, May 4, 1970, on staying out of Laos and Cambodia.

3   "You know . . . I have only one eye": Carola Oman, *Nelson,* New York, 1946, p. 446.

5   Number of servicemen not old enough to vote: the Federal Voting Assistance Program, *Sixth Report,* p. 5, and *Seventh Report,* p. 6. (Dept. of Defense.) Opinion studies on youth and the war: DSAOS, May 20, 1970, pp. 1, 3.

7   450 colleges and universities on strike: NYT, May 12, 1970, p. 19. WS, May 16, 1970, p. 1, reported 282 of the nation's 1500 four-year colleges on strike. Both gave as a source the strike information center at Brandeis University. There were several other reports during May, with numbers running between 250 and 300, but qualifications such as type of college, degrees of strike, and strike durations were not clear.

7   Reactions abroad: among the most interesting, that of Mao Tse-tung, who said, "Nixon's fascist atrocities have kindled the raging flames of the revolutionary mass movement in the United States. The Chinese people firmly support the revolutionary struggle of the American people."

8   Dependence of all modern governments on consent: Barber, pp. 84–
     85. Public opinion and the Nazis: Aryeh L. Unger, "The Public
     Opinion Reports of the Nazi Party," in POQ, Winter, 1965–66,
     pp. 565–82. Votes of confidence for Mr. Nixon: AIPO, May 9,
     1970; Harris, May 25, 1970. Public tendency to support Presidents
     in time of crisis: Barber, pp. 118–19. Reaction of blacks: WP,
     May 7, 1970, p. A2; WS, May 15, 1970, p. 1; *The National
     Observer*, June 29, 1970, p. 1.

11   Amendment . . . to cut off funds: the Senate approved the Cooper-
     Church amendment on June 30, 1970. By then the American
     ground troops were out of Cambodia. The House refused to en-
     dorse the amendment.

12   Heads of three large corporations condemn extension of the war: John
     T. Connor, chairman of the board, Allied Chemical Corp., on May
     8; Thomas J. Watson, Jr., chairman of the board, IBM Corp., on
     June 2; and Charles B. McCoy, president of E. I. du Pont de Nem-
     ours & Co., on June 4. (L. L. L. Golden in *Saturday Review*, Sept.
     12, 1970, p. 95.)

12   Harris survey on flag decals: Oct. 23, 1969.

13   Reaction of leftist labor press to Wall St. demonstrations: *Bulletin*,
     weekly organ of the Worker's League, May 18, 1970, p. 2.

14   "If those kids want to be against the war . . .": *The National Ob-
     server*, May 18, 1970, p. 8.

14   *Newsweek* poll in mid-May: by AIPO, May 25, 1970. Public opinion
     on Chicago demonstrations: John P. Robinson, "Public Reaction to
     Political Protest: Chicago 1968," in POQ, Spring, 1970, pp. 1–9.

15   Keniston's comment on protest-prone campuses: Keniston, pp.
     310–11.

16   Controversy at high school: this was John F. Kennedy High School in
     Wheaton, Md., where Allison Krause graduated June, 1969 (WP,
     May 6, 1970, p. 1).

16   Reactions to war among clergy: Harold E. Quinley, "The Protestant
     Clergy and the War in Vietnam," in POQ, Spring, 1970, pp.
     43–52.

17   Reactions of Catholics, Protestants: POQ, Spring, 1970, part of data
     on p. 150.

17   Disagreements in Connecticut churches: *The New Haven Register*,
     May 20, 1970, p. 88.

17   Concerned Officers' Movement: WS, June 1, 1970, p. B1.

17   Hints of mutiny, revolt in Vietnam: Huntley Brinkley Report, NBC-TV, May 6, 1970; CBS-TV Evening News, May 6, 1970.

17   Draft troubles: CBS-TV Evening News, May 24, 1970; WS, May 13, 1970, p. A4; *Philadelphia Inquirer*, May 4, 1970, p. 4 (UPI, May 3); Mel Ziegler, "Selective Service Meets Massive Resistance," in *New York*, June 29, 1970, pp. 28–29.

18   McGeorge Bundy comment: NYT, May 17, 1970, p. 8.

19   "It's not his country!": Bowdoin College News Service Bulletin, May 7, 1970, p. 2.

19   "My God! We're Losing a Great Country!": NYT, May 12, 1970, p. C19.

20   "SMASH THE STATE!" . . . "SMASH AMERICA!": these were part of the aftermath of the demonstrations at Yale, May 2–3, 1970, concerned with the imprisonment and trial of Black Panthers.

21   Wilson speech: made in Philadelphia, May 10, 1915, reported in NYT, May 11, 1915, p. 1.

CHAPTER TWO: GOD AND/OR COUNTRY

23   Stonewall Jackson's opinion of CO's: Brock, p. 807.

24   Civil War policy on CO's: Clark, p. 7.

24   Incident of Mennonites: Brock, pp. 889–92.

24   CO's in WWI: Stone, pp. 255–67, 271.

27   "Judicial surgery": Harlan, p. 7.

28   Seeger case: Clark, pp. 2–3.

28   Welsh case: Black, pp. 2–3, 6–9; "lobotomy," Harlan, p. 8.

CHAPTER THREE: WHEN PATRIOTS WERE REBELS

33   Grodzins's thesis: Grodzins, *The Loyal and the Disloyal*, pp. 7–8, 25–26, 28–29, 81–102.

34   Washington's flag: Cleveland H. Smith and Gertrude R. Taylor, *Flags of All Nations*, New York, 1946, p. 13.

35   "In many hearts": Curti, p. 19.

36   War of 1812: Morison, pp. 3–6; Wirth, pp. 245–47; Upton, pp. 6, 96, 98.

37   Webster speech: *The Writings and Speeches of Daniel Webster Hitherto Uncollected*, Boston, 1905, Vol. 14, pp. 61–62.

38   Artemus Ward on Washington: *Vanity Fair*, November 17, 1860, p. 243.

40   Close to a million blacks . . . did not qualify: 757,208 according to 1790 census (Bennett, p. 364).

40   Jefferson's condemnation of the slave trade: Julian P. Boyd, *The Declaration of Independence: the Evolution of the Text as Shown in Facsimiles of Various Drafts by its Author, Thomas Jefferson*, Princeton, N.J., 1945, pp. 20–21, 33, 37.

41   Albert Gallatin's warning: in his *Peace With Mexico*, New York, 1847, p. 13.

CHAPTER FOUR: ABRAHAM LINCOLN'S TONKIN GULF

43   Estimate of Civil War cost: Beard, pp. 280–81.

44   Slavery as a religious issue: Charles C. Cole, Jr., *The Social Ideas of the Northern Evangelists*, New York, 1954, pp. 205, 218.

44   "So you're the little woman . . .": Carl Sandburg, *Abraham Lincoln, The War Years*, New York, 1939, Vol. II, p. 201.

45   Edmund Ruffin and firing on Ft. Sumter: *Dictionary of American Biography*, New York, 1963, Vol. VIII, Part 2, p. 216; Bruce Catton, *The Coming Fury*, Garden City, N.Y., 1961, pp. 311–15. According to Catton, Ruffin's was not the first shot fired but was among the first.

45   Convening of 1861 Congress: CG, 37th Congress, 1st Session, p. 1.

46   Equivalent of Tonkin Gulf Resolution: ibid., p. 16; this was designated S. No. 1.

46   Breckinridge speech: ibid., pp. 137–40, July 16, 1861.

46   Senator Kennedy's statement: ibid., p. 42, July 10, 1861.

47   Lincoln's speech to Congress: CG (Appendix) 30th Congress, 1st Session, pp. 93–5, January 12, 1848.

47   Senator Howe's statement: CG, 37th Congress, 1st session, pp. 393, 395, August 2, 1861.

48   Senator Lane's statement: ibid., p. 142, July 16, 1861.

48   Breckinridge, "I am quite aware that in the present temper of Congress . . .": ibid., p. 142, July 16, 1861.

49 "I claim not to have controlled events . . .": Helen Nicolay, *Personal Traits of Abraham Lincoln,* New York, 1913, p. 350.

CHAPTER FIVE: BULLETS AND BALLOTS:
A UNIQUE TEST OF PATRIOTISM

51 Colby College: Marriner, pp. 71, 73.

52 "You remember better than I": ibid., p. 153.

52 Zemro Smith letter: to Charles Emery, July 14, 1862. Colby College Library.

53 N. B. Coleman letter: to Charles Emery, November 10, 1862. Colby College Library.

53 Ames and 20th Maine flag: Pullen, p. 170.

54 Lincoln-McClellan political situation, 1864: ibid., pp. 229–30.

55 "Things look cheering to us": Zemro Smith to Charles Emery, September 16, 1864. Colby College Library.

55 1st Maine Heavy Artillery: William E. S. Whitman and Charles H. True, *Maine in the War for the Union,* Lewiston, Maine, 1865, pp. 468–69.

55 Provisions for soldier voting in the 1864 election: *DOD Pam 5–10,* p. 3.

56 Number voting in the armed services 1968: 1,142,600. (The Federal Voting Assistance Program, Department of Defense, *Seventh Report,* p. 5.)

56 Veteran who offered to pay to get back in the Army: Charles O. Fernald of Winterport, Maine. His letter of July 10, 1863, is in the Maine Adjutant General's Civil War Correspondence, Vol. 39.

57 Vote cast by the 20th Maine, Fifth Corps, and Army of the Potomac: Pullen, p. 231.

57 Chamberlain's comment on the election: Joshua L. Chamberlain, *The Passing of the Armies,* New York, 1915, pp. 12–13.

58 Comments of private in the 20th Maine: Pullen, p. 230.

58 Vietnam veteran's comment on an antiwar resolution: *The New Haven Register,* May 20, 1970, p. 88.

60 Further history of soldier voting: *DOD Pam 5–10,* pp. 3–4. (The Federal Voting Assistance Program, Department of Defense, *Sixth Report,* p. 19, and *Seventh Report,* pp. 2–6.)

CHAPTER SIX: PATRIOTISM IN SONG, STORY, AND FRATERNITY

63   War deaths: Bell I. Wiley estimated more American servicemen died in Civil War than in *all* other American wars, as of 1963.

64   Union veterans initially not inclined to forgive: Davies, pp. 237–38, 249–80.

64   Gettysburg, 1938 reunion: Jack McLaughlin, *Gettysburg: The Long Encampment,* New York, 1963, pp. 222–33. This is a most interesting book on Gettysburg and its memories, including accounts of the reunions of 1913 and 1938.

65   Vivien Leigh as Scarlett: Subject of an AIPO survey, February 20, 1939.

68   Society of the Cincinnati: Davies, p. 2. According to the 1970 *Encyclopedia of Associations,* it still had 2,450 members.

68   Military Order of the Loyal Legion: Davies, p. 29.

68   G.A.R.: Davies, pp. 31, 36, 44, 75, 217–41, 353–55. According to an AP story of February 14, 1953, the last member of the G.A.R., William A. Magee, died January 23, 1953, at the age of 106. Other veterans still alive were not G.A.R. members.

69   Hereditary societies: information on those mentioned is from *Enclycopedia of Associations,* pp. 967, 973.

69   G.A.R. medal and Medal of Honor: John J. Pullen, *A Shower of Stars,* Philadelphia, 1966, pp. 140–41 and photographs.

69   "Until these old veterans began to totter . . .": *Proceedings of the Congress of Constructive Patriotism,* p. 317.

70   Patriotic societies and social unrest, "Americanization": Davies, pp. 44–48, 281–90, 353–57; Curti, pp. 189–90.

CHAPTER SEVEN: NATIONALISM, IMPERIALISM, AND VOICES OF DISSENT

74   Henry George's warnings: his *Social Problems,* New York, 1953, pp. 5, 75–76, 164–66.

74   State of pacifism following Civil War: Brock, pp. 689, 869, 920; Davies, p. 339.

75   Revolt at Bowdoin: Willard M. Wallace, *Soul of the Lion: A Biography of General Joshua L. Chamberlain,* New York, 1960, pp. 236–40.

75   Spanish-American War: Freidel, pp. 70–74; Smith, pp. 283–84.

77 Senator Beveridge's speech: CR, 56th Congress, 1st Session, p. 711, January 9, 1900.

78 Charles Denby's comment: his "Shall We Keep the Philippines?" in *The Forum*, November, 1898, p. 281.

79 "If you have an empire . . .": Smith, p. 285.

79 Senator Hoar's comment: CR, 55th Congress, 3rd Session, p. 496, January 9, 1899.

79 "Hard and selfish men": Morrison I. Swift, *Imperialism and Liberty*, Los Angeles, 1899, pp. 34, 375.

79 Troubles in Philippines, dissatisfaction with imperialism: Freidel, pp. 88, 92–95; Sullivan, pp. 8–11, 56, 536–40; Wirth, p. 596.

CHAPTER EIGHT: PATRIOTISM SHOWS ITS DARKER SIDE
81 Tolstoy and American pacifist disciples: Brock, pp. 934–35.

81 "It is a terrible thing to say . . .": Tolstoy, p. 76.

81 "The everlastingly deceived . . .": ibid., p. 30.

82 Americans' information on Europe: Millis, pp. 42–43, 47–56; Adams, pp. 367–69.

82 WWI a mistake: Erskine, "The Polls," pp. 135–36.

82 WWI propaganda: Millis, pp. 62–66; Adams, p. 370.

84 "Organized" patriotism: Curti, pp. 224–26.

84 Preparedness campaign: Millis, pp. 93–96, 148–50, 208–11, 254–55.

84 National Security League: *Proceedings of the Congress of Constructive Patriotism,* pp. 4–6, 172.

85 Pacifists: Millis, p. 103.

85 Socialists: Adams, p. 379.

85 Intolerance toward pacifists, socialists, German-Americans: Curti, pp. 227–28.

87 "In times of peace many a good patriot . . .": Mathews, pp. 2–3.

88 WWI activities at Colby: Marriner, pp. 303–9.

CHAPTER NINE: FOREIGN AND INTERNAL FOES
89 Patriotism and *status quo:* Curti, p. ix, with reference to "Americanism."

89   Fear of Bolshevism: Adams, pp. 390–91.

90   The American Legion: Curti, pp. 236–37; *The American Legion Through the Years*, undated booklet issued by national headquarters of the Legion, pp. 1–2, 7, 10, 12–16; information on number of members, posts, from National Membership Director, 1970; Gellermann, pp. 13, 14, 20, says one reason the American Legion was founded was that national leaders were worried about radical unrest and feared that returning servicemen might otherwise form a Bolshevistic organization. He notes, p. 130, that the American Legion's hostility to subversive doctrines has been continuous.

91   New type of patriotic societies such as foundations, etc.: Hapgood, pp. 2–37, notes their rise since the beginning of WWI—also, p. 113, their tendency to form friendly ties with the military.

92   Meanings of "liberal" and "conservative": Free and Cantril, pp. 2–5.

92   Poll on socialism in 1942: Cantril, p. 802, Socialism, No. 2.

92   Ambivalence of public—ideology vs. practice: Chase, pp. 361–64; Free and Cantril, pp. 13–17, 31–33, with comments, pp. 174–81, on the relationship of principle and pragmatism in America, its historical background, and the need for a restatement of American ideology to make it more understandable in view of its apparent conflict with operational realities.

94   Polls on economic vs. "Freedom" values: AIPO, August 28, 1946, May 7, 1948, and September 10, 1949.

95   Allegiance to federal government strengthened in the Depression: Curti, p. 243.

95   Gallup Polls on "big government," "big labor," and "big business": AIPO, May 7, 1941, and August 18, 1968.

96   "I'm afraid of the government": WS, May 13, 1970, p. A4.

96   Computerized federal surveillance system: NYT, June 28, 1970, p. 1; bombings, *N.Y. Daily News*, July 16, 1970, p. 2; system recommended, *Report of the President's Commission on the Assassination of President John F. Kennedy*, Washington, D.C., 1964, pp. 461–69.

97   Isolationism in America: Chase, p. 359; Manfred Jonas, *Isolationism in America 1935–1941*, Ithaca, N.Y., 1966, pp. 4, 32, 77, 98, 123–25, 218.

98   WWII least "mistaken": Erskine, "The Polls," pp. 134–50. Also, AIPO, June 27, 1970.

99   Oxford balloting: Winston Churchill, *The Gathering Storm*, Boston, 1948, p. 85.

99   WWI considered "a mistake" (in descending order): AIPO, April 4, 1937, by 70 per cent; November 8, 1939, by 68 per cent; December 15, 1940, by 39 per cent.

99   Favor for preparedness: Cantril, p. 458, Military Service, Compulsory, No. 4, shows a sharp increase in favor for the draft and p. 462, No. 15, shows 85 per cent in favor of calling up the National Guard in July, 1940.

99   Odd mood in approach to WWII: AIPO, January 29–30, 1939, showed 57 per cent thinking U.S. would be drawn in and August 20, 1939, 76 per cent thought so; yet AIPO, December 8, 1939, showed public against entering the war 27 to 1 and May 29, 1940, against it 13 to 1.

100   "War referendum" idea: Whitney H. Shepardson and William O. Scroggs, *The United States in World Affairs 1938*, New York, 1939, pp. 152–57, also reporting the results of the Gallup Polls bearing on this subject.

100   Battle of organizations, public opinion prior to WWII: John W. Masland, "Pressure Groups and American Foreign Policy," in POQ, Spring, 1942, pp. 115–22.

102   NYT editorial on F.D.R.: April 12, 1970, p. E12.

102   Gallup Polls in support of F.D.R.'s war measures: typical AIPO polls show majorities favoring the following courses of action—February 10, 1939, all-out aid to England, France; September 24, 1939, changing neutrality law; September 5, 1940, destroyer transfer; January 22, 1941, lend-lease; September 26, 1941, shoot on sight at U-boats; November 14, 1941, stopping Japan even at risk of war.

102   People 8-to-1 against entering the war in March, 1941: AIPO, March 21, 1941. Churchill's reaction to the news of Pearl Harbor: Winston S. Churchill, *The Grand Alliance*, Boston, 1950, pp. 607–8.

103   WWII at Colby: Marriner, p. 541.

103   People dissatisfied with war production, willing to work harder: AIPO, January 5–6, 1941, January 19–20, 1941.

103   Public leading Congress in advocacy of war measures: AIPO, March 11, 1942, December 6, 1942.

103   Satisfaction with fairness of the draft: Cantril, p. 462, Military Service, Compulsory, No. 20.

104 Majorities favoring registering for war work, taking directions from government: Cantril, p. 113, Civilian Defense, Nos. 21 and 22.

105 Attitudes of soldiers toward the war: Star, pp. 430–47.

CHAPTER TEN: ON THE ROAD TO VIETNAM

107 Attitudes toward Russia: Almond, pp. 93, 98–99; AIPO, July 14, 1944.

108 Attitudes toward domestic communists: typical are NORC, June 30, 1953, and AIPO, April 18, 1947, December 5, 1947, May 23, 1948, August 15, 1948, and August 26, 1949.

110 Truman Doctrine: *U.S. Commitments,* p. 65.

110 News of Korean invasion, Truman considers action: Truman, pp. 331–33.

112 Truman commits forces, informs Congress: Truman, pp. 337–38.

112 Truman and A-bomb: Truman, pp. 395–96.

112 Majorities in favor of stopping Russian aggression: typical are AIPO, August 27, 1950, and NORC, June 29, 1951, February 5, 1952, and May 18, 1954.

112 Internationalist sentiment predominates: this is consistently shown by a long series of polls by AIPO, NORC, Roper, and others, 1942–69. Free and Cantril, pp. 63–66, reports the public in 1964 was only 8 per cent isolationist, 27 per cent mixed, 65 per cent internationalist.

113 Students' attitudes toward the Korean War: Edward A. Suchman, Rose K. Goldsen, and Robin M. Williams, Jr., "Attitudes Toward the Korean War," in POQ, Summer, 1953, pp. 171–84.

113 Public attitudes in general toward the Korean War: AIPO release of June 27, 1970, shows these compared with attitudes on the Vietnam war. Opinion that Congress should control troop commitments, AIPO, February 9, 1951, and April 4, 1951. Concern about cost of living, AIPO, May 11, 1951.

114 Decline in Truman's popularity: GOI, February, 1970, p. 9.

115 "Low blow" on Korea: Truman, p. 501.

115 Eisenhower's attitude toward National Security Council system: Hilsman, pp. 18–20.

115 Appraisal of Eisenhower years: Hughes, pp. 56, 162–63, 166, 262–63, 297–306.

116 Kennedy reduces NSC group: Hilsman, p. 23.

116 Fulbright's accidental involvement in Bay of Pigs deliberations: Fulbright, pp. 47–48.

117 Hilsman's impression of Kennedy's Vietnam policy: Hilsman, pp. 415, 536–37.

118 Impressions of L.B.J.: Eric F. Goldman, *The Tragedy of Lyndon Johnson*, New York, 1969, pp. 20–21, 378.

118 Public more concerned about international than domestic affairs: Free and Cantril, p. 57.

118 Polls on aid to Asian countries: typical are NORC, June 30, 1953, August 21, 1953, November 25, 1953, June 30, 1954, October 6, 1955, November 15, 1956.

119 College-educated more internationalist: Free and Cantril, pp. 66–67.

119 Internationalism had a slight liberal tinge: ibid., pp. 67–68.

119 Decline of support for Vietnam war: AIPO release of June 27, 1970.

119 Decline of President Johnson's popularity: GOI, February, 1970, pp. 14–16. Eisenhower record, pp. 10–12; Kennedy's, pp. 12–13. Johnson actually registered higher than Eisenhower initially.

119 Johnson vs. Nixon and Romney: Erskine, Collection of Poll Figures, pp. 26–27.

119 Johnson's decision not to run: George E. Reedy, *The Twilight of the Presidency*, New York, 1970, pp. 68–69, says people close to L.B.J. told him he would have to make an extraordinary effort even to win the nomination.

120 Irving Kristol's comment: "American Intellectuals and Foreign Policy," in *Foreign Affairs*, July, 1967.

120 Decline of support by college-educated: Erskine, "The Polls," p. 135.

121 Better educated far better informed: Free and Cantril, p. 61.

121 SRC study of college-educated attitudes on Vietnam: Converse and Schuman, pp. 23–25.

122 Most Americans' disenchantment with war not based on moral reasons: ibid., noted, p. 24. Also, GOI, June, 1967, p. 6.

123 Clarence Darrow changes his mind: Brock, pp. 936–37.

125 Purpose of Senate Committee on Foreign Relations hearings: *U.S. Commitments*, p. 1; Fulbright, p. 56.

125   Use of executive agreements by the President: *U.S. Commitments*, pp. 15, 28, 242, 285–86.

126   Katzenbach testimony: ibid., pp. 140–41, 170.

126   Idea of impeachment: ibid., pp. 314–16.

CHAPTER ELEVEN: "CHUCK HIM OUT, THE BRUTE!"

129   General Sherman as a storyteller: Melville O. Landon, *Thirty Years of Wit*, New York, 1891, pp. 20–30.

129   Douglas statement: William O. Douglas, *Points of Rebellion*, New York, 1970, p. 41.

129   Marquis Childs comment: WP, March 13, 1970, p. A25.

130   DOD Share-of-budget figures: CD, March 28, 1970, p. 2.

131   Cost overruns: *The Wall Street Journal*, March 4, 1970, p. 4.

131   Armed forces strength, military and civilian: CD, February 7, 1970, p. 2; *Armed Forces Management*, April, 1970, p. 53.

133   R.O.T.C.—Decline in enrollments: NYT, March 3, 1970, p. 13. Attacks on buildings, *U.S. News & World Report*, June 29, 1970, p. 20. As source of officers: this apparently varies from year to year and service to service; according to GCR, p. 71, in 1965 the newly commissioned officers accounted for by R.O.T.C. were about 60 per cent for the Army, 35 per cent for the Air Force, 15 per cent for the Navy, and 7 per cent for the Marine Corps. Dropouts: Michael Getler, "Pentagon Says Unrest Isn't Curtailing ROTC," in WP, September 17, 1970, p. A6.

134   Attacks on draft boards: *Congressional Quarterly*, April 3, 1970, p. 930; NBC-TV, September 3, 1970.

134   Draft counseling: WP, March 8, 1970, p. A4.

135   Hostile soldiers, underground papers: *Army*, January, 1970, pp. 22–27; NYT, June 21, 1970, p. 1.

135   Decline in respect for the uniform: *Congressional Quarterly*, April 3, 1970, p. 931.

135   Retention of personnel problem: ibid., pp. 930–31.

135   West Point graduate objector: *NYT Magazine*, July 5, 1970, p. 15.

135   Decline of military prep school enrollments: NYT, March 25, 1970, p. 49.

136   Senator McCarthy said military unfairly blamed: WS, May 29, 1970, p. A5.

137   George S. Patton III (then a colonel) portrayed as brutal in Vietnam: Seymour M. Hersh, *My Lai 4*, New York, 1970, pp. 9–11.

137   Senator Smith's comments: "Defense Spending: Changing Attitudes," in *Defense Management Journal*, Winter, 1970, p. 5.

CHAPTER TWELVE: "WHY ME?"

139   Washington on patriotism: quoted in Curti, p. 20.

140   President's instructions to Gates Commission: GCR, p. vii.

140   All-volunteer force said possible by July 1, 1971: GCR, p. 8.

140   Reception of the report, distribution: Stockstill.

141   "The United States has relied throughout its history . . .": GCR, p. 6.

141   Low between-wars strength: Brit, Vol. 22, pp. 760–61.

141   War of Independence fought "almost entirely by volunteers": GCR, p. 160.

141   Imminence of draft, weakness of bounty system in War of Independence: Brit, Vol. 6, p. 285; Upton, pp. 35–41, 66.

142   "While the patriotism of a people, taken collectively . . .": Upton, p. 35.

142   Upton's conclusions on the draft: Upton, p. 67.

142   Congress rejects universal service and draft in 1790: GCR, p. 160.

142   Establishment and role of militia: Upton, pp. 84–85.

143   Conscription in Europe: Brit, Vol. 6, pp. 283–84.

143   Voluntary enlistment fails in Civil War, both North and South: Brit, Vol. 6, p. 285.

143   "The Civil War . . . largely fought by volunteers . . .": GCR, pp. 161–62.

144   Civil War manpower problems, draft used as threat: Upton, pp. 439–40, 443; Murdock, pp. 4–15.

145   Draft riot in New York: ibid., pp. 1–2.

146   Civil War draft authorities' advice to successors: ibid., p. 15.

146   Numbers drafted, use of draft in WWI and WWII: *Statistical Abstract of the United States*, 1962, p. 257; Brit, Vol. 6, pp. 285–87.

146 Public approval of draft in WWII: Cantril, p. 458, Military Service, Compulsory, No. 4, and p. 462, No. 20.

146 Draft violations in WWII: Brit, Vol. 6, p. 287.

147 Statements on lapse of draft, 1947–48: GCR, p. 165; L. James Binder, "Military Service Is Not a Commodity," *Army*, April, 1970.

147 Polls indicating more sympathy for young men opposed to draft: Harris, November 13, 1969, and December 29, 1969.

149 $3.2 billion estimate for added cost of all-volunteer force: GCR, p. 7.

149 Size of force interpreted as 2.5 million: WP, April 24, 1970, p. A10.

149 Higher estimates of cost: Stockstill.

149 All-volunteer forces in Canada, England: GCR, pp. 169–72.

149 Projections of force sizes: CD, February 7, 1970, p. 2, and February 14, 1970, p. 8.

150 Future build-up role for Guard, Reserves: WP, September 9, 1970, p. 1.

150 Goal of zero draft call by 1973 and conditional aspects: news briefings at the Pentagon, Sec. of Defense Melvin R. Laird, October 12, 1970; and Roger T. Kelley, Asst. Sec. of Defense (Manpower and Reserve Affairs), October 14, 1970; speech by Army Chief of Staff William C. Westmoreland to Association of the U.S. Army, October 13, 1970.

151 Gallup Poll on universal service: AIPO, July 4, 1970.

153 Only 4 per cent volunteer for combat: Roger T. Kelley, news briefing, October 14, 1970.

CHAPTER THIRTEEN: THE RAMPARTS WE WATCH

155 Exchange of toasts: *U.S. Commitments*, p. 67.

155 Various forms of commitments: ibid., pp. 15, 52–71.

156 Senate resolution to define commitment: *Issues*, pp. 4, 11.

156 List of countries: ibid., pp. 16–19; *U.S. Commitments*, pp. 51–71.

156 Relationship with Cuba: ibid., pp. 52, 62.

157 Protocol for Laos, Cambodia: ibid., p. 57.

157 Commitment to the Middle East: ibid., p. 65.

158 Flexibility of treaty language: *Issues*, pp. 3, 10.

158 Relevant wording of NATO, SEATO treaties: *U.S. Commitments,* pp. 55, 57–58.

159 President has sent troops 150 times: *Issues,* p. 12.

162 List of military installations: DOD, "Major Military Installations or Activities Outside the U.S., August 4, 1969."

162 "The United States will keep . . . We shall provide . . .": Nixon, p. 55.

163 National Security Council system described: ibid., pp. 17–23.

164 Editorial comment on Nixon Doctrine: DSAOS, March 4, 1970, and July 30, 1970.

165 There was more time for deliberation in recent crises: opinion of Senator J. William Fulbright expressed in *U.S. Commitments,* p. 3.

165 Jefferson statement: quoted in *Issues,* p. 12.

166 Quarter of American people not aware of fighting in Vietnam, 1964: Free and Cantril, pp. 59, 61.

166 Almond opinion on informing public: Almond, pp. 4, 6–7, 227.

167 Findley statement: *U.S. Commitments,* pp. 226–27.

167 Case statement: ibid., pp. 187–88.

168 Extent of domestic programs: "Efficiency of Executive Reorganization," WP, July 1, 1970, p. A19.

CHAPTER FOURTEEN: VALOR IN VIETNAM

171 "Primary groups": Grodzins, *The Loyal and the Disloyal,* pp. 39–45; Edward A. Shils, "Primary Groups in the American Army," in *Continuities in Social Research: Studies in the Scope and Method of "The American Soldier,"* Eds. Robert K. Merton and Paul F. Lazarsfeld, Glencoe, Ill., 1950, pp. 16–39.

172 Medal of Honor men, statistics: with the exception of the story about John Levitow, which appeared in *Air Force Magazine,* July, 1970, pp. 56–57, this information is from records accumulated by Flint O. DuPre and the author in the form of official citations, press releases, from the services and newspaper clippings.

176 Mike Ransom's letters: *Letters From Vietnam,* see Bibliography.

177 "All of a sudden, he's challenged . . .": Col. Granville A. Sharpe, C.O., The Student Brigade, at Fort Benning, Georgia, to the author who, as it happened, visited there in the fall of 1967, about three

months after Mike Ransom had graduated from Infantry O.C.S. Impressions of O.C.S. are from this visit as well as the author's experience in O.C.S. in WWII.

CHAPTER FIFTEEN: PRO PATRIA AND PRO PEOPLE

183 "Hour of Decision: God *or* Country?": NYT, July 5, 1970, p. 32, said this sign was held up by a group of Mennonites from Pennsylvania who were protesting the fusion of church and state in the exercises.

184 Sale of flags doubled: NYT, June 28, 1970, p. 65.

184 50,000 flag decals: CBS-TV Evening News, July 3, 1970.

184 Mathews on flag: Mathews, p. 1.

185 60 per cent to 90 per cent of the people "turned off" by protesters . . . ethnic patriots: Andrew N. Greeley, program director, NORC, "Turning Off 'The People,' " in *The New Republic*, June 27, 1970, pp. 14–16.

186 Evacuation of Japanese: Grodzins, *Americans Betrayed*, pp. 1, 2, 93, 175, 232, 325–48, 357, 387; Cantril, p. 380, Japanese in the U.S., Nos. 1, 2; Brit, Vol. 5, p. 743.

187 32 states pass laws: NYT, June 28, 1970, p. 41.

188 Black's record in America: Bennett, pp. 56, 364.

188 Polls on blacks, other than ORC: NORC, June 20, 1942; Harris-*Newsweek*, August 22, 1966.

189 Estimate on blacks in cities: *Newsweek*, August 3, 1970, pp. 16, 21.

190 GOI, June 1969: pp. 5, 6.

190 GOI, Jan. 1970: pp. 23, 24.

191 Gallup on differences, beards, etc.: GOI, June 1969, pp. 5, 17.

192 "Malevanism": Tolstoy, p. 17.

193 Attitudes on sovereignty, UN force: AIPO, May 24, 1950, May 2, 1951, April 8, 1957; NORC, March 1, 1951, April 24, 1951, May 24, 1951.

195 Dr. Keniston's book: on stage of youth development, pp. 239–47; on New Left, pp. 16–19; on antiacademic attitude, pp. 178–81; on attitude toward basic American principles, pp. 220–21, 234, 301; on flexibility, pp. 276–81; on nonviolence, p. 285; "If a growing number . . .", p. 234.

197   Six out of ten believing war a mistake also view protesters negatively: noted by Converse and Schuman, p. 24, reporting on SRC study.

197   Young radicals not doctrinaire: Keniston, pp. 177–78.

198   Yankelovich finding on patriotism: *Fortune,* June, 1969, p. 73.

200   Faculty members urging colleges to "take a position": NYT, July 19, 1970, p. 1, on study by Carnegie Commission on Higher Education reporting more than a third of the institutions surveyed had an increase in the proportion of faculty members urging this policy.

200   "Neither the government . . .": Fulbright, p. 160.

200   "It is a curious thing . . .": ibid., p. 162.

202   Hijackers: NYT, March 17, 1970, p. 1, March 18, 1970, p. 1, and March 26, 1970, p. 16; *Time,* March 30, 1970, p. 17.

202   Nuremberg trials: Woetzel, pp. 1–3, 7–15, 96–121, 274–75.

203   Yamashita article: James B. Reston, Jr., "Is Nuremberg Coming Back to Haunt Us?", *Saturday Review,* July 18, 1970, pp. 14–17, 61.

205   "The ultimate test": Stone, p. 269.

205   Kennedy speech: CR, 88th Congress, 1st Session, p. 22824.

Index